Getting Results
in Nonprofits and Philanthropy

Key Lessons in Strategy, Funding, and Leadership

Photo Credits:
Front Cover: Top left photo by Jason Steinberg for National Academy Foundation
Back Cover: Photo by John Rae for ACCION International

The Bridgespan Group would like to thank Our Piece of the Pie, ACCION International,
and National Academy Foundation for the photos used on the cover of this book. We also
would like to thank the *Stanford Social Innovation Review*, the *Harvard Business Review*,
and *The Nonprofit Quarterly* for their permission to reprint articles in this compilation.
We sincerely appreciate their help.

Contents

Foreword

Strategy

1   "Galvanizing Philanthropy," Susan Wolf Ditkoff and
Susan J. Colby, *Harvard Business Review,* November 2009

10   "Delivering on the Promise of Nonprofits," Jeffrey L. Bradach,
Thomas J. Tierney, and Nan Stone, *Harvard Business Review,*
December 2008

25   "More Bang for the Buck," Alex Neuhoff and Robert Searle,
Stanford Social Innovation Review, Spring 2008

36   "Zeroing in on Impact," Susan J. Colby, Nan Stone, and
Paul Carttar, *Stanford Social Innovation Review,* Fall 2004

50   "Going to Scale," Jeffrey L. Bradach, *Stanford Social
Innovation Review,* Spring 2003

Funding

67   "The Nonprofit Starvation Cycle," Ann Goggins Gregory and
Don Howard, *Stanford Social Innovation Review,* Fall 2009

77   "Ten Nonprofit Funding Models," William Foster, Peter Kim,
and Barbara Christiansen, *Stanford Social Innovation Review,*
Spring 2009

95   "Money to Grow On," William Foster, *Stanford Social Innovation Review,* Fall 2008

107   "How Nonprofits Get Really Big," William Foster and Gail Fine [Perreault], *Stanford Social Innovation Review,* Spring 2007

128   "Should Nonprofits Seek Profits?" William Foster and Jeffrey L. Bradach, *Harvard Business Review,* February 2005

Leadership

143   "Leadership Priorities: What Facets of Management Shouldn't You Delegate?" Jeffrey L. Bradach and Kirk Kramer, *The Bridgespan Group,* February 2010

152   "Finding Leaders for America's Nonprofits," David Simms and Carol Trager, *The Bridgespan Group,* April 2009

174   "Strongly Led, Under-managed," Daniel Stid and Jeffrey L. Bradach, *The Bridgespan Group,* July 2008

185   "Who Decides? Mapping Power and Decision Making in Nonprofits," Jon Huggett and Caitrin Moran [Wright], *The Nonprofit Quarterly,* Fall 2008

195   "The Leadership Deficit," Thomas J. Tierney, *Stanford Social Innovation Review,* Summer 2006

212   Author Biographies

213   Endnotes

Foreword

What kinds of knowledge would nonprofit leaders and their funders find most useful? And how could such knowledge achieve the reach, relevance, and influence required to help shape their thinking and improve their organizations' results? These questions have animated Bridgespan since our founding. The articles collected here reflect some of the ways in which we've sought to answer them. We'll say more about that in a moment; but first, a little context.

From the outset, Bridgespan aimed to multiply the impact of organizations tackling society's most important challenges and opportunities. Conversations that led to Bridgespan's creation quickly zeroed in on the power of knowledge to contribute to that goal. In fact, our first round of funding came with the expectation that creating and sharing knowledge would be a core part of the business model, alongside direct consulting and advisory services. To this end, we learned to view collaborations with clients as shared opportunities not only to help navigate their critical issues in the here and now, but also to identify insights that could help others. As a result, we also learned the value of balancing action with reflection—a mindset that continues to be a hallmark of Bridgespan's culture.

Because case studies allowed—and disciplined—us to write about what we knew, that's where our knowledge work started. As our experience deepened, cross-cutting strategic challenges, such as scaling and aligning programs with mission, moved onto our research agenda. "Going to Scale" and "Zeroing in on Impact," published in *Stanford Social Innovation Review (SSIR)*, were the first fruits of this research, which was further developed in "Delivering on the Promise of Nonprofits" and "Galvanizing Philanthropy," both published in *Harvard Business Review (HBR)*.

Bridgespan's body of work on social capital markets and funding models was similarly grounded in multiple client engagements. Their real-world challenges were the catalyst for the research that led to "How Nonprofits Get Really Big" and "Ten Nonprofit Funding Models." These articles engendered enormous interest from *SSIR* readers, as did "The Nonprofit Starvation Cycle," which demonstrated the value of "good overhead" and triggered ongoing conversations among private and public funders about how to evaluate effectiveness. "The Leadership Deficit," which projected a huge shortfall of senior management talent, had a comparable impact on discussions within the sector.

Follow-on studies, such as "Finding Leaders for America's Nonprofits," provided additional data to illuminate the problem, while articles like "Strongly Led, Under-managed" offered insights on developing stronger management and leadership teams.

Looking forward, Bridgespan's knowledge agenda continues to be driven by our mission: to "strengthen the ability of nonprofit organizations to achieve breakthrough results in addressing society's most important challenges and problems." To deliver on this imperative, we are developing ideas and insights for specific fields, such as education, the environment, and philanthropy; exploring levers for scaling impact, such as field-building and advocacy, that go beyond the work of single organizations; and embracing new ways to expand our reach and deepen our relevance and influence through multimedia outreach, cohort learning, and other forms of engagement (both virtual and face-to-face) with communities of social-sector constituents.

Being asked to assemble a tenth-anniversary collection of Bridgespan knowledge work is both a blessing and a curse: a blessing because it affords a wonderful opportunity to reflect and remember. A curse because there is so much to choose from that any selection is inevitably incomplete. We hope that when you close these pages, you will open the virtual library on www.bridgespan.org and not only enjoy the wealth of content available there, but also add to it, by sharing your thoughts and insights on how we all can do more good, better, day by day.

Nan Stone and Katie Smith Milway, Bridgespan Knowledge Partners
May 2010

Strategy

What impact will we hold ourselves accountable for? How will we achieve it and grow it, and what will it cost?

This article originally appeared in the November 2009 issue of the Harvard Business Review.

Galvanizing Philanthropy

To strengthen their impact in the world, philanthropic investors need to rigorously define their goals, be realistic about how to achieve them, and commit to continual, systematic improvement.

By Susan Wolf Ditkoff and Susan J. Colby

Creating lasting environmental, social and economic change requires discipline—a concept with which many foundations, grant makers, and committed wealthy individuals (well intentioned as they may be) have traditionally struggled. Exempt from the accountability imposed on business by the markets or on government by voters, philanthropy is free to experiment and take risks. But with few external parties offering candid feedback or calling them to account, philanthropic investors (and their boards) have had insufficient experience objectively assessing their own performance and making hard decisions about programs and people.

The consequences of this inability to optimize resources and organizational outcomes are even greater in the current economy: Foundation assets that collectively once topped $680 billion have dropped by 20% to 40% from their highs in 2007. Many philanthropic investors are dissatisfied with how much social change they've been able to create; they're helping fewer children and families than intended, or influencing climate change less than they'd hoped. Most of the 75,000 foundations in the United States (like their counterparts worldwide) know they must change, but they're not sure how.

In our experience, developing a philanthropic strategy is an iterative process, regardless of the economic climate. It requires the internal discipline to ask—and rigorously answer—three fundamental questions: How do we define success? What will it take to make change happen? How can we improve our results over time? We think of this process as *getting clear, getting real, and getting better.* In the following pages we'll explore how leaders at the James Irvine Foundation, the Bill & Melinda Gates Foundation, the Annie E. Casey Foundation, the David and Lucile Packard Foundation, and the Edna McConnell Clark Foundation have wrestled with these questions, made tough decisions, and dramatically increased the effect they've had in their communities and globally. They share a commitment not just to finding promising grantees and declaring victory in their annual reports but also to maximizing their impact. And although they are large, well-established institutions, the lessons they've learned apply to any philanthropic investor or organization hoping to create significant, lasting change.

Getting Clear: How Do We Define Success?

In philanthropy there is rarely a "right" answer to the question "What should we be doing?" Philanthropic investors can't make new investments, however, without setting boundaries around what to fund and defining success within them. Thus it's useful for leaders to select a few strategic anchors—the people, problems, places, pathways, or philosophies that they really care about—and use them to guide subsequent decisions about programs, initiatives, and grantees. To further clarify their goals, philanthropic investors need to consider both hard evidence (what do we know?) and softer values and beliefs (what do we care about?).

The James Irvine Foundation did just that several years ago, when it undertook its first comprehensive strategic-planning effort in more than a decade. Its leaders continued to embrace the broad mission that had been set by the real estate magnate James Irvine in 1937: to promote the welfare of the people of California. Over time, however, this inspirational statement of purpose had led to a sprawling portfolio of grants, and the foundation's leaders had come to recognize that it was far too open-ended to be useful in making program and funding decisions. To decide where the foundation could have the most lasting impact, they commissioned research on a broad range of issues facing Californians, including education, health, and the environment.

The senior team was soon awash in data. Some findings leaped out—the significant challenges facing California's youth, for one. But given the magnitude of the state's needs, the team quickly realized that numbers alone could justify a large variety of funding decisions. So it homed in on three critical organizational values: addressing root causes rather than crises; enabling Californians to help themselves; and working on problems that might attract like-minded partners or funders. Guided by both values and data, the team selected youths aged 14 to 24 as the primary beneficiaries of its funding, and education as the primary lever for change. Saying yes to those criteria meant exiting other investments in, for example, civic culture and sustainable communities. It was a difficult choice.

The Irvine Foundation had to make some hard decisions: What, for instance, should it do about its long-standing commitment to the arts? The arts did not emerge from the data as a critical challenge, but decades of investment there had given Irvine unique assets in the form of reputation and relationships. Furthermore, its exit would have a disproportionately harsh impact on the field. So the foundation's leaders continued arts funding, albeit at a much lower level.

The Pacific Northwest Initiatives (PNW) team at the Bill & Melinda Gates Foundation faced a different challenge in refining its strategy for combating homelessness among families in the Puget Sound region of Washington State. From 2000 to 2007 the foundation's Sound Families Initiative, a $40 million public private partnership, provided funding support for almost 1,500 affordable housing units with on-site support services. Its investment prompted another $200 million in funding from other sources. Nevertheless, the number of homeless families in the region didn't drop significantly. The PNW team began a strategic analysis to understand why.

The initial results were promising: Of families served, 75% had successfully completed the transitional housing program and 89% of those had moved into permanent housing. More than 90% of the latter were still in permanent housing one year later. But what about the other 25%? Further investigation showed that they were more likely to face multiple barriers, including domestic violence, mental illness, and substance abuse, and therefore needed more-intensive support. The team realized that one-size-fits-all services weren't an optimal use of scarce resources: Some families were getting less support than they needed, while others were being offered relatively expensive services to help overcome barriers they didn't necessarily face. The PNW team had to make a choice: to define success as building housing units (which it had done well) or as ending homelessness (which it had done less well). It chose to recommit to its mission of ending homelessness, and changed its strategy and grant making to promote more-focused services to families according to their needs.

Coordinating evidence with values is both a necessity and a common roadblock for philanthropic investors, which is why it's critical to beware of two subtle traps:

Relying too much on evidence too early in the process. Thoughtful investors typically want evidence to inform their decisions as they set boundaries and try to define success. But the truth is that some issues simply don't lend themselves to that kind of analysis. For example, is it "better" to fund clean-air projects or early-childhood education? It may be more useful if investors ask: How do we believe change happens? What role do we want to play in tackling this issue? Do we prefer market-based approaches, policy-based approaches, or neither? Do we favor a vibrant field of volunteer-led organizations or a few larger, professionally managed ones? Early discussions about underlying beliefs, values, and assumptions are imperative and must be actively managed. Consider the additional work required if, later in the process, even one major stakeholder disagrees with a foundation's selected beneficiaries or goals.

Relying too much on values and beliefs too late in the process. Philanthropy is inherently personal and values-driven, even in professional funding institutions. But overreliance on personal preferences, particularly late in the decision-making process, can have negative consequences for the donor's reputation and for the field. For example, an investor that values entrepreneurship but enters a field where what is critically needed is money to grow already successful programs risks alienating the very community it's trying to help. After certain boundaries have been established, investors must be realistic about the resources and time required to bring about the change they desire. This is where targeted data can be of greatest help—by translating "what matters most" into concrete, specific goals.

Getting Real: What Will It Take to Make Change Happen?

Unless a funding institution operates its own programs, its ability to create change will depend largely on the work of its grantees, its partners, and policy makers. Some philanthropists, especially small ones, may make individual grants to support great initiatives yet have no overarching theory of change. Others may dedicate resources to multiple prongs of a strategy designed to attack a central challenge, such as keeping teens in high school. Still others may invest in innovation, funding multiple new approaches to solving social problems across a range of issues. Whatever their bent, decision makers need candid feedback from the field, both to craft and to reality-check their strategy.

Consider how the Annie E. Casey Foundation is tackling K–12 program reform. Its vision? That "all young people, especially those in tough neighborhoods, will graduate from school with the knowledge and skills they need for adult success"— a grand goal indeed, given the well-documented crisis in U.S. education. To make progress toward this objective, Bruno Manno, the director of the foundation's education program, and his team create "proof points" by improving educational results in specific neighborhoods. They share this evidence with critical decision makers, such as civic and education leaders, policy makers, and families; and motivate other financial supporters of education reform to back quality educational options and community partnerships.

This is not a unique approach. What distinguishes Manno is *how* he makes decisions within each of those areas. Take the choice of where to generate proof points. Even if the Casey Foundation's annual budget were 100 times larger than it is, the education program would need to selectively invest its resources to generate national impact. So Manno decided to focus on cities where the foundation was already investing and to leverage its previous work. Many philanthropists want to create initiatives that others will join. Manno seeks out and joins the efforts of others if that means increasing the likelihood that his program will succeed. Strategic partnerships and innovative collaborations with grantees and other funders are an explicit part of his strategy.

Why aren't most philanthropic investors similarly realistic about how to make change happen? They may be falling into these traps:

Being too optimistic about what limited resources can accomplish. When crafting their strategies, philanthropists understandably aim high, often targeting the most intractable problems with the newest interventions and structures. This impulse can make them fall prey to wishful thinking. More often than not, the resources allocated to an initiative are simply inadequate. For instance, some investors believe that if they launch a successful pilot project—one that involves, say, 1,000 children in a creative new after-school program—other groups will quickly adopt the model and thus revolutionize education. Pilot projects are important but hardly sufficient. If they do succeed, the investor should then ask: What will it take to get others involved in this project? Who are the right people to influence? How will they learn and—here's the hard part—actually use the lessons to create further change? Unless investors candidly and critically examine these questions from the outset, they may squander precious resources that could have supported realistic strategies.

Hiring people and creating processes that don't fit the strategy. Obviously, philanthropic investors should fund activities that advance their ambitions and disinvest from those that don't; this affects decisions about people, processes, and organizational structures. Surprisingly, these elements often aren't aligned with a foundation's strategy: Skills are mismatched, and investors inadequately address their own underperformance. Like others, philanthropic investors need the right people in the right jobs at the right time. So their leaders should ask: Does our strategy require academics, policy experts, or generalists? Must all these skill sets be on staff, or can we partner with grantees or contractors? What cultural and operating principles must we follow to bring our values and beliefs to life?

Lacking market pressures and operating in an insular environment, some investors become overly cautious and focus on minutiae. For instance, their approval processes require endless costly paperwork from grantees—reports that are rarely read or acted upon. No single grant-approval process is best: Investors making big, long-term bets will want rigorous due diligence from potential grantees, including business plans, milestones, and evaluations. Investors taking a "seeding the field" approach with lots of small grantees may find so much oversight unnecessary. But philanthropies simply can't allow processes to proliferate unchecked; they need feedback from grantees and other interested parties. Leaders should think about cost and complexity and ask: Have we created clear, respectful mechanisms for sourcing, selecting, supporting, and sustaining grantees?

Getting Better: How Can We Improve Over Time?

When you build a museum or a laboratory, it's easy to see where the investment has gone: The concrete and equipment offer tangible proof. It can be much harder to track the results of grants that, say, try to improve the sustainability of sea life— much less to feel confident in claiming credit for whatever positive results do ensue.

If they can't track results, investors have trouble improving outcomes over time. One way around this problem is to assess a foundation's entire funding strategy, not just the performance of individual grantees or programs. Unfortunately, few philanthropists do the hard work of learning and adapting as they go. The experience of the David and Lucile Packard Foundation shows why it is vital to do just that.

Packard has long supported conservation; the goal of its marine fisheries program is to improve the health of ocean ecosystems and wild fish stocks. In 1999 the foundation launched Seafood Choices, an initiative to increase the demand for and supply of sustainable seafood. Because there was little evidence to indicate which elements of this program would be most effective, Packard experimented: It seeded the field and supported a host of organizations engaged in activities ranging from raising consumer awareness to encouraging fishermen worldwide to adopt sustainable practices.

Packard has a culture of continual improvement and strong leadership, so it stepped back in 2004 to evaluate these early efforts. It listened to academics, researchers, and critical industry players, and pored over media, market, and funding reports. Among the most important findings was that sustainability was increasingly prominent globally—particularly among large seafood retailers and wholesalers—even if consumer behavior didn't yet reflect that. The finding validated and strengthened Packard's efforts to influence the buying practices of large U.S. retailers. It also prompted the foundation to shift some of its resources away from costly consumer-education efforts to promoting fishery certification, where they could have a much greater impact.

Investors don't have access to as many "truth tellers" as they should.

Three years later the foundation embarked on another round of evaluation and reflection. Once again, the findings both affirmed the wisdom of existing efforts and pointed to the need for course corrections. The number of fisheries that were either certified or in full assessment had increased from 13 in 2003 to 117 in 2007, and interest in sustainability was rising sharply among North American retailers. Wal-Mart, for example, gave the issue a huge push in 2006 when it announced a commitment to sourcing sustainable seafood. But important as the role of large retailers was in creating a market for sustainable fish, it wasn't enough. The suppliers and processors that link fishermen to buyers had to be part of any change effort— which meant that Packard would have to bring in new partners and experiment with new ways of investing.

Why aren't more philanthropic investors getting better as they go? They must beware of the following traps:

Failing to solicit outside perspectives. As noted earlier, philanthropic decision makers lack genuine feedback mechanisms. Although this liberates them to make innovative long-term investments, it also prevents them from knowing if those investments go off track or are misdirected from the start. Investors don't have access to as many "truth tellers" as they should. Because they hold the purse strings, just about everyone has a vested interest in telling them they're doing a great job—even while complaining privately. Voices from the field—and from the beneficiaries—are often missing in the decision-making process. Investors that want the unvarnished truth about their results must go out of their way to get it. Good sources are third-party agencies such as the Center for Effective Philanthropy, which can collect anonymous input from grantees.

Underestimating the power of nonfinancial assets. Philanthropic investors often fail to accurately assess their own capabilities and what they uniquely bring to the table. Money is the primary resource, of course, but long-term commitments generate less-tangible assets such as reputation, relationships, and expertise that can help an organization get better over time. Many investors have considerable convening power: The Gates, Clinton, and Rockefeller foundations can pull in heads of state; others are influential within their cities or sectors. But not even the Gates Foundation is rich enough to solve complex world problems alone. Particularly under the current economic constraints, investors must leverage their nonfinancial assets—offering grantees not just funding but such critical services as expertise in strategic planning and capacity building, access to partnerships, and public support or advocacy. Some creative philanthropic investors even provide grantees with back-office technology and support for core functions such as marketing and HR, to help maximize their programs' impact.

* * *

Developing a strategy for social change that is both ambitious and realistic is without question hard work. It's also true that many philanthropic investors haven't been rigorous enough in their pursuit of such strategies. But when they are, the results can be game changing, as the experience of the Edna McConnell Clark Foundation (EMCF) demonstrates. For the past nine years EMCF has been committed to promoting the growth of youth-development nonprofits with evidence-based programs. Consciously avoiding the traps discussed above, its leaders have adjusted the foundation's grant-making approach and realigned its staff and processes. The payoff for this self-imposed commitment to maximizing impact? After learning from grantees and its own analysis that finding sustainable funding was the primary roadblock to further growth, EMCF was able to partner with 19 other funders to create an innovative $120 million growth capital fund to support the expansion of three of its grantees with proven outcomes: Nurse-Family Partnership, Youth Villages, and Citizen Schools.

By embracing the disciplined approach we've outlined, other philanthropic investors, too, can freely explore breakthrough ideas for social change and also demonstrate how seriously they view their public trust. But this pursuit of excellence *must* be self-imposed.

STRATEGIC DECISIONS INVESTORS FACE

Funding organizations committed to continual improvement need
to ask themselves rigorous questions such as:

- What mission, vision, and values will guide our work?

- What program areas will we invest in, and how will we allocate resources?

- What leaders will we hire, and what authority will they have?

- Which principles and approaches must be consistent throughout our institution, and which should be at a program's discretion?

- Which program strategies will we pursue?

- How will we set annual goals for programs and initiatives, and how will we respond to emerging opportunities?

- How will we cultivate grantees and partners?

- How will we handle external communications and the brand?

- How will we determine our positions on public policy or controversial topics?

- How will we flag and approve risky grants?

Harvard Business Review

This article originally appeared in the December 2008 issue of the Harvard Business Review.

Delivering on the Promise of Nonprofits

Nonprofit leaders face unique challenges in achieving results, but a growing number are showing it can be done—by rigorously confronting questions related to strategy, capital, and talent.

By Jeffrey L. Bradach, Thomas J. Tierney, and Nan Stone

Ending violence in inner-city communities, educating disadvantaged children, stemming the loss of rain forests or marine wildlife—U.S. nonprofits are being asked to take on an increasing share of society's most important and difficult work. At the same time, the expectations being placed on these organizations to show results—by their staff members, their boards, and public and private donors—are rising. How are nonprofits responding? By being much more explicit about the results they intend to deliver and the strategies and organizations they'll create to achieve those outcomes.

Consider the following example. Ten years ago, Rheedlen Centers for Children and Families had a $7 million budget and a truly herculean mission: to improve the lives of poor children in America's most devastated communities. It provided New Yorkers with family support networks, a homelessness-prevention program, a senior center, and a host of programs to meet the needs of troubled and impoverished children and teenagers. Among them was the Harlem Children's Zone, a fledgling neighborhood initiative based in a 24-block area in south-central Harlem.

Despite Rheedlen's many good programs, however, the prospects for Harlem's children appeared to be getting worse, not better. For Geoffrey Canada, the nonprofit's longtime CEO, the imperative was clear: To help the greatest possible number of kids lead healthy lives, stay in school, and grow up to become independent, productive adults, Rheedlen would have to step up its performance. So in 2002, it changed its name and sharpened its focus. Now simply called the Harlem Children's Zone (HCZ), the agency linked its original mission to a very concrete statement of the impact it intended to have: namely, that 3,000 children, ages 0 to 18, living in the zone should have demographic and achievement profiles consistent with those found in an average U.S. middle-class community.

With support from the board and major funders, particularly the Edna McConnell Clark Foundation, Canada and his team discontinued or transitioned out of activities that were no longer in line with HCZ's intended impact (such as homelessness prevention programs outside the zone) and took on new ones (such as a Head Start program and a charter elementary school). They also diversified HCZ's funding, shook up and expanded its management ranks, and invested precious dollars in evaluating results. By 2004, HCZ had more than doubled in scope, encompassing 60 square blocks that housed some 6,500 children. In 2007, the organization added another 37 square blocks—housing 4,000 kids—to the zone. Over the same five-year period, its budget grew from $11.6 million to $50 million. Civic and nonprofit leaders in other cities have expressed interest in replicating HCZ's approach.

HCZ's is not an isolated case. During the past eight years, we have worked with more than 150 nonprofits whose executive directors and boards are committed to increasing their organizations' social impact. We have yet to find one "best way" to do that, and we wouldn't expect to. Every organization faces unique challenges and opportunities, and the decisions its leaders make necessarily reflect those realities. The one constant, however, is a willingness to rigorously confront a few essential, interdependent questions:

• Which results will we hold ourselves accountable for?

• How will we achieve them?

• What will results really cost, and how can we fund them?

• How do we build the organization we need to deliver results?

Together, these questions create a framework that executive directors can use in candid conversations with stakeholders and in developing pragmatic, specific plans for making a tangible difference, whether that is measured in more high school graduates or in healthier oceans. Although the questions look easy and generic, answering them—and acting on the recommendations—is remarkably hard for many reasons. Ironically, the dynamics driving the nonprofit sector actually undermine its organizations' ability to focus on results, despite the mounting pressure to do just that.

The Challenge of Delivering Results in the Nonprofit Sector

A day in the life of an executive director is filled with fund-raising, board tending, and "fire" extinguishing. Meanwhile, staff members work long hours in bare-bones facilities. These are stereotypes, sure, but like most stereotypes, they contain a kernel of truth. Leaders and employees of nonprofit organizations are constantly being pulled in different directions to serve multiple constituencies. This "scatterization" is as much a function of how the nonprofit sector is organized as it is of how the organizations themselves operate.

In the business world, market forces serve as feedback mechanisms. Companies that perform well are rewarded by customers and investors; underperformers are penalized. Performance is relatively easy to quantify through quarterly earnings, ROI, customer loyalty scores, and the like. Moreover, such metrics can be calibrated and compared, ensuring that the companies producing the best results will attract capital and talent. Managers are encouraged to invest in the people, systems, and infrastructure needed to continue delivering superior performance. And internal feedback mechanisms, from up-to-the-minute operating data to performance reviews, keep everyone focused on critical activities and goals.

In the nonprofit world, missions, not markets, are the primary magnets attracting essential resources—from donors inspired by organizations' audacious goals; from board members, who not only volunteer their time and expertise but also often serve as major funders; and from employees, who accept modest paychecks to do work they care passionately about. But missions are typically better at providing inspiration than direction. So it is not uncommon for key stakeholders to have deeply felt but divergent views about what the organization's chief priorities ought to be—and for those differences to be masked by the broad aspirations of the mission statement.

Assessing and comparing performance is also a more subjective and values-driven exercise for nonprofits than for companies. Given the diversity of the goals nonprofits pursue, there is no single quantitative or qualitative metric against which performance can be evaluated and ranked. Even when several organizations are aiming for the same goal—reducing school dropout rates, say—the absence of standard outcome measures makes it impossible to compare their performance.

Quirky, too, are the sector's funding flows, which often fail to reward high performance and are seldom reliable enough to justify significant investments in organizational capacity. A nonprofit's very success can provide an excuse for donors to stop giving, because the organization no longer "needs" their money. Both public and private funders overwhelmingly want to support programs (especially new ones) rather than overhead. So program proliferation trumps investment in existing programs, and the organization is strained on every front: Management ends up being undercompensated and overstretched. Operating systems and technology are often rudimentary.

Committing to deliver a defined set of results may sound unremarkable, but it is not easy for nonprofits given these dynamics. It involves forging new relationships with the external stakeholders who provide the funding and with the internal stakeholders who do the work—changes as profound and revolutionary as those that U.S. business leaders experienced when they embraced the quality movement decades ago.

Which Results Will We Hold Ourselves Accountable For?

The most fundamental—and perhaps most difficult—decision a nonprofit can make is to define the results it must deliver in order to be successful. That process entails translating the organization's mission into goals that are simultaneously compelling enough to attract ongoing support from stakeholders and specific enough to inform resource allocations.

One approach is for nonprofit leaders to formulate and agree upon what we call its *intended impact*. A strong intended-impact statement identifies both the beneficiaries of a nonprofit's activities and the benefits the organization will provide—that is, the change in behavior, knowledge, or status quo its programs are designed to effect. Such specificity gives decision makers a powerful lens to use when they have to make trade-offs among worthy, competing priorities. To see the difference between a mission and an intended-impact statement, consider this example from Larkin Street Youth Services, a San Francisco–based nonprofit that is nationally recognized for its work with homeless and runaway youths. Larkin Street's mission is "to create a continuum of services that inspires youth to move beyond the street. We will nurture potential, promote dignity, and support bold steps by all." The intended-impact statement drills down further: Help homeless youths, ages 12 to 24, in the San Francisco Bay area develop the self-sufficiency and skills to live independently.

Discussions about an organization's intended impact tend to be iterative, inclusive (drawing in board as well as staff members), and incredibly hard. One source of difficulty: Legitimate needs invariably outstrip any single organization's ability to meet them. So by clarifying its strategy and scope, the nonprofit is also determining what it will *not* do. Should the Natural Resources Defense Council's oceans program work to block offshore oil drilling or to promote more responsible management of fisheries? Should STRIVE, a job training organization, focus on the chronically unemployed, who are the most difficult to serve, or on those with the best chance of rapidly reentering the workforce? These are tough choices, without "right" answers. But only by making them can a nonprofit align its limited resources with the activities that will have the greatest impact.

There is no standard template for an intended-impact statement, but organizational values, data, and a willingness to make tough decisions are all part of the mix.

Organizational values. An especially helpful way to begin a discussion about intended impact is to identify an anchor that is embedded in the organization's values and history. Four types exist: target population (in Larkin Street's case, homeless youths, ages 12 to 24), target outcomes (self-sufficiency), geography (San Francisco), and approach (continuum of care). The organization ultimately must address all these dimensions—who, what, where, and how—in order to develop an intended-impact statement that can be acted on. But it helps to have one fixed starting point on which all the stakeholders can agree.

Data. Objective information plays an equally critical role in developing a realistic intended-impact statement: What is the magnitude and nature of the need for our activities? What are our relative strengths and weaknesses? What resources are required to achieve the outcomes we hope for, and how likely are they to be available? Bringing hard data to bear on questions like these promotes better decision making and builds consensus. Although Larkin Street's decision to keep its direct services focused on the Bay area may have been rooted in the organization's history, it was solidly reinforced by statistics showing that there were nearly four times as many homeless youths in San Francisco as there were providers to help them.

Making tough choices. Because hard choices, especially those with tangible human costs, need to be made, nonprofit leaders must be able to build agreement among stakeholders while avoiding the paralysis of endless discussions about what the organization should be doing. When the Harlem Children's Zone decided to hand the management of its senior center over to another agency, it was extremely difficult for many staff members—not so much because of the effect on them personally but because of the effect on the people they would no longer be assisting. What ultimately made it possible for everyone to rally around was analysis showing how much of HCZ's discretionary funding the center was absorbing—dollars that could be reallocated to help kids.

How Will We Achieve Results?

When time and money have to be allocated among various programs and activities, identifying the most effective initiatives isn't easy. Nor is the logic supporting those decisions likely to be transparent. That is why *theory-of-change work*—explaining how the organization, working alone or with others, will achieve its intended impact—is so critical. The process ensures that stakeholders understand why strategic decisions are being made as they are; it also unearths assumptions about programs and services that can then be tested and revised as necessary. A strong theory of change is broad enough to show the scope of an organization's beliefs about how social change occurs (including, where appropriate, the activities of others) but specific enough to allow decision makers to map programs and resources against it. (See the exhibit "One Blueprint for Delivering Results," next page.)

Like intended-impact work, theory-of-change discussions are iterative, and several options may be plausible for achieving a given set of results. For example, teacher training, curriculum reform, an extended school day, and personalized instruction might all be levers for improving graduation rates among disadvantaged youths in urban high schools. The "right" approach will depend in part on what the leaders of an organization believe they ought to be doing. An even bigger factor will be what they learn as they analyze their organization's capabilities and economics, and gather information about what others are doing—for example, whether similar programs already exist and which ones are being funded by whom.

Several issues pop up routinely in theory-of-change work. One is the question of proof: Which elements have been shown to create positive results? Formal evaluations, which document the link between a particular program or activity and a set of positive outcomes, are time-consuming, costly, and difficult to get funded, so most organizations can't answer this question definitively. Even so, many fields do have a growing body of academic research about what really works—for instance, studies on climate change or early childhood development. Decision makers need to be familiar with any such information, especially since what may look like a nuance—whether a tutor meets with a child once a week or twice, for example—can be central to a program's success.

Another challenge is determining where one organization's work begins and ends relative to the work of others. Jumpstart, a national nonprofit that mentors young children in Head Start programs who are falling behind, offers a good illustration. Jumpstart focuses on providing tutors who are well trained to support the intellectual and emotional development of their tutees. But should the organization also develop programs focused on the children's families? Jumpstart's leadership had to wrestle with that question because the organization's intended impact is school readiness, and it is abundantly clear that families are crucial in helping children succeed in school. But given Jumpstart's limited resources, and the fact that it couldn't drive change on both fronts, the organization decided to stay focused on increasing the number of kids it could serve.

ONE BLUEPRINT FOR DELIVERING RESULTS

Since its founding in 1984, San Francisco–based Larkin Street Youth Services has become a model of innovative and effective service provision for homeless and runaway youths. The organization's theory of change, refined in 2007 and presented here, articulates its beliefs about how Larkin Street can achieve its intended impact.

Mission
"To create a continuum of services that inspires youth to move beyond the street. We will nurture potential, promote dignity, and support bold steps by all."

Theory of Change
Larkin Street's continuum of care raises the hope, optimism, and self-esteem of youths by:

• making homeless youths aware of services through outreach
• meeting youths where they are and addressing immediate needs
• providing a stable living situation and supportive environment
• increasing life skills and connecting youths with jobs and education

This continuum of care is continually refined through collaboration across programs and access to evaluation data.

Larkin Street disseminates best practices and informs thought leaders through presentations, publication of brief reports, and advocacy activities.

Direct Impact
Larkin Street helps homeless youths ages 12 to 24 in San Francisco to live independently.

Indirect Impact
Other organizations employ Larkin Street's best practices for serving homeless youths.

Thought leaders and policy makers envision and enact better policies for homeless youths.

Finally, theory-of-change work highlights gaps between what is supposed to happen and what is actually occurring. It is not unusual to find, for instance, that the people using a nonprofit's services are not the intended beneficiaries. Or an organization may discover a discrepancy between what its leaders think is required for its programs to be effective (the length of time that people participate, say) and how the programs are being delivered. This was the case for Expeditionary Learning Schools (ELS), which trains teachers to educate students through real-world projects called learning expeditions.

Multiple evaluations by independent researchers showed that the ELS model could improve student learning and performance when implemented with fidelity. For a low-performing school, that meant having ELS staff members work on-site with its leadership and faculty 30 days a year for at least three years. In 2004, ELS received significant funding from the Bill and Melinda Gates Foundation to extend its work to new small high schools in needy areas. Before expanding, however, ELS leadership wanted to assess the existing network. The results were bracing: Few of the schools were as highly engaged as they needed to be to achieve excellent results. After several soul-searching conversations, the ELS leadership team and board made the painful decision to exit schools unwilling to devote the time required to implement the nonprofit's curricular approach. Although that decision initially reduced the size of the network by nearly 25%, within three years the addition of new schools, excited by the model's rigor and thoughtfulness, had more than compensated for the loss.

Constraining overhead inhibits the very systems and staff the nonprofit needs to achieve its intended impact.

What Will Results Really Cost, and How Can We Fund Them?

A theory of change that can't be funded isn't real. And yet nonprofits almost never have enough money to cover everything they are already doing, let alone surplus funds to support new activities and investments. So hard choices inevitably appear as leaders determine which outcomes they can reasonably achieve given current and potential levels of support. If they are to make the necessary trade-offs, reaching financial clarity has to be their first order of business: This entails understanding the full costs of current programs and how each is affecting the organization's overall financial health. Does the program cover its own costs? Does it require a subsidy? Generate a surplus? Although it might seem as though such information ought to be obvious, the environment in which nonprofits operate tends to make it opaque.

What do things cost? Nonprofits' financial systems typically are rudimentary. Much of Finance's time goes to preparing individual reports for multiple funders about their specific program grants or contracts. Moreover, grants and contracts usually set arbitrary limits—invariably too low—on how much of the money can be used for overhead. This pattern of constraining overhead, which we will talk more about later, both obscures the real costs of essential activities and inhibits investments in the very systems and staff that would enable the nonprofit to achieve its intended impact.

Financial clarity often leads to surprising insights. For example, a youth-development nonprofit launched a culinary enterprise, which involved building a commercial kitchen and hiring local kids to work in it. Believing that a bottle of salad dressing cost $3.15 to produce, the organization sold it for $3.50, yielding a putative 35-cent profit. However, that estimate captured only direct expenses. When indirect expenses such as the kitchen manager's salary, facility expenses, and organizational overhead were appropriately allocated, the cost shot up to $90. What looked like a money maker was in fact a dramatic money loser.

Financial clarity also allows decision makers to assess the impact of their programs on both the organization's mission and its margins. (See the exhibit "Strategic and Financial Clarity.") The objective is not to do away with those that aren't earning their keep: Many essential programs cannot fully cover their own costs. Rather, it is to determine whether discretionary dollars are being used to support activities with the greatest potential to help the organization achieve its intended impact. It's not uncommon for nonprofits to discover—as HCZ did—that they are subsidizing programs lacking such potential. Or, conversely, to find that programs not completely aligned with the strategy are nonetheless worth maintaining because they throw off cash that can be applied to other areas.

Where does the money come from? In the for-profit sector, customers drive an organization's performance. If no one is willing to pay for a product or service, we say, "The market has spoken," and shut down the product line or even the organization. In the nonprofit sector, weak market forces exist—donors do decide whom to support, for example. But funders' choices are often influenced by personal relationships or the emotional appeal of the mission rather than by organizational performance. People will give millions of dollars to their alma maters without requiring clear evidence of performance. Yet they may stop funding organizations delivering demonstrable results when their personal interests shift, a phenomenon called donor fatigue.

As a consequence, nonprofits can be quite fragile financially. For example, a Bridgespan study of 17 well-known and successful youth-serving organizations found that two-thirds experienced at least one year of declining revenues between 1999 and 2003. Nearly one third dipped twice—and setbacks unrelated to performance led half to lay off staff and 45% to cut entire programs.

STRATEGIC AND FINANCIAL CLARITY

Once a nonprofit's leaders hone their organization's intended impact and get an accurate picture of its finances, they can use the matrix below to classify their programs and identify strategic options.

Alignment with intended impact (strategy)		negative	positive
	high	These programs **require funding**. Pursue opportunities for additional funding and/or cost improvements.	These programs are **self-sustaining**. Invest in and grow them.
	low	These programs are **potential distractions**. Find ways to improve them, or reconsider participation.	These programs **generate income**. Pursue them unless they become a management distraction.

**Financial contribution
(revenue minus cost)**

How can nonprofit leaders develop a reliable funding base? There is no simple answer, but they can begin by bringing their funding and their strategies into better alignment. We have seen them do that in several ways.

First, they very clearly articulate what the organization needs financial support for, and they identify appropriate sources to meet those needs. Larkin Street relies extensively on government funding, which has accounted for two-thirds of its revenues for many years. In contrast, HCZ relies heavily on individual contributions. The activities nonprofits pursue may lend themselves to one financial model or another (and the model may change as an organization gets larger), so it is important to invest over time in building the capabilities to attract and manage appropriate types of funding. Cultivating private donors requires capabilities very different from those needed to apply for government grants and respond to RFPs, for example.

Nonprofit leaders also must look hard at the true costs—both tangible and intangible—associated with potential revenue. Will accepting proffered funds mean executing on the donor's strategy instead of the organization's own? Will the value of the funding be reduced by the donors' excessive reporting requirements, overly long and unpredictable decision processes, or aversion to covering appropriate overhead?

Perhaps most important, both nonprofit leaders and funders need to stop pulling punches—with themselves and others—and confront the reality of what it will cost to deliver results. Knowing that a new program will require $500,000 to implement, raising one-fifth of that, and then attempting to initiate it with the hope that "more will come in later on" or that "something is better than nothing" is standard operating procedure among too many nonprofits. That is a recipe for disappointment and disillusion all around.

How Do We Build the Organization We Need to Deliver Results?

When it comes to delivering and sustaining results, having the right people in the right positions trumps having the right strategy or even a reliable source of capital. In this respect, many nonprofits are fortunate. Their leaders are passionate, entrepreneurial, and hardworking. Their ranks are filled with dedicated people motivated more by the opportunity to help others than by personal economic incentives.

But while nonprofits tend to be strongly led, they also tend to be undermanaged. As a result, they are often marked by persistent confusion about roles and responsibilities and by opaque decision making. These issues play out at every level of the organization: between the board and the executive director, between the executive director and the staff, and, in larger networks, between the center and the affiliates. As the executive director of Communities in Schools observed before bringing in a chief operating officer, "There were a whole series of issues around who had access to decisions, who would get money, who wouldn't....We had absolutely no framework for defining what were reasonable expectations and what were not."

Such confusion leads to the repeated reinvention of virtually every process, especially in organizations filled with volunteers whose institutional memory can be very short. The costs show up both in a weakened ability to achieve results for beneficiaries and in burnout among volunteers and staff members. As Rob Waldron noted when he was the CEO of Jumpstart, "We have to muscle everything we do, and eventually you just get tired!"

Creating better processes. Staff members may feel passionate, but in Bridgespan surveys they also report feeling undersupported and underdeveloped professionally. The absence of processes for setting employees' goals and obtaining feedback, for instance, disconnects individuals and their performance from the organization's strategy. In one nonprofit that pairs mentors with disadvantaged kids, staff members were repeatedly told that the organization's priorities extend beyond the number of matches made to include other dimensions, such as their quality and presence in hard-to-serve communities. But when the time came for performance reviews, staffers were assessed and rewarded only on the first, most easily quantifiable metric. Recognizing this problem, senior leadership redesigned the process to include data and qualitative feedback on the other dimensions and began to reward people who performed well against all the priorities. This story is an exception, however. Few nonprofit directors devote so much energy to improving processes.

Building leadership capacity. Although nonprofits are growing in scale and facing increased pressure to perform, they're not doing nearly as much as they must to attract, retain, and develop a cadre of leaders and managers. A recent study by the Eugene and Agnes E. Meyer Foundation and CompassPoint Nonprofit Services reported that three-quarters of the executive directors surveyed planned to leave their positions within five years. Among the reasons, anxiety about fundraising and shaky financial sustainability—their organizations' and their own—loomed large. And even though many organizations need executives with specialized skills (such as chief operating and chief financial officers) to implement their strategies, the comparatively low compensation levels in the nonprofit sector can be a significant barrier to filling those positions—and to retaining talented people more generally. That is why the willingness to provide fair pay in exchange for topflight executive performance will be a key differentiator between nonprofits that can deliver great results consistently and those that cannot.

Distinguishing between good and bad overhead. The phenomenon most to blame for inefficiencies in nonprofits is something we noted earlier: resistance by just about everyone, including the general public, to supporting overhead. The word itself is disparaging, suggesting wasteful or unnecessary expenses. But there is a difference between good overhead and bad. Investing in an IT system that can track program results is good; paying excessive rent for opulent office space is bad. Attempts to limit all overhead blur this distinction and severely undermine nonprofits' ability to invest in the people and HR processes necessary to deliver great results year after year.

Nonprofits' most common and pernicious response to this phenomenon is to both underinvest in infrastructure and underreport what they've spent—thereby reinforcing external expectations about what is (and isn't) appropriate. In the short run, staff members may be able to "do more with less," but ultimately the organization's beneficiaries suffer.

Nonprofit leaders who understand the link between developing capacity and achieving results are pushing back—by identifying the positions and infrastructure that will be required to implement their strategies, by making those needs transparent to funders, and by communicating the logic that supports those investments throughout their organizations and to their boards.

***

No question, a nonprofit's journey from aspirations to impact is a challenging one. Moreover, this pursuit is largely self-imposed, as nonprofits do not typically confront the customer defections, market-share battles, and quarterly earnings reports that shape executive behavior in the for-profit world. There is still a lot of voluntarism in these organizations: Board members donate both time and money. Executives serve a cause rather than maximizing their own compensation. Philanthropists donate their hard-earned wealth. Legions of community members contribute their time. So the executive director of a nonprofit cannot simply impose her or his perspective on this diverse group of personally motivated stakeholders.

Instead, the discipline of leadership must replace the discipline of markets. The executive director shoulders the heavy burden of engaging key stakeholders in a rigorous consensus-building process, in which all parties confront the fundamental questions in this article—and fully embrace the subsequent answers.

When such leadership is complemented by donors, board members, and staff members who are equally committed to excellence, the results—whether measured in clearer skies, fewer homeless families, or more college graduates—can be outstanding.

HOW DONORS CAN HELP NONPROFITS ACHIEVE RESULTS

The basic imbalance between philanthropists and nonprofits—one group has the money the other group desperately needs—gives donors enormous power. Whether their money actually helps the recipients deliver greater results depends on how they give it, not just how much they give. To that end, here are four guideposts for individual donors and foundations.

Understand that the results aren't "ours." Donors can influence the behavior of the nonprofits they fund, but when they impose their own priorities, they risk compromising the nonprofits' ability to deliver results. Achieving impact through nonprofit organizations thus demands a shared understanding of priorities between donors and recipients. Such consensus building takes time and effective collaboration. Personal opinions must yield to data, and personal motivations must take a backseat to common goals.

Realize that everything takes longer and costs more. Like nonprofits, philanthropists have an alarming tendency to underestimate what it costs to produce results. Instead of placing appropriately sized bets on well-defined strategies, donors often spread too little money among too many recipients. Sophisticated donors recognize when nonprofits are ripe for deeper investment in the form of more money over longer periods of time.

Invest in good overhead. B-level leadership teams will not deliver A-level results. Yet donors are inclined to fund programs while minimizing overhead, including essential expenses such as basic infrastructure and leadership development. Donors must be willing to invest in capacity building for the organizations they support and hold them clearly accountable for generating results.

Remember that excellence is self-imposed. Philanthropy exists in a world without marketplace pressures. Donors don't actually have to do much good in order to feel good. Nor do foundations go out of business because they miss their numbers in consecutive quarters. Quite the contrary: Thanks to the unfailingly positive feedback donors receive, mediocrity is easily perpetuated. Those who are serious about making a real impact must first establish the results for which they will hold themselves accountable and then align their grant making appropriately.

IDEA IN PRACTICE

In response to the growing pressure for nonprofits to demonstrate that they are achieving results, their leaders should be able to answer the following key questions:

Which results will we hold ourselves accountable for? Example: Despite the variety of programs Rheedlen Centers for Children and Families (now the Harlem Children's Zone) offered to help inner-city youths, outcomes for kids weren't improving. So the organization revamped itself around a very concrete set of goals: namely, that 3,000 children, ages 0 to 18, living in a 24-block area in south-central Harlem should have demographic and achievement profiles consistent with those found in an average U.S. community.

How will we achieve results? Example: Expeditionary Learning Schools (ELS) trains teachers to educate students through real-world projects. To achieve results in a low-performing school, ELS staff members must work on-site 30 days a year for at least three years. When the organization assessed its existing network, it found that few schools were as engaged as they needed to be to attain excellent results. ELS made the painful decision to exit sites unwilling to devote the time required to implement its curricular approach.

What will results really cost, and how can we fund them? Example: Larkin Street Youth Services relies heavily on government funding. Because grants and contracts often set arbitrary limits on overhead, obscuring the real costs of essential activities, the organization has had to clearly articulate what it needs financial support for and identify appropriate sources to meet those needs.

How do we build the organization we need to deliver results? Example: Geoffrey Canada, CEO of Harlem Children's Zone, actively engaged staff members and funders in a disciplined process of organizational change. In drawing up their plan, the CEO and his team were willing to question just about every aspect of the organization: They discontinued some activities, diversified funding, shook up and expanded management ranks, and invested money in new IT systems. After doing that, Canada was able to secure multiyear financial commitments from several major funders.

This article originally appeared in the Spring 2008 issue of the Stanford Social Innovation Review.

More Bang for the Buck

Scores of pundits have written books, research reports, and articles about how business leaders extracted greater productivity from their companies. Yet few have paid attention to this topic in the nonprofit sector. Recognizing that increasing productivity could be a powerful way for nonprofit organizations to multiply the impact of their work, the authors explore how three nonprofits succeeded in reducing costs without sacrificing the quality of their services.

By Alex Neuhoff and Robert Searle

In virtually every for-profit industry, stiff competition breeds economic efficiency. Success hinges on producing more goods or services at a lower cost without compromising quality—that is, on increasing productivity. The classic example of the benefits of productivity gains is Henry Ford's adoption of the assembly line, an innovation that allowed his company to build more reliable cars at a faster pace and at a lower cost—transforming the automobile from a plaything for the wealthy to an everyday tool for ordinary Americans.

But in the nonprofit world, organizations have few external incentives to operate more efficiently. Indeed, many people are actually suspicious of efforts to increase nonprofit productivity. At a recent meeting of 20 nonprofit leaders, for example, we presented some of the Bridgespan Group's findings about the growth in size of nonprofits that serve young people. When we broached the topic of economies of scale—that is, the idea that larger organizations can produce more goods and services for less—most attendees said that they simply could not increase their productivity without compromising the quality of their services.

If these skeptics are correct, then the only way that nonprofits can increase their impact is by raising and spending more money. Yet for-profit companies routinely preserve and even improve the quality of their goods and services without increasing their costs. If nonprofits could be equally savvy about how they spend their existing dollars—that is, if they could increase their productivity—they could get more bang for their buck.

Some nonprofits, such as Teach for America, have achieved exactly this result. Since its inception in 1989, the organization has recruited and trained 17,000 college graduates to teach in some of the country's neediest schools. Between 2001 and 2005, the cost to develop each Teach for America teacher increased 12 percent each year. But at the same time, the percentage of Teach for America teachers who hit their performance benchmarks increased about 24 percent each year. And so although the organization's cost per teacher increased during this period, its cost per *successful* teacher decreased by approximately 10 percent each year.

Teach for America is not the only nonprofit that has increased its productivity. Our recent study reveals that Jumpstart and Year Up, two other nonprofits serving young people, have also found ways to deliver the same or better services without increasing their costs. (See "Three Productive Nonprofits" for more information about these organizations.)

So productivity gains can happen—nonprofits can increase their efficiencies. But they don't *just* happen. Productive nonprofits standardize their best practices, invest in essential people and processes, manage their costs, and measure their progress. Adopting these practices is not easy, because of the nature of nonprofits' work and prevailing funding practices. Nevertheless, Teach for America, Jumpstart, and Year Up all managed to overcome these obstacles and multiply their impact.

Not surprisingly, these findings largely dovetail with those of researchers who have examined productivity in other sectors. But although there are scores of studies related to productivity in the for-profit sector, we have not been able to identify comparable studies in the nonprofit sector. We hope this small study sparks many more.[1]

THREE PRODUCTIVE NONPROFITS

	Jumpstart	Teach For America	Year Up
Year founded	1993	1989	2000
Revenue (2005)	$11.3 million	$40.5 million	$5.5 million
Mission	Working toward the day every child in America enters school prepared to succeed	To enlist our nation's most promising future leaders in the movement to eliminate educational inequality	In the future, every urban young adult will have access to the education, experiences, and guidance required to realize his or her true potential
Program description	Corps members establish one-to-one relationships with preschool students and work with families to help them incorporate language and literacy into the daily activities of their children	TFA recruits and trains college graduates and places them in two-year teaching roles in some of the country's highest-need schools	Urban young adults ages 18 to 24 engage in an intensive training program, focused on a combination of technical and professional skills, college credits, and a paid corporate apprenticeship
Output measure	Number of students	Number of teachers (as a proxy for the number of students)	Number of students
Outcome measure	Number of students with greater gains in school readiness than comparison group	Number of teachers whose students achieve significant gains	Number of students placed in livable-wage jobs
Average annual change in cost per outcome	-6% (2000-04)	-10% (2001-05)	-9% (2001-05)

Two Paths to Productivity

Measuring productivity can be a tricky matter, even in the for-profit sector. Companies often have to go beyond tracking cost per widget produced. A classic example is that of the tire manufacturer. When a consumer buys a tire, he or she typically takes into account not just the cost of the tire but also the number of miles it will travel. Technological advancements may increase the cost of each tire, but decrease the cost of each mile traveled on it—and the latter is the metric that matters most to the consumer. The tire company that focuses on cost per tire is likely to be bested by one that grasps the true *unit of value* to the consumer and focuses on tire cost per mile traveled.

This same concept of value applies to the work of nonprofits. It's not cost per output (such as a youth served) that provides a window into productivity, but rather cost per outcome (a youth who achieves the results targeted by the organization). Here's where things get more complicated for nonprofits, though. Although it's relatively easy to calculate tire cost per mile (i.e., the tire's total cost divided by the number of miles it will go), it's far harder to calculate dollars required for a nonprofit to achieve an outcome, for reasons we will explore below.

Let's back up and define some terms. *Outputs* are the amount of work a nonprofit does—in other words, the quantity of the programs or services it delivers. In the case of Year Up, this would be the number of students participating in the program. *Outcomes,* in contrast, are the *results* of the nonprofit's work—in other words, the benefits for participants during or after their involvement with the organization. At Year Up this would be the number of graduating students placed in livable-wage jobs. Finally, the *success rate* reflects the number of outputs that turn into outcomes—for example, the ratio of students in the program to those who go on to get jobs paying a livable wage.

As the equation below illustrates, there are two paths to increasing a nonprofit's productivity: reduce the costs of producing each output, or increase the number of outputs that turn into outcomes—in other words, increase the success rate. In practice, as these nonprofits show, organizations typically work on both facets of the equation.

Cost per output		**Success rate**		**Cost per outcome**
$\dfrac{\text{Cost}}{\text{Output}}$	X	$\dfrac{\text{Outputs}}{\text{Outcome}}$	=	$\dfrac{\text{Cost}}{\text{Outcome}}$

Jumpstart improved its productivity by decreasing its cost per output while holding its success rate steady. Jumpstart's mission is to work toward the day when every child in America will enter school prepared to succeed. To this end, corps members work one-on-one with preschool students and their families to incorporate language and literacy into daily activities. The organization's output is the total number of students with whom corps members work, and its outcome is the number of students who achieve greater gains in school readiness than a comparison group.

At Jumpstart, staff salaries are the greatest expense. In 2002 management noticed that the organization's Boston site had twice as many staff members as its other sites, yet the other sites still turned out similar numbers of children ready for school. Armed with these data, Jumpstart could reduce the number of its Boston-region staff by almost half without worrying that it would be compromising the quality of its outcomes.[2] In other words, Jumpstart reduced its cost per output by halving the number of salaries it paid at its Boston site while serving the same number of children equally well.

Year Up likewise increased its productivity by reducing its cost per output. But the organization first had to spend money to save money. As part of its intensive training program, Year Up pays its students a biweekly stipend for the hours they have worked at their internships. Historically, Year Up gathered time sheets manually and processed the checks internally—a time-intensive process. Seeing more growth and expense on the horizon, the organization invested in a centralized mechanism for collecting student data at all of its sites. An automated process then translates the data into a format accessible for a payroll outsourcing partner, providing a scalable solution to a potentially expensive challenge.[3] And so the organization is able to train the same number of young people for less cost.

Teach for America, in contrast, improved its success rate. It did so by increasing the number of its recruits who turned into truly effective educators. As this example illustrates, efficiencies sometimes come from spending more money, not less: Spending more on each teacher increased the number of teachers who later proved successful in front of their classrooms. By spending more money on *outputs*, organizations may wind up spending less on *outcomes* because they increase their success rates.

The converse is also true. Reducing the cost per output can increase the cost per outcome if the measures taken to cut costs hurt the organization's success rates. Consider, for example, a youth development organization that assigns youths to case workers. If its leaders decide to try increasing caseloads as a cost saving measure—say by having case managers work with six youths each instead of its past standard practice of working with four—they could very well be disappointed. The larger caseloads could decrease the effectiveness of workers' interactions, with the resulting decline in the organization's success rate more than trumping the salary cost savings. Such unintended consequences are one of the reasons that it is unwise to focus exclusively on either reducing costs or increasing success rates. Organizations have to consider the impact of their efforts on both variables to achieve the desired results.

How to Increase Productivity

Increased productivity doesn't just happen. Jumpstart, Teach for America, and Year Up observed four management basics: standardize best practices; invest in staff and critical activities; manage costs aggressively; and measure progress.

Standardize Best Practices. All three organizations discovered and spread their most cost-effective practices throughout their organizations.[4] Jumpstart, for example, has standardized every aspect of its program and made these practices available in hard copy guidebooks as well as on its intranet. Corps members can sign into the system at any time and get lesson plans and curricula. Teach for America has created a centralized information system to capture and share best practices. This sort of standardization helps to keep costs down by increasing efficiency: Staff spend less time reinventing the wheel and more time executing effective practices. It also ensures that all sites are using the practices that have been shown to lead to the best outcomes, which can have a positive effect on the organization's success rate.

Invest in Staff and Critical Activities. All three organizations invested more in the activities most important to the success of their programs and the sustainability of their organizations. For example, in 2000 Teach for America embarked on an ambitious five-year growth plan. The organization knew that in order to attract the best college graduates it would have to invest more in on-campus recruiting. It also added staff positions to its teacher training and support teams, invested in better data management and communications systems across regions, and made a commitment to pay higher salaries to attract and retain better talent. Teach for America's leaders point to highly qualified and well-resourced teachers as propelling the organization's healthy success rate, and strong teacher retention as offsetting recruiting and training investments.

Jumpstart also invested in building its management capacity, noting that when it comes to salaries, "paying more costs less." Although this may sound counterintuitive, the logic holds: Better compensation reduces turnover, increases the average experience level of the staff, and builds institutional knowledge.[5]

Manage Costs Aggressively. All three organizations paid a great deal of attention to managing their costs, particularly with respect to major costs like salaries. At Year Up, overhead and training stipends—for both the participating students and the companies that provide them with internships—are the organization's two biggest costs. To manage overhead, Year Up constantly monitors its administrative and personnel ratios to keep them as low as possible, even as class sizes grow. Training stipends receive similar scrutiny. Year Up analyzes and experiments with stipend levels at each of its four sites to determine the minimum level necessary to secure target student and company participation levels, thus ensuring that its cost per output remains low.

Measure Progress. All three organizations established performance measurement systems to give them timely feedback about their costs, outputs, and outcomes. Year Up, for example, has created a set of PowerPoint performance dashboards for reporting regularly on six critical areas of its work: recruiting and retaining talented staff, cultivating a solid student pipeline, teaching marketable skills, providing high-quality service to corporate partners, positioning students for ongoing success, and creating a sustainable program infrastructure. The management team then sets performance benchmarks and rates its progress against each benchmark.

Take the critical area "positioning students for ongoing success," for example. Year Up breaks this area down into three metrics: average starting wage, graduate employment, and college attendance by class. The associated dashboard charts the data in these three subareas and then rates the performance of each relative to the benchmark goals, using a green, yellow, or red traffic light icon.[6]

Why Nonprofits Don't Calculate Productivity

The three organizations in our study all tracked costs and measured outcomes. Yet none had brought its data together to calculate cost per outcome, even though all appreciated the value of this metric. One reason for this oversight is that as each organization accumulated experience, it refined its definition of a successful outcome, complicating the process of tracking the metric. Consider Jumpstart, which uses a tool called the "School Success Checklist" to assess its students' language, literacy, initiative, and social skills. As Jumpstart learned more about its programs and participants, it changed the checklist. In the 2001-02 school year Jumpstart increased the number of items from 10 to 15, and in 2003 it revised the ratings and subscales for each item yet again. To participate in our study, Jumpstart staff had to dig back into its historical data and restate them in terms of its new school success checklist.[7]

Another challenge to tracking cost per outcome is the lag between the time when an organization incurs program costs and the time when it can measure outcomes. For example, Jumpstart cannot possibly know whether students have improved until the end of the school year. In contrast, the organization can readily calculate cost per output (specifically, cost per tutor hour), a more immediately useful measure that helps Jumpstart's managers understand what is happening right now. As a result, the internal pressure to monitor costs naturally points people toward cost per output rather than cost per outcome.

The time lag between when an organization incurs costs and when it realizes outcomes is even more pronounced when it makes a large investment in its program or infrastructure, because these costs may all show up in one year. The benefits, in contrast, may take years to appear. For example, Teach for America's cost per outcome actually increased for several years while its investments were taking hold, only to decrease in the longer term.

Matching expenses to the outputs and outcomes of one specific cohort of youth is also difficult. For example, Teach for America's costs for a given fiscal year include the cost to support teachers who are already in the classroom and the costs to recruit and train new teachers, who will not teach until the following year. To calculate Teach for America's cost per outcome for this study, we had to break down and reassemble its cost, output, and outcome data.

Productivity Blocks

Without broader-based research, we cannot say how widespread reductions in cost per outcome are in the nonprofit sector. Nevertheless, on the basis of Bridgespan's work over the years with more than 100 nonprofits, we suspect that nonprofits do not regularly or fully realize such reductions. The reasons are many, but several additional barriers (besides the ones already mentioned) stand out in particular.

One of the impediments to achieving increased productivity is the lack of funding for nonprogram expenses. Building information systems to track outputs, outcomes, and costs requires money. The staff time needed to analyze the data is also not cheap. Many nonprofits simply do not have the money to make these investments, and foundations and other donors are often unwilling to provide the funding. As a result, many nonprofits have only a rudimentary understanding of what their true costs per outcome and output are.

A second reason why nonprofits do not pay more attention to productivity is that they face little pressure to do so. Some of the organizations in our study cited an internal desire to decrease their cost per outcome, but none of them mentioned any external pressure to do so. Businesses face unrelenting external pressure from customers and competitors to reduce prices while maintaining quality. Companies are also under pressure from investors to increase their earnings per share, which they can often achieve by increasing productivity.

When funders and other stakeholders do focus on nonprofits' costs, they most often scrutinize cost per output, not cost per outcome. Year Up, for example, usually reports the cost per participating student, not the cost per student placed in a living wage job. Similarly, Teach for America usually reports the cost to recruit, train, and place a teacher, not the cost to recruit, train, and place a *successful* teacher. Some funders even provide a fixed amount of funding per output. This focus on cost per output can be counterproductive if it is not married to a focus on maintaining or improving outcomes.

The difficulty of achieving scale presents another challenge. In the for-profit sector, building economies of scale is a well understood and oft-practiced way to increase efficiency. Although scale does not automatically decrease cost per outcome, it often allows an organization to spread fixed costs over more activities and to accumulate experience faster. And so growth can help an organization reduce costs and learn more quickly. The three organizations we studied are larger than average, but none is among the largest in the sector. Given the fragmented nature of the nonprofit sector, with the vast majority of organizations having annual budgets under $1 million, it may be hard for the average nonprofit to achieve economies of scale.[8]

Yet another barrier is the failure to sustain activities long enough to decrease their costs or improve their success rates. Foundations have a reputation for being more interested in supporting the next exciting idea than in continuing to support a proven idea or program. Accordingly, nonprofits that depend primarily on foundation support may find it difficult to sustain a given program—and therefore to accumulate the kind of experience that can lead to savings. The fact that two of the three organizations we studied received more funding from public sources than from foundations may not be entirely coincidental.[9]

Jumpstart, Teach for America, and Year Up all give real-world proof that maintaining quality while reducing cost is not only a theoretical goal but also a practical possibility. We hope that this research will inspire more nonprofits to track and manage their cost per outcome. We also hope that it will encourage more funders to shift their focus from cost per output to cost per outcome and to provide nonprofits with the long-term unrestricted support that will enable them to do the same.

We recognize that changing the rules of the funder-grantee game is never risk-free. Wrongly applied, external pressure on nonprofits to focus on cost per outcome could simply become yet another reporting burden on capacity-strapped organizations. Foundations may also be tempted to compare two organizations' cost per outcome without taking into account important differences between them, such as the populations they serve or the kinds of overhead that they have to bear.[10] Equally, it could lead nonprofits to shift their costs, to serve less needy populations, or to make unsustainable cost cuts.

Done right, however, reducing cost per outcome will lead to more bang for the nonprofit buck—a greater impact across the whole range of issues that nonprofits grapple with on society's behalf. And impact, after all, is the true bottom line of nonprofit work.

The authors thank the nonprofit executives of the profiled organizations for sharing their experiences and data. We also thank our colleagues from the Bridgespan Group— Jeff Bradach, Meghan Gouldin, Jennifer Lee, Gail Perreault, and Nan Stone—for their thoughtful contributions.

OUR RESEARCH METHODS

We addressed two general questions in our study: Have any nonprofits maintained, or even improved, their outcomes while reducing costs? If so, how did they do it?

We first identified nonprofits with a reputation for achieving results and managing costs. To keep the analysis simple, we focused on single program, direct-service nonprofits in the fields of youth development and education. Three organizations emerged from our preliminary investigations—Jumpstart, Teach for America, and Year Up. For each organization we collected and analyzed a minimum of five years worth of cost, output, and outcome data. We also conducted detailed interviews with the organization's executive director, chief financial officer, director of research and evaluation, and other key people. Finally, we compared our findings to secondary research on efficiency studies in the public sector and in for-profit service companies.

In light of the composition and small size of our sample and the preliminary nature of the research, our findings are, at best, suggestive. Nevertheless, they do shed light on the central question of whether nonprofits can maintain, or even improve, the quality of their outcomes while reducing costs.
–A.N. & R.S.

Stanford SOCIAL
INNOVATION REVIEW

This article originally appeared in the Fall 2004 issue of the Stanford Social Innovation Review.

Zeroing in on Impact

In an era of declining resources, nonprofits need to clarify their intended impact.

By Susan J. Colby, Nan Stone, and Paul Carttar

Many nonprofit organizations have Goliath-sized aspirations.

Habitat for Humanity, a nonprofit that has built more than 150,000 homes in the United States and abroad since its founding in 1976, constructs a new house every 26 minutes, but its ultimate goal is even bigger—to "eliminate poverty housing and homelessness from the world, and to make decent shelter a matter of conscience and action."[1] The Natural Resources Defense Council, an environmental action organization with 1 million members and online activists, seeks to arrest global warming on an annual budget of $39 million,[2] just 1 percent of what the major car companies spend on advertising alone each year.[3] Harlem Children's Zone (HCZ), a nonprofit community-based organization that provides programming for more than 7,500 at-risk children in New York City, strives to "improve the lives of poor children in America's most devastated communities"—on an annual budget of less than $15 million.[4]

Developing practical, workable ways to achieve audacious and inspiring missions like these has always been a key ingredient in successful nonprofit leadership. And the challenge of mapping limited resources against seemingly unlimited needs is especially critical today, given declining government funding and the slowed growth of private contributions to nonprofits.[5]

Getting critical resource decisions right—allocating time, talent, and dollars to the activities that have the greatest impact—is what "strategy" is all about. Yet relatively few nonprofits have strategies in this pragmatic sense of the word.

The consequences of this financial squeeze are increasingly evident throughout the nonprofit sector. From small neighborhood organizations to large multiservice agencies, nonprofit leaders and their boards are reordering priorities and reducing programs and staff. The premium on ensuring that the right choices are made is great, and the stakes are high—for the individuals these organizations serve, and for society overall.

Getting critical resource decisions right—allocating time, talent, and dollars to the activities that have the greatest impact—is what "strategy" is all about. Yet relatively few nonprofits—even the most successful—have strategies in this pragmatic sense of the word. They have missions that define their reason for being. And they have programs and services that contribute toward the fulfillment of their missions. But when resource-allocation decisions have to be made among these activities, all of which do some good, determining those that will do the *most* good can be a difficult, often contentious task. Revising the organization's mission, so that it is narrowly focused on a finite set of objectives, is one way to resolve this dilemma. Another approach, and in our experience a better one,[6] is to help an organization's decision makers develop clarity, not about mission, but about what we call "intended impact" and "theory of change."[7]

Clarifying What Success Looks Like

A nonprofit's mission is essentially its reason for being, and it often encompasses ambitious—even visionary—goals. Consider Larkin Street Youth Services, a $9 million San Francisco-based nonprofit founded in 1984 that works with homeless youth. Larkin's mission is concise but sweeping: "to create a continuum of services that inspires youth to move beyond the streets."[8]

By 2003, the nonprofit was serving more than 2,000 youth through 18 programs at 10 sites across the city. That year, nearly 80 percent of the young people enrolled in its case management services exited life on the street. The breadth of Larkin's mission contributed significantly to its success by giving the organization the room to innovate and to expand programming in response to the evolving needs of homeless youth. This record of purposeful growth, in turn, has allowed Larkin to attract and retain high-caliber staff, as well as raise funds for its continued impact.

Larkin's management and board were eager to maintain this healthy cycle of service, innovation, and growth over the next five years. At the same time, the national economic downturn was casting an ever-darker shadow, and it was likely Larkin would have more opportunities to expand its impact than funding to support those opportunities. Faced with this prospect, Larkin's leadership, in conjunction with the Bridgespan Group, a nonprofit consulting firm, decided to clarify the agency's priorities in the context of intended impact and theory of change.

Intended impact and theory of change provide a bridge between a nonprofit's mission and its programmatic activities. Intended impact is a statement or series of statements about what the organization is trying to achieve and will hold itself accountable for within some manageable period of time. It identifies both the *benefits* the organization seeks to provide and the *beneficiaries*. Larkin leadership decided that their intended impact was to help San Francisco Bay Area homeless youth between the ages of 12 and 24 exit life on the street permanently. By specifying *which* youth the agency will focus on and the outcome that will constitute success, this intended impact clarifies Larkin's strategic priorities in a way the mission statement does not.

Theory of change explains how the organization's intended impact will actually happen, the cause-and-effect logic by which organizational and financial resources will be converted into the desired social results. Often an organization's theory of change will take into account not only its own resources but also those that others bring to bear. Larkin's leaders identified a theory of change premised on the belief that young people need to rebuild (or build) hope, optimism, and self-esteem to take advantage of the educational and employment opportunities that will allow them to exit life on the street. To help homeless youth develop this inner strength, Larkin provides a *continuum* of services, which includes reaching out to kids on the street; addressing their immediate needs for food, medical care, and emergency housing; offering transitional housing and case management; and building life skills. While Larkin's theory of change entails a broad range of programmatic activities, all of its programs are focused on meeting the specific needs of Larkin's target beneficiaries.

Although the terms intended impact and theory of change may sound abstract, the effect of using them is anything but. By enabling an organization's leaders to clarify what "success" will look like in the near-to-medium term, intended impact and theory of change create a coherent framework for making tradeoffs that are truly strategic—tradeoffs that reflect the aspirations of the organization's mission as well as the constraints of its bottom line. To illustrate, consider two decisions that Larkin's management team made while developing the nonprofit's business plan.

Guided by Larkin's theory of change, which emphasizes not only meeting youth where they are on the streets, but keeping them engaged until they are able to leave the streets, the management team decided to develop an innovative new residential facility for youth with both mental health and substance abuse problems. But the question remained: Should the facility serve youth with the most extreme disorders or should it concentrate on those with less severe troubles, who have a better shot at leaving the streets? Both options had strong support within the organization, but each population required a different sort of program and Larkin didn't have the resources to support both. To resolve the issue, Larkin's management turned to its newly clarified intended impact statement: The facility would serve less-troubled youth, because they had a better chance of ultimately transitioning to independent living.

HOW DO YOU KNOW YOU'VE ARRIVED?

An actionable intended impact...

- Links in a compelling way to your mission and vision for social change.
- Specifies the outcomes you seek to create for your beneficiaries.
- Affords sufficient control over outcomes to enable real accountability.
- Is realistic and achievable, given your capabilities.
- Is measurable on an accurate, timely basis.
- Provides an effective platform for making strategic tradeoffs, especially those related to program focus and resource-allocation decisions.

A coherent theory of change...

- Identifies the most important needs of your chosen beneficiaries.
- Articulates the most important leverage points to meet those needs.
- Links your solutions to your beneficiaries' needs through a chain of cause-and-effect relationships.
- Is empirically plausible if not proven.

Intended impact and theory of change work is an iterative process, informed by an organization's values and beliefs as well as by hard data—its operations and economics, and about the activities of other organizations addressing the same issues or problems. One question inevitably leads to another, and the discussions often cycle back and forth between intended impact and theory of change, as participants engage in the messy work of clarifying what, specifically, will constitute success. Some organizations will start by identifying their intended impact, while others might arrive first at their theory of change. Not surprisingly, therefore, it is usually most helpful to begin the process with one or more open-ended questions.

To get at intended impact, for example, nonprofit leaders can start with questions such as: Who are our beneficiaries? What benefits do our programs create? How do we define success? What *won't* we do? What would make us obsolete?

Nonprofits can clarify their theory of change by asking questions like: What is the cause-and-effect logic that gets us from our resources (people and dollars) to impact? Where are the gaps or leaps of faith in that logic chain? What are the most important elements of our programs' content and structure? What assumptions led us to choose these particular program elements? Are there other ways in which we could achieve the desired outcomes? What is the minimum length of time our beneficiaries need to be engaged to achieve these outcomes? What else do our beneficiaries need to achieve these outcomes?

To illustrate how one nonprofit used this process to clarify its strategy, consider the experience of Harlem Children's Zone.

'We Had Reached the End of Our Ability to Manage Growth'

The Harlem Children's Zone was founded in 1970 as Rheedlen Centers for Children and Families to combat truancy on Manhattan's Upper West Side. The organization grew rapidly during the 1990s under the leadership of Geoffrey Canada, its second executive director. By the end of the decade, Rheedlen had grown into a $10 million agency, serving 6,000 children. It was sponsoring 16 different programs, ranging from its highly regarded Beacon Schools, which offer educational, recreational, and youth development services during afternoon and evening hours, to a senior center, family support networks, and a program to prevent homelessness. Among its most prominent activities was the "Harlem Children's Zone," an initiative launched in 1997, which included seven programs ranging from "baby college" classes for new parents to a neighborhood revitalization effort—all located in a 24-block "zone" of central Harlem.

In 2000, the nonprofit was experiencing both the rewards and the challenges of this remarkable growth. Canada and his colleagues had been extremely successful in developing a diverse set of programs to advance Rheedlen's long-standing mission: "to improve the lives of poor children in America's most devastated communities." External interest in these programs was running high among experts in the youth-development field and among potential funders as eager as Canada himself to see the organization expand geographically and programmatically.

At the same time, the bevy of disparate programs was straining Rheedlen's organizational capacity, management systems, reporting structure, and finances. The agency simply didn't have the economic or managerial resources to accomplish everything it was trying to do. It was becoming increasingly apparent to Canada that if Rheedlen's impact were to continue to grow, he and his management team would need to make some hard choices about their activities and programs.

"We wanted to grow," Canada said. "We planned to grow. But we had reached the end of our ability to manage growth. I didn't want the limit on our future to be the fact that we weren't able to think strategically."

To develop strategic clarity, in March 2000 Canada and his team joined forces with the Edna McConnell Clark Foundation, a longtime Rheedlen funder with expertise in evaluation, and a team of consultants from the Bridgespan Group. Together they engaged in a series of discussions designed to clarify what Rheedlen aspired to achieve and how the organization would deliver those results.

As the Rheedlen team began to talk about the organization's intended impact and theory of change, the question of ends and means immediately arose. Which was their intended impact: improving the lives of poor children or rebuilding the social fabric of devastated communities? Since the agency's existing program portfolio pointed in both directions, and the management team's resource-allocation decisions going forward would be shaped by the answer, the question represented a critical fork in the road. Putting themselves on the hook for improving kids' lives would lead to very different program priorities than taking responsibility for rebuilding neighborhoods would. For Canada and his colleagues, the answer was clear: The core of Rheedlen's mission, and thus the primary focus of its intended impact, was "to improve the lives of poor children."

At the same time, Canada was convinced that without the social infrastructure that brings a community together, it is difficult, if not impossible, to rear healthy children. Heroic efforts might help a handful of children escape from devastated neighborhoods like those of central Harlem, but saving the next generation would require a critical mass of adults versed in the techniques of effective parenting and engaged in common activities. As a result, while the neighborhood wouldn't be Rheedlen's primary target, it would become a critical element in its emerging theory of change.

As noted earlier, intended impact and theory of change work is an iterative process. Accordingly, Canada and his team went back and forth between the two, as they discussed which children would be their target beneficiaries, what benefits they would strive to create for the youth, and how they would effect these changes. Would the nonprofit target participants in specific programs, all children of a certain income status, or all residents of a specific community? What kind of improvement did Rheedlen's leadership want to see in the children? Did they want to ensure a smooth transition to the next stage of development, say, from infancy to early childhood, or was the ultimate goal to help children become successful adults? And how would all of this come about? Which programs and activities would have the greatest impact?

The answers the management team arrived at were summed up by the decision, in April 2002, to rename Rheedlen the "Harlem Children's Zone."

Heroic efforts might help a handful of children escape from devastated neighborhoods like those of central Harlem. But saving the next generation would require a critical mass of adults versed in the techniques of effective parenting and engaged in common activities.

HCZ adopted an intended impact statement that reads, in part: "Over the next decade, Harlem Children's Zone's primary focus will be on children aged 0–18 living in the Harlem Children's Zone project, a 24-block area of central Harlem. …

Harlem Children's Zone's objective will be to equip the greatest possible number of children in the HCZ project to make a successful transition to an independent, healthy adulthood, reflected in demographic and achievement profiles consistent with those in an average middle-class community."[9] This statement moves beyond the mission statement by specifying *which* poor children will be served, in *which* communities, and *what* benefits they will receive—within a specified time frame.

HCZ adopted a theory of change that rests in part on two pillars: "First, critical mass: Success in raising healthy children entails rebuilding the institutions and functions of a normal, healthy community, something that has been undermined in central Harlem by years of neglect, disinvestments, and demographic upheaval. Building such a community requires the participation of a critical mass of parents and children in common undertakings, including both effective child rearing and community building.

"Second, early and progressive intervention: Effective early intervention pays long-term benefits by making later interventions less necessary for many young people, and by making those interventions more likely to succeed when they are needed."

The theory of change goes on to outline target participation rates: 80 percent of children between birth and age 2, 70 percent of kids between ages 3 and 4, 60 percent of kids between ages 5 and 11, 40 percent of adolescents between 12 and 13, and 30 percent of teens between 14 and 18.

These are compelling statements of HCZ's intended impact and theory of change. The links to Rheedlen's mission and values are apparent, yet the statements are focused enough to inform strategic tradeoffs and resource-allocation decisions. They also establish a definition of success and a time frame that will enable HCZ's leaders to track and evaluate their performance, and be held accountable for the results (sidebar page 48).

The Biggest Surprise

Equipped with this new level of strategic clarity, the management team could evaluate how well each of HCZ's existing programs was contributing to the social impact they aspired to have. To inform their decision making, however, they also needed an equally clear understanding of each program's economic impact on the organization's financial condition. With the help of Bridgespan analysts, HCZ staff assembled financial analyses that mapped each program's full costs against its related revenues.

The purpose of these evaluations was not to identify money losers; virtually all of the programs were receiving less in program-specific funding than they incurred in program-specific costs. Rather, it was to illustrate where HCZ was investing its unrestricted revenues and managerial capacity, so that the management team could determine whether it was allocating these resources to the most mission-critical activities. Unrestricted revenue and senior management talent are usually the scarcest and most precious resources in a nonprofit. How that revenue is allocated, and how senior management allocate their time, should reflect the organization's highest priorities. Often, however, they don't.

Informed by these evaluations and newly committed to concentrating HCZ's resources on programs that aligned with intended impact (focusing on children, particularly the youngest ones, residing in the 24-block zone) and theory of change (which assumes that early childhood intervention and a critical mass of involved parents are essential to help kids transition successfully to adulthood), Canada and his managers made a number of strategic decisions. For example, they resolved to transfer two existing programs—the senior center and a dropout prevention program (located outside the zone)—to other qualified agencies, and to discontinue a homelessness-prevention program (also outside the zone) that had lost its government funding. All three programs were contributing to improving the lives of individuals, and the decision to relinquish operating control was painful.

"The biggest surprise was to discover just how much money was going into programs that didn't meet our core mission—that was a big epiphany," Canada said. "The local senior center that was very dear to a lot of people here just didn't correlate to helping poor kids. We made the decision to find another appropriate nonprofit organization to run it. It was tough, but doing so has made resources available to other mission-related programs."

"The biggest surprise was to discover just how much money was going into programs that didn't meet our core mission. The local senior center that was very dear to a lot of people here just didn't correlate to helping poor kids."

At the same time, Canada and his management team reiterated their commitment to the existing Beacon School centers, even though the facilities housing them were located in host schools outside the 24-block zone. Offering educational, recreational, and youth-development programs during the nonschool hours of the day and evening, the Beacon centers drew children from all over Harlem, including youth living in the zone, and thus contributed directly to HCZ's intended impact.

The new level of clarity about HCZ's priorities also shaped Canada's plans for the nonprofit's programmatic growth. For example, many youth development experts believe that preschool programs such as Head Start (the federally funded program for 3-, 4-, and 5-year-old at-risk children designed to prepare them for success when they enter K-12 programs) and a sound elementary education are essential factors in bringing poor children to parity with their middle-class peers. Yet there was neither an adequate supply of Head Start spaces nor a good primary school within the boundaries of the zone. Addressing these gaps, in conjunction with the city, would have to be part of HCZ's agenda if Canada and his team were to achieve their goals. This realization led to an HCZ initiative to open two new Head Start programs (projected to serve more than 200 children) by 2005.

Achieving Strategic Clarity

Developing strategic clarity—making mission strategic—is a process of inquiry and analysis, not a formula. The only universal answer to the question "What is the right degree of focus for our activities?" is "It depends"—on the impact the organization aspires to have; on assumptions and beliefs about how that impact can be generated; and on the actual resources, human and economic, the organization can marshal to do the work.

Consider two organizations, located in the same city and dedicated to the same goal: ensuring that disadvantaged youngsters succeed in school. Both provide individual tutoring, but one concentrates on building reading skills while the other serves breakfast, offers afterschool activities, and runs a drop-in center in addition to its academic services. Although we can say with certainty that the first organization has a more limited set of activities than the second, we can't say whether it is more appropriately focused. That would depend on its intended impact and theory of change, its resources, and the presence or absence of other organizations in the community providing complementary services.

The practical reason to engage in a series of discussions about intended impact and theory of change is to develop a set of strategic priorities that are focused enough to be actionable and broad enough to reflect the organization's mission. Often, one of the most challenging aspects of the process is finding the best place to start. Based on our experience with nonprofits in a variety of fields, we see three potential ways to anchor these discussions. One is to begin with the beneficiaries the organization seeks to serve. Another is to start with the social benefits it strives to create. The third is to help an organization articulate its theory of change by making the logic underlying its current programs transparent. Determining which option is best usually depends on the organization's mission and institutional history as well as on the passions and values of its leadership, present and past.

The willingness of an organization's leaders and board to set and hold themselves accountable for objectives that reflect their strategic priorities is the dynamic that transforms an intended impact statement and theory of change from expressions of good intentions into strategic decision-making tools. HCZ, for example, established ambitious targets for the number of children in the zone it would serve—including 80 percent of children under 2 over the 10-year period.

Establishing priorities can be wrenching on several dimensions, not least in that it compels nonprofit leaders to say what their organizations won't do as well as what they will.

And yet, as HCZ's experience demonstrates, establishing priorities can be wrenching on several dimensions, not least in that it compels nonprofit leaders to say what their organizations *won't* do as well as what they will. By choosing to focus on a specific set of children and families, Canada and his management team were also "choosing" not to serve seniors, or equally needy children living in other parts of the city. "The seniors were very upset that we were severing our relationship with them. And my staff was stunned," Canada said. "[But] if you are focused on children, would you make an investment in seniors or in children? That became a much easier conversation to have with staff."

Questions about what's in—and out—of the scope of an organization's activities are among the thorniest that nonprofit leaders committed to developing strategic clarity have to confront. As an organization matures and the scope of its activities expands, the links between particular programs and the mission often get lost in the mists of institutional history. Everyone genuinely believes that they are advancing the organization's chief priorities and working on the most important tasks, and yet their decisions lack cohesive force. Intended impact and theory of change discussions can be particularly helpful under these circumstances, because they enable the leadership at complex organizations to create a common language for discussing what they are trying to achieve and a common set of criteria for evaluating choices and making tradeoffs. As a result, the management team is in a better position to make decisions that are consistent with the organization's overall goals.

Strategic clarity can also provoke discomfort. Some staff and key constituents may have to practice new behaviors, more aligned with the organization's intended impact or theory of change. Others may have to adopt new priorities or ideas. A few are likely to feel, and may actually be, disempowered by changes in programs and norms. Decisions to terminate existing programs that aren't well-aligned with the intended impact and theory of change can be hard for emotional reasons, since these programs inevitably do *some* good, and may be legacies from the organization's past, or staffed by loyal employees and volunteers. And these decisions can be difficult for financial reasons, because eliminated programs that are attached to steady funding streams can mean reduced funding in the short term.

Not deciding is also a decision, though, and seldom a particularly good one. It is hard to argue that organizations engaged in the important work most nonprofits undertake shouldn't try to maximize the good they can do with their always-limited economic and organizational resources.

Yet, practically speaking, this is the very path many nonprofit leaders run the risk of taking, if they cannot explain clearly, to themselves and to their supporters, what their priorities are, why the organization's programs and services contribute to these larger goals, and how they know that they are making progress.

HARLEM CHILDREN'S ZONE: GAINING STRATEGIC CLARITY

A nonprofit's **mission statement** defines its reason for being. HCZ's mission statement: "To improve the lives of poor children in America's most devastated communities."

Intended impact is a statement or series of statements about what the organization is trying to achieve and will hold itself accountable for within some manageable period of time. It identifies both the benefits the organization seeks to provide and the beneficiaries.

HCZ's intended impact statement reads, in part: "Over the next decade, Harlem Children's Zone's primary focus will be on children aged 0-18 living in the Harlem Children's Zone project, a 24-block area of central Harlem bounded to the south and north by 116th and 123rd streets, and to the east and west by Fifth and Madison avenues. Harlem Children's Zone's objective will be to equip the greatest possible number of children in the HCZ project to make a successful transition to an independent, healthy adulthood, reflected in demographic and achievement profiles consistent with those in an average middle-class community."

Theory of change explains how an organization's intended impact will actually happen, the cause-and-effect logic by which organizational and financial resources will be converted into the desired social results. Often an organization's theory of change will take into account not only its own resources but also those that others bring.

HCZ's theory of change reads, in part: "The organizing principles of [our] plan are: First, critical mass: Success in raising healthy children entails rebuilding the institutions and functions of a normal, healthy community, something that has been undermined in central Harlem by years of neglect, disinvestments, and demographic upheaval. Building such a community requires the participation of a critical mass of parents and children in common undertakings, including both effective child rearing and community building.

"Second, early and progressive intervention: Effective early intervention pays long-term benefits by making later interventions less necessary for many young people, and by making those interventions more likely to succeed when they are needed."[1]

Using its intended impact and theory of change, the Harlem Children's Zone made the following decisions:

• Transfer the senior center, located outside the zone, to another agency.

• Transfer the dropout prevention program, located outside the zone, to another agency.

• Discontinue a homelessness prevention program, located outside the zone.

• Reiterate a commitment to the Beacon School centers, located outside the zone, not least because the schools provide safe havens for youth and families inside the zone.

• Open two new Head Start programs, to prepare at-risk 3-, 4-, and 5-year-olds inside the zone for elementary school.

1 Harlem Children's Zone, Inc. Growth Plan FY2001-FY2009.

This article originally appeared in the Spring 2003 issue of the Stanford Social Innovation Review.

Going to Scale

Replicating a nonprofit's proven programs is one important way it can extend its impact. But to make replication successful and broaden the footprint and impact of the program, leaders of nonprofits should carefully think about the process, evaluating the decisions they'll need to make across their organizations and the steps they'll need to take to ensure the success of new sites. The following looks at the challenge of replicating social programs.

By Jeffrey L. Bradach

Homelessness, illiteracy, chronic unemployment: nonprofits struggle to address society's most intractable problems. And yet, as Bill Clinton noted, in reviewing school reform initiatives during his presidency, "Nearly every problem has been solved by someone, somewhere." The frustration is that "we can't seem to replicate [those solutions] anywhere else."[1]

With a few exceptions, the nonprofit sector in the United States is comprised of cottage enterprises—thousands upon thousands of programs, each operating in a single neighborhood, in a single city or town. Often, this may be the most appropriate form of organization, but in some—perhaps many—cases, it represents a substantial loss to society overall. Time, funds, and imagination are poured into new programs that at best reinvent the wheel, while the potential of programs that have already proven their effectiveness remains sadly underdeveloped.

One impediment to replication is the prevailing bias among funders to support innovative, "breakthrough" ideas.[2] Another is the fact that, for many people, the concept conjures up images of bureaucracy and centralized control. Such images are uninviting in any sphere, but they are especially problematic in the nonprofit sector, where local "ownership" by donors and volunteers plays such an important part in organizational success. Add in the fact that for many social entrepreneurs, autonomy is an important form of psychic income, and it becomes easy to understand why implementing someone else's dream tends not to be nearly as satisfying as building one's own.

In practice, however, replication is anything but a cookie-cutter process. The objective is to reproduce a successful program's *results,* not to slavishly recreate every one of its features. At the heart of replication is the movement of an organization's theory of change to a new location. In some cases, this might entail transferring a handful of practices from one site to another; in others, the wholesale cloning of the organization's culture. Whatever the specifics, the right choice— including whether to replicate at all—will be strongly influenced by the complexity of the organization's theory of change and the degree to which it can be articulated and standardized.[3]

Time, funds, and imagination are poured into new programs that at best reinvent the wheel.

Before turning to replication in the social sector, however, it is worth spending a moment on its for-profit sector analogue, franchising. Born in the 1920s, the franchise has become one of the dominant organization forms of our time, accounting today for roughly 50 percent of all U.S. retail sales. Franchise organizations align the energy and investment of local entrepreneurs with the strength of a network that may encompass hundreds or even thousands of units operating under the same trademark in different locations. While there are sharp differences between the for-profit and nonprofit sectors, which limit the analogy, franchising offers some thought-provoking lessons for social enterprises seeking to grow.[4]

First is the value of a proven program. Leveraging the knowledge developed by someone else can enable a new site to increase the speed of implementation and the odds of obtaining the desired outcomes. Independent start-ups in the for-profit sector face a much higher failure rate than new units in a franchise chain. The Small Business Administration estimates that approximately half of all small business start-ups fail within five years. The comparable rate for franchise units is half that, or about 25 percent. Quite simply, replication can reduce the risk of failure.

Adopting a recognized model can also make it easier to attract resources. A well-known franchise will attract customers even in a new market, because they associate the brand name with deliverables they know they can count on. Comparable benefits can accrue in the nonprofit sector. For example, prospective Habitat for Humanity volunteers know what the organization is trying to do, what to expect when they volunteer, and what the results of their work will be. Likewise, prospective donors, who want to be sure their gifts will have an impact, know that the organization is building on the experience of others who have used the same program successfully.

Finally, by virtue of being part of a larger system, local programs may gain access to resources and expertise in areas such as fundraising, human resources, and legal services that might be unaffordable for a single unit. They will also be able to tap into ideas and knowledge generated by other sites. A network provides a natural environment for experimentation and learning. McDonald's Big Mac, Filet-O-Fish, and Egg McMuffin were all innovations conceived by local franchisees. Similarly, City Year's Young Heroes program, which engages middle-school students in service and has spread throughout the system, was developed in Providence, R.I., not at the organization's headquarters in Boston.

The core of a franchise is a proven (which is to say a profitable) business idea that can be replicated in multiple sites. What makes replicating social ideas so complicated, and how can the key issues be addressed?

Is Replication a Reasonable and Responsible Option?

Replicating programs that do not produce results is at best a waste of precious social resources and at worst a source of active harm to the participants. For this reason, the first question to ask is whether there is enough substantive evidence of success to justify replication.

What constitutes "enough" will vary, depending on the nature of the program, its longevity, and the scope of the contemplated replication. Expanding from 10 sites to 100 requires more proof of demonstrated success than opening a second location, while programs that truly break new ground need more evidence that the desired results can be sustained over time than those whose methods are tried-and-true.[5] At a minimum, however, an organization has to be able to show that its theory of change is strong, that its initial outcomes are encouraging, and that it has systems in place to track key performance data going forward.

Acquiring evidence of success can be challenging, not least because much of the work nonprofits do involves social interventions, where outcomes are notoriously hard to define and the full effects can take years to see. Nevertheless, the issue of demonstrable results must be dealt with head-on if good decisions about investing resources in creating social change are to be made. The ability to assess (through direct measures or meaningful proxies) whether a program is generating value for its key constituents is an essential prerequisite for any discussion about replication.

Equally important is the ability to articulate the organization's theory of change, which reflects both its view of why its program works and its understanding of the activities required to produce successful outcomes for its key constituents—recipients, donor funders, staff, and volunteers. To illustrate, consider the problem of early-childhood literacy. An organization with a strong theory of change will be able to specify not only how it is going to affect its participants' reading ability (through one-on-one tutoring, say), but also which of its activities are essential to create positive outcomes and how those activities must be executed. Answers to questions such as "How will the tutoring be delivered? How often? and By whom?" are, in essence, the organization's social technology. And it is this core technology that will have to be replicated in new sites.

In some nonprofits, the organization's culture is a key element in its theory of change. City Year is a Boston-based organization that brings together young people, ages 17 to 21, for a yearlong stint of community service in urban areas. Its culture embraces individual differences and embodies the belief that individuals can change their communities.[6] This worldview, which is both an outcome of the program and a key element in making the program work, is primarily a byproduct of how the organization operates—its structures, systems, and processes, reinforced by the purposeful efforts of City Year's leaders. Replicating the culture of an organization is a far more complicated undertaking than replicating a few program elements.

One of the key dimensions on which theories of change vary is their degree of complexity, as measured by the number of activities required to create the desired outcomes. For organizations seeking to produce value on a broad array of dimensions, identifying the requisite interventions and ensuring that they are all in place is a complex undertaking. Helping to stabilize troubled families, for example, might entail the provision of counseling, day care, and housing support, as well as economic assistance and job training.

Yet even in organizations that provide seemingly simple services, the level of inherent complexity can be significant. Habitat for Humanity builds houses, but its theory of change goes well beyond construction, as Eric Duell, one of its international partners explains:

"Habitat has not chosen the easiest way to build houses! The easiest way is like the construction companies do it, with paid skilled labor and lots of it. Habitat does not work this way because the ultimate goal is...not the house but the people who participate in the building of that house, the families who will live in that house, the society that they are a part of, and [the volunteers] participating in so many different ways."[7]

The more complex an organization's theory of change, the more difficult it is to replicate, which is why its leaders' ability to specify the activities that create their program's value is so important. The principle that should guide the analysis is *minimum critical specification,* defining the fewest program elements possible to produce the desired value. In an organization like City Year, which aspires to create value for the corps members, the community, and the private sector sponsors, many elements need to be in place. But does it matter, for example, whether all corps members wear red jackets, or companies sponsor individual teams? These were key elements of the original program, but what needs to be considered is whether they are critical to the results City Year achieves.

One way to identify the core elements of a theory of change is to ask whether varying an element would diminish the value the program creates. Consider D.A.R.E., a 15-week program taught by police officers to fifth-graders that focuses on resisting the use of drugs.[8] D.A.R.E. began in Los Angeles, and as other cities became interested in it, some sites sought to change the targeted grade level (D.A.R.E. approved this). Another city wanted to reduce the length of the program to five weeks (D.A.R.E. disapproved). Yet another sought to eliminate police officers as trainers (D.A.R.E. disapproved).

A STRONG THEORY OF CHANGE...

1. Is as simple as can be—as many elements as needed but as few as possible.

2. Uses systems thinking—shows causes and effects among the parts of the operating model, and predicts how changes in one element affect another.

3. Is one in which both the theory and activities necessary to produce results can be articulated clearly and concretely.

With a clear understanding of its theory of change, an organization may discover that what needs replication is a piece of the program, not the entire program or the organization itself. Earth Force aims to build young people's civic skills so that they make lasting changes in the environment and their communities. Its original growth strategy focused on creating full programs in franchise sites, but a clear-eyed picture of its theory of change led to a different approach: "packaging" a handful of tools (such as how to create and maintain youth councils) that others can use to replicate the organization's desired outcomes.

Without a strong theory of change, replication becomes extremely difficult, because it is impossible to determine what is working and why. One of the most daunting management challenges that nonprofit executives face is determining whether the complexity of their programs is justified, or whether there is a simpler way to create the same value. And even if some dilution of value were to occur with simplification, would that be offset by the increased ease of replication? Serious thought and ongoing experimentation are essential to determine which of a program's elements really create value and which might have little to do with results.

Going to Scale

If an organization has a clearly articulated theory of change, the potential for replication is likely to rest on the degree to which its key activities and the key components of its operating model can also be articulated and standardized. As a general principle, the greater the number of elements that can be standardized, the more likely it is that replication will succeed.

In the for-profit sector, a critical success factor in franchising is the ability to standardize the key activities in the founder's business model. At fast-food restaurants, for example, everything from preparing the food to sweeping the floors to greeting the customers is well documented, and the knowledge required to perform those activities is codified into prescribed routines.

In the nonprofit sector, where critical knowledge is often tacit, this process is far more challenging, as the STRIVE program demonstrates. STRIVE provides three weeks of job training, focused on improving attitudes and job-readiness, to the hard-core unemployed. For those who graduate from the grueling three-week program, STRIVE provides job placement and follow-up for two years.

Half of all small business start-ups fail within five years—the comparable rate for franchise units is half that.

A part of the original model was the "tough-but-fair" approach taken by the trainers during the program. According to Frank Horton, STRIVE's first director of training:

"It takes the right kind of person to do this training. There are different ways, it's not a formula—but you know it when you see it in person. Then you can mold it and shape it. The STRIVE method has been spread like an African folk tale—a combination of watching others, hearing about it, and doing it yourself. You're not really a STRIVE trainer until you have been doing it for 18 months."[9]

If this type of training truly is integral to STRIVE's success, the organization either has to specify the characteristics its trainers must possess and standardize the process of recruiting and developing them (as it ultimately did, after allowing some of the initial expansion sites to experiment with a less "in-your-face" style of training) or accept the fact that the program will replicate very slowly.

Making the knowledge lodged in an operating model explicit is crucial to being able to transfer the model to new locations. Jumpstart matches young children who are struggling in preschool with college students (called corps members) for a one-year relationship. A program guide for corps members specifies how to develop a customized curriculum for each child and offers a range of reading activities associated with each developmental need. Jumpstart's ability to standardize the instruction process into teachable routines, while still leaving wide degrees of latitude for individual improvisation, has been instrumental in enabling it to add new sites rapidly.

People. The skills of local site managers are often a critical ingredient in making replication work. Finding the right people to fill new positions depends on two distinct activities: (1) proper selection, and (2) training and socialization.

Selection entails having a clear understanding of the skills required to manage a site and implement the theory of change. As with the theory of change itself, this involves being explicit about what is required. Training can then be used to fill any skill gaps and/or to inculcate the culture of the program into new managers. The importance of acculturation often leads organizations to believe they must promote from within, since "people from the outside just don't get the *it* of our program." Oftentimes, however, an organization's reliance on insiders reflects nothing more than the fact that the tacit knowledge in its operating model has not yet been made explicit.

Context. Every program starts off somewhere, and the effectiveness of its operating model is often context dependent. Summerbridge prepares talented youngsters from diverse backgrounds to succeed in school. The intensive summer program was initially hosted in independent schools, and when the organization tried to present it in public schools, the model proved difficult to implement.[10] Board members debated the causes and consequences; some worried that the public schools' bureaucracy and thin resources would constrain the program, while others believed the independent schools' attractive campuses were part of the program's allure. Still others believed that the budgeting process would put the program at risk to a variety of political and financial forces. Ultimately, the board decided that although it would continue to experiment with alternate venues, the centerpiece of its efforts would be independent schools. Effective replication often depends on holding constant—standardizing— the context within which a program will operate.

Financial structure. A critical aspect of standardizing a program is making its underlying economics—costs as well as revenues—transparent. Programs that struggle to stay afloat, bootstrapping people and resources, and living on the edge, are not good candidates for replication, however impressive their results. Neither are organizations that cannot articulate—and replicate—the unit cost of their theory of change (the cost per child served, for example, or the cost per house built). The fact that funders are increasingly asking for performance metrics that reflect the true cost of providing programs may not only encourage such economic clarity, but also have an unintended benefit—underscoring the fact that results never come for free.

Establishing a reliable source of funding—standardizing the flow of money— increases the odds of success for two reasons. First, new leaders can direct their time and energy to building the program instead of finding new ways to raise funds. Second, it can help to minimize the pressures created by funders' varying interests. In the case of Jumpstart, for example, some funders are interested primarily in engaging older youth in the community, while others focus on literacy (and thus the preschool tutees). The cumulative effect of such pressures can be program drift or variations in the model that may diminish results.

Sometimes standardization is possible. Habitat has a financial model that lays out how to finance construction, what can be acquired through in-kind contributions, and how to attract funds from local individuals. Similarly, City Year has clear expectations about the percentages of funding that will come from government, business, and the local community. Within the business segment, there is a standardized model for how corporate sponsors will support teams of corps members.

Service Recipients. Most theories of change are designed to affect a specific set of recipients: seventh-graders, alcoholics in recovery, homeless, working poor. The consequent tight alignment between the organization's operating model and these intended beneficiaries makes it difficult to serve other groups unless the model is modified at the same time. STRIVE's core job-training program is tailored to meet the needs of the hardest to employ, and its leadership monitors the performance metrics of local sites closely to see that this focus is maintained. Given its intended beneficiaries, STRIVE expects that 10 to 15 percent of the participants will drop out of the program and that, of those who complete it, only 80 percent will be placed in jobs. Higher percentages in either category would raise the possibility that a less difficult set of clients was being served. Program leaders must be careful not to drift into serving recipients to whom their theory of change does not apply.

Replicating the Operating Model

Replication requires answers to three critical questions: (1) where and how to grow; (2) what kind of network to build; and (3) what the role of the "center" needs to be. While the right answers require both good data and careful analysis, replication is basically a process of planned evolution. Many replication efforts begin with expansion to a handful of sites, which can then provide useful lessons for broader initiatives. Learning from the planned—and unplanned—experiments that occur along the way is an important part of the implementation process.

Defining the Growth Strategy. Identifying the potential demand for a program and determining where the critical ingredients for success can be found are early challenges of implementation. In developing its growth plan, STRIVE examined statistics from the 50 largest cities across the United States to identify those with (1) the highest concentration of unemployed people; (2) lack of alternative job-training providers; and (3) interested local funders. This detailed analysis led it to redouble its efforts in some of its existing markets, where there was unmet demand, as well as to prioritize new markets where there were both potential funders and an absence of alternative providers. A key element in Jumpstart's model is the availability of Federal Work Study money, which is used to compensate the corps members. Recognizing this, Jumpstart prioritized college campuses according to the size of their work-study budgets and now has programs on 31 campuses, 20 of which are in the top 200 in terms of work-study funding. For City Year, a key criterion might be the size of a city's business base, since corporate sponsors are an integral part of the model.

Often, careful analysis will reveal that a program has underpenetrated its current markets. While there are sometimes compelling reasons to go "national" (appealing to a corporate sponsor, for example), it is important not to overestimate the benefits—or underestimate the risks—associated with expanding to new sites. The Steppingstone Foundation is a Boston-based program that prepares motivated urban fourth- and fifth-graders for admission to and success at top independent and public-exam schools. After 10 years of operation—and the opening of a second site in Philadelphia—it was considering further expansion, until analysis demonstrated a compelling opportunity to double the size of the program at home, in Boston.

Leveraging existing networks by identifying partners who can supply essential resources is an important way to facilitate rapid growth. Citizens Schools, an innovative after-school program that addresses community needs while building student skills through hands-on experiential learning activities, is pursuing a partnership with the YMCA to replicate its program. Rather than develop stand-alone "retail" programs, a partnership with the YMCA will enable it to engage in "wholesale" distribution of the concept. Similarly, Jumpstart has been able to replicate its model quickly by working through networks of university presidents and administrators.

The fact that dollars seldom follow success is one of the most vexing challenges nonprofit leaders face. Proven solutions to pressing problems do not spread.

Even with clarity about where a program might best be replicated, it is still crucial to find local champions, who will exert the necessary energy and garner essential resources. Sometimes a program can "sell" its model to new locations by meeting with local people who can become its champions. Alternatively, local champions will sometimes identify themselves once they learn about a successful program in another city. Some of the most notable replication stories of the last decade were built on the visibility provided by public figures (Jimmy Carter's involvement with Habitat for Humanity, for instance, and Bill Clinton's interest in City Year) or media exposure (STRIVE, for example, was featured on 60 Minutes).

In the nonprofit sector, it is very difficult to pursue pure "push" strategies—literally taking a program to a city without local involvement and support. At the same time, even in cases where there is massive demand for the program, as was the case for STRIVE, it is vitally important that the organization has great clarity about the critical elements of its theory of change, so that it can select new sites effectively.

Designing the Network. The relationship among local affiliates and between affiliates and the national office can range from "tight" to "loose." In a loose network, local sites operate with very little direct involvement from the center: STRIVE's affiliates are independent entities that contract to follow certain program guidelines and meet once a year at a conference. City Year is at the other extreme: All the sites operate under one 501(c)(3) organization, and the local executive directors are all City Year employees. Extensive training, field visits, and regular participation in City Year events make this a tight network characterized by a high degree of involvement between a local site and the national organization.[11]

The key dimension driving the shape of the network is the degree to which the operating model can be standardized. The greater the standardization, the looser the network can be, since people are able to grasp the model quickly, and it is easy for local and national leaders to identify deviations. Conversely, when culture is an important part of the model, a tighter network is likely to be required. This does not necessarily mean that control has to emanate from the network's center, but it is apt to involve substantial interaction between the local office and the center and among the programs (as it does, for example, at City Year).

A variety of tools, ranging from the network's legal status to its reporting requirements to the existence—or not—of training manuals, can be used to structure the relationship between local sites and the center. Ideally, networks would be self-organizing, given the desire of most local managers to operate as autonomously as possible and the fact that central activities require additional resources. In practice, however, the challenge is to design a network that is as loose as possible yet maintains fidelity to the concept and produces results.

Striking the right balance between loose and tight is a matter of constant experimentation. There are no simple rules. Jumpstart started with an organization model similar to City Year's and then shifted to a looser network, which relies on its university partners to manage local sites. Conversely, STRIVE started with a very loose network and then shifted to a somewhat tighter system governed by a well-defined contract. What is crucial is that the organization constantly reflect on what it is learning about replicating the theory of change and producing results.

The Role of National. However a network's founders choose to organize its members, sooner or later they will need to confront three challenging issues: (1) ensuring quality; (2) facilitating learning; and (3) providing central services.

Ensuring quality and protecting the brand. Once a few sites have been developed, a network begins to share a common public identity, or brand. Since brands invite generalization—for good or ill—network leaders have an interest in ensuring that all the members are delivering consistent results. Dorothy Stoneman, the founder of YouthBuild, recounted the evolution of her program:

"Our initial desire was to get a good idea out there. We wanted it to become a generic concept like a library or day care. We were just trying to get resources and ideas to people. Eventually the sites told us that we needed to protect the brand. Everyone said we needed to tighten up the system."

YouthBuild now conducts a thorough audit every two years that includes a site visit and an assessment of more than 100 indicators of operational performance. A crucial element in ensuring quality is to have a data collection system that provides evidence that a local program is delivering the theory of change with fidelity and that the program is producing results.

Facilitating learning throughout the network. The opportunity to learn from other people is one of the great benefits of a network. At Jumpstart, local executive directors talk on a conference call every week to discuss their challenges and share new ideas. At City Year, a daily newsletter reports on the events at different sites and highlights innovations across the network. Many organizations have annual meetings where peers can learn from peers. The center plays a critical role in facilitating these interactions, and local leaders tend to value them highly. Indeed, for some, it is the reason they joined the network as well as the way in which the system positions itself to improve.

Nevertheless, tension between local sites and the center is almost inevitable, because the particularities of local conditions are rarely 100 percent aligned with the national model. Sooner or later, these discrepancies will create some conflict in the system. The key question is whether the conflict is constructive—producing learning—or destructive.

Providing centralized services. The center can also play a critical role in providing functional expertise and services that local sites might not otherwise be able to obtain. Training is an important benefit for many local sites, for example, as is centralized purchasing. Similarly, the ongoing development of the program—in essence, the research and development function—is typically the province of the center.

There is a natural life cycle to the center-affiliate relationship, which makes it challenging for the center to continue to deliver value as the network evolves. The first year in which affiliates are part of the network, they cannot believe the "smarts" at national. With a year of experience under their belts, affiliates typically feel they have all the answers and begin to wonder what national has done for them lately. Over time, the center must find ways to contribute to the success of local sites.

The Paradox of Success in the Nonprofit Sector

The failure to replicate innovative social programs is usually attributed to problems of strategy and management. Much of the time, it is simply a problem of money. The fact that dollars seldom follow success is one of the most vexing challenges nonprofit leaders face. At precisely the moment when large amounts of capital would flow to a proven idea in the for-profit sector, funders in the nonprofit sector frequently back away. There are many reasons—donor fatigue, a belief that equity requires spreading money around, hesitance to make "big bets"—but the consequence is that proven solutions to pressing problems do not spread.

There are two dimensions to the economic challenges of replication. First, each new site needs resources to develop the model. Given the difficulty of raising capital, it is not surprising that there are few instances in which the center was able to provide the capital for building local sites. (In the for-profit sector, by contrast, entire chains of retail outlets, department stores, and grocery stores are funded, built, and managed by one company.) This is why successful models often build in a template for the financial structure of their new sites.

While private funders will sometimes provide seed money to stimulate the development of local programs (a $50,000 matching grant for the first two years of a site's development, for example), they rarely supply the capital to build a network of sites. The one exception to this rule is the federal government, which sometimes supports the proliferation of successful programs. YouthBuild is a line item in the Housing and Urban Development budget, and over the past seven years more than $300 million has been devoted to supporting YouthBuild programs. Not surprisingly, many high potential nonprofits pursue strategies that involve tapping into government funding streams.

The second economic challenge is funding the national office. Local sites pay fees to the center in many networks (at Jumpstart the fee is $5,000 per year, per site), and this represents an important indicator of whether the local sites value the center. But even in loosely managed networks, these fees rarely cover the costs of the center's operations,[12] and funders are notoriously reluctant to provide support for non-programmatic activities. From a social welfare perspective, the opportunity cost of this underinvestment is huge: tens or hundreds of sites serving thousands of people without the support and management discipline that might enable them to execute more powerfully.

If replication is to occur and proven ideas are to spread, strong organizations are required both at the local level and at the center. Yet, for the most part, the funding patterns of the nonprofit sector—small grants, for short durations, focused on program work—conspire against building strong organizations. There are a few examples of funders that are supporting replication and providing adequate capital for well-conceived strategies, but many more are needed if the challenges facing our society are to be addressed.

Funding

What funding model will sustain our mission, its impact, and future growth?

Stanford SOCIAL INNOVATION REVIEW

This article originally appeared in the Fall 2009 issue of the Stanford Social Innovation Review.

The Nonprofit Starvation Cycle

A vicious cycle is leaving nonprofits so hungry for decent infrastructure that they can barely function as organizations—let alone serve their beneficiaries. The cycle starts with funders' unrealistic expectations about how much running a nonprofit costs, and results in nonprofits' misrepresenting their costs while skimping on vital systems—acts that feed funders' skewed beliefs. To break the nonprofit starvation cycle, funders should take the lead.

By Ann Goggins Gregory and Don Howard

Organizations that build robust infrastructure—which includes sturdy information technology systems, financial systems, skills training, fundraising processes, and other essential overhead—are more likely to succeed than those that do not. This is not news, and nonprofits are no exception to the rule.

Yet it is also not news that most nonprofits do not spend enough money on overhead. In our consulting work at the Bridgespan Group, we frequently find that our clients agree with the idea of improving infrastructure and augmenting their management capacity, yet they are loath to actually make these changes because they do not want to increase their overhead spending. But underfunding overhead can have disastrous effects, finds the Nonprofit Overhead Cost Study, a five-year research project conducted by the Urban Institute's National Center for Charitable Statistics and the Center on Philanthropy at Indiana University. The researchers examined more than 220,000 IRS Form 990s and conducted 1,500 in-depth surveys of organizations with revenues of more than $100,000. Among their many dismaying findings: nonfunctioning computers, staff members who lacked the training needed for their positions, and, in one instance, furniture so old and beaten down that the movers refused to move it. The effects of such limited overhead investment are felt far beyond the office: nonfunctioning computers cannot track program outcomes and show what is working and what is not; poorly trained staff cannot deliver quality services to beneficiaries.

Despite findings such as these, many nonprofits continue to skimp on overhead. And they plan to cut even more overhead spending to weather the current recession, finds a recent Bridgespan study. Surveying more than 100 executive directors of organizations across the country, we found that 56 percent of respondents planned to reduce overhead spending. Yet decreasing already austere overhead spending (also called *indirect expenses*) may jeopardize organizations' very existence—not to mention their ability to fulfill their missions. And although the Obama administration's stimulus package may fuel rapid growth among some nonprofits, many will lack the infrastructure to manage the windfall and may well be crushed under the weight of all those well-intended funds.

Why do nonprofits and funders alike continue to shortchange overhead? To answer this question, we studied four national nonprofits that serve youth. Each organization has a mix of funding, including monies from government, foundation, and individual sources. We also interviewed the leaders and managers of a range of nonprofit organizations and funders, as well as synthesized existing research on overhead costs in the nonprofit sector.

Our research reveals that a vicious cycle fuels the persistent underfunding of overhead.[1] The first step in the cycle is funders' unrealistic expectations about how much it costs to run a nonprofit. At the second step, nonprofits feel pressure to conform to funders' unrealistic expectations. At the third step, nonprofits respond to this pressure in two ways: They spend too little on overhead, and they underreport their expenditures on tax forms and in fundraising materials. This underspending and underreporting in turn perpetuates funders' unrealistic expectations. Over time, funders expect grantees to do more and more with less and less—a cycle that slowly starves nonprofits.

Although several factors drive the cycle of nonprofit starvation, our research suggests that taking action at the first stage—funders' unrealistic expectations—could be the best way to slow or even stop the cycle. Changing funders' expectations, however, will require a coordinated, sector-wide effort. At a time when people need nonprofit services more than ever and when government is increasingly turning to nonprofits to solve social problems, this effort is necessary to keep nonprofits healthy and functioning.

Funders' Unrealistic Expectations

The nonprofit starvation cycle is the result of deeply ingrained behaviors, with a chicken-and-egg-like quality that makes it hard to determine where the dysfunction really begins. Our sense, however, is that the most useful place to start analyzing this cycle is with funders' unrealistic expectations. The power dynamics between funders and their grantees make it difficult, if not impossible, for nonprofits to stand up and address the cycle head-on; the downside to doing so could be catastrophic for the organization, especially if other organizations do not follow suit. Particularly in these tough economic times, an organization that decides—on its own—to buck the trend and report its true overhead costs could risk losing major funding. The organization's reputation could also suffer. Resetting funder expectations would help pave the way for honest discussions with grantees.

Many funders know that nonprofit organizations report artificially low overhead figures, and that the donor literature often reflects grossly inaccurate program ratios (the proportion of program-related expenses to indirect expenses). Without accurate data, funders do not know what overhead rates *should* be. Although for-profit analogies are not perfect for nonprofits, they do provide some context for thinking about how realistic—or not—average overhead rates in the nonprofit sector are. As the figure below shows, overhead rates across for-profit industries vary, with the average rate falling around 25 percent of total expenses. And among service industries—a closer analog to nonprofits—none report average overhead rates below 20 percent.

THE REAL COST OF DOING BUSINESS
Most for-profit industries spend far more on overhead than the 10 to 20 percent norm in the nonprofit sector.

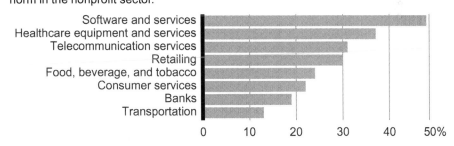

Selling, administrative, and general expenses as % of sales (2005)

SOURCE: Compustat; Standard & Poor's Global Industry Classification Standard Structure

In the absence of clear, accurate data, funders must rely on the numbers their grantees report. But as we will later discuss, these data are riddled with errors. As a result, funders routinely require nonprofits to spend unhealthily small amounts on overhead. For instance, all four of the youth service organizations that we studied were managing government contracts from local, state, and federal sources, and none of the contracts allowed grantees to use more than 15 percent of the grant for indirect expenses (which include operations, finances, human resources, and fundraising).

Some foundations allot more money for indirect costs than do government agencies. Yet foundations are quite variable in their indirect cost allowances, with the average ranging from 10 percent to 15 percent of each grant. These rates hold true even for some of the largest, most influential U.S. foundations. And foundations can be just as rigid with their indirect cost policies as government funders.

Many times, the indirect allowances that grants do fund don't even cover the costs of administering the grants themselves. For example, when one Bridgespan client added up the hours that staff members spent on reporting requirements for a particular government grant, the organization found that it was spending about 31 percent of the value of the grant on its administration. Yet the funder had specified that the nonprofit spend only 13 percent of the grant on indirect costs.

Most funders are aware that their indirect cost rates are indeed too low, finds a recent Grantmakers for Effective Organizations (GEO) study. In this national survey of 820 grantmaking foundations, only 20 percent of the respondents said that their grants include enough overhead allocation to cover the time that grantees spend on reporting.[2]

Individual donors' expectations are also skewed. A 2001 survey conducted by the Better Business Bureau's Wise Giving Alliance found that more than half of American adults felt that nonprofit organizations should have overhead rates of 20 percent or less, and nearly four out of five felt that overhead spending should be held at less than 30 percent. In fact, those surveyed ranked overhead ratio and financial transparency to be more important attributes in determining their willingness to give to an organization than the success of the organization's programs.

Not only do funders and donors have unrealistic expectations, but the nonprofit sector itself also promotes unhealthy overhead levels. "The 20 percent norm is perpetuated by funders, individuals, and nonprofits themselves," says the CFO of one of the organizations we studied. "When we benchmarked our reported financials, we looked at others, [and] we realized that others misreport as well. One of our peer organizations allocates 70 percent of its finance director's time to programs. That's preposterous!"

In this context, nonprofits are reluctant to break ranks and be honest in their fundraising literature, even if they know that they are fueling unrealistic expectations. They find it difficult to justify spending on infrastructure when nonprofits commonly tout their low overhead costs. For example, Smile Train, an organization that treats children born with cleft lip and palate conditions, has claimed that "100 percent of your donation will go toward programs...zero percent goes to overhead." Nevertheless, the fine print goes on to say that this is not because the organization has no overhead; rather, it is because Smile Train uses contributions from "founding supporters" to cover its non-program costs.

This constellation of causes feeds the second stage in the nonprofit starvation cycle: pressure on nonprofits to conform to unrealistic expectations. This pressure comes from a variety of sources, finds the Nonprofit Overhead Cost Study. The survey found that 36 percent of respondents felt pressure from government agencies, 30 percent felt pressure from donors, and 24 percent felt pressure from foundations.[3]

Underfed Overhead

In response to pressure from funders, nonprofits settle into a "low pay, make do, and do without" culture, as the Nonprofit Overhead Cost Study calls it. Every aspect of an organization feels the pinch of this culture. In our consulting work with nonprofits, for example, we often see clients who are unable to pay competitive salaries for qualified specialists, and so instead make do with hires who lack the necessary experience or expertise. Similarly, many organizations that limit their investment in staff training find it difficult to develop a strong pipeline of senior leaders.

These deficits can be especially damaging to youth-serving organizations, notes Ben Paul, president and CEO of After-School All-Stars, a Los Angeles-based nonprofit organization that provides after-school and summer camp programs for at-risk youth nationwide. "It is clear to anyone who has led an organization that the most important capital in a company is the human capital," says Paul. "In after-school we have a saying: Kids come for the program, but stay for the staff. If we don't hire the right people, we might as well not run after-school programs."

Meanwhile, without strong tracking systems, nonprofits have a hard time diagnosing which actions truly drive their desired outcomes. "The catch-22 is that, while organizations need capacity-building funding in order to invest in solid performance tracking, many funders want to see strong program outcome data *before* they will provide such general operating support," says Jamie McAuliffe, a portfolio manager at the New York-based Edna McConnell Clark Foundation.

Take the case of a well-respected network of youth development programs. To protect the identity of this organization, we will call it the Learning Goes On Network (LGON). Poised for a huge growth spurt, LGON realized that its data systems would be hopelessly inadequate to accommodate more clients. An analysis showed that program staff spent 25 percent of their time collecting data manually. One staff member spent 50 percent of her time typing results into an antiquated Microsoft Access database.

Staff members can become so accustomed to their strained circumstances that they have trouble justifying even much-needed investments in overhead, our interviews revealed. "We [had] known for a long time that a COO was vital to our growth but [hadn't] been able to fund one," relates the CEO of one of the four youth development organizations that we studied. But when his organization's board finally created the COO position, the rest of the staff resisted. "They had lived so long in a starved organization that the idea of hiring a COO was shocking to them."

Misleading Reporting

The final driver of the cycle that starves nonprofit infrastructure is nonprofits' routine misrepresentation of how much they actually spend on overhead. The numbers that nonprofits report on their financial statements "[defy] plausibility," finds the Nonprofit Overhead Cost Study. Upon examination of more than 220,000 nonprofit organizations, researchers found that more than a third of the organizations reported no fundraising costs whatsoever, while one in eight reported no management and general expenses. Further scrutiny found that 75 percent to 85 percent of these organizations were incorrectly reporting the costs associated with grants.

Our study of the four youth-serving nonprofits likewise reported discrepancies between what nonprofits spent on overhead and what they reported spending. Although they reported overhead rates ranging from 13 percent to 22 percent, their actual overhead rates ranged from 17 percent to 35 percent.

Many factors support this underreporting of nonprofit costs. According to a survey conducted by *The Chronicle of Philanthropy* in 2000, a majority of nonprofits say that their accountants advised them to report zero in the fundraising section of Form 990.[4] Limited surveillance of nonprofits' Form 990 tax reports only exacerbates the problem: The IRS rarely levies the $50,000 penalty for an incomplete or inaccurate return, and generally applies it only when an organization deliberately fails to file the form altogether. According to the *Chronicle* study, "Improperly reporting these expenses is likely to have few, if any, consequences."

The IRS' ambiguous instructions likewise lead to error, report several sources. For example, nowhere does the IRS explicitly address how to account for nonprofit marketing and communications. As a result, many organizations allocate all marketing and communications expenses to programs when, in most cases, these expenses should be reported as administrative or fundraising overhead.

Government agencies likewise have varying and ambiguous definitions of indirect costs. The White House Office of Management and Budget, for example, defines indirect costs as "those that have been incurred for common or joint objectives and cannot be readily identified with a particular final cost objective." It then goes on to say that "because of the diverse characteristics and accounting practices of nonprofit organizations, it is not possible to specify the types of cost that may be classified as indirect cost in all situations."[5]

There is some good news. Currently, the U.S. Government Accountability Office (GAO) is conducting a study of various federal grantors' definitions of indirect costs. As Stan Czerwinski, the director of strategic issues for GAO, explains, "The goal is to achieve consistency, so that when nonprofits go in for funding, they have clarity (as do funders) about what they're actually going to get reimbursed for." The study is in the early stages, but as Czerwinski notes, the need is clear: "We don't find anybody telling us that we're barking up the wrong tree."

Proper Care and Feeding

Although the vicious cycle of nonprofit starvation has many entry points and drivers, we believe that the best place to end it is where it starts: Funders' unrealistic expectations. Foundations and government funders must take the lead because they have an enormous power advantage over their grantees. When funders change their expectations, nonprofits will feel less need to underreport their overhead. They will also feel empowered to invest in infrastructure.

The first step that funders should take is to shift their focus from costs to outcomes. In the nonprofit world, organizations are so diverse that they do not share a common indicator of program effectiveness. In the absence of this indicator, many funders try to understand an organization's efficiency by monitoring overhead and other easily obtained yet faulty indicators. Funders need to refocus their attention on impact by asking "What are we trying to achieve?" and "What would define success?" In so doing, they will signal to their grantees that impact matters more than anything else. Even focusing on approximate or crude indicators (for example, "Are we getting an A or a C on our impact goals?") is better than looking at cost efficiencies, as focusing on the latter may lead to narrow decisions that undermine program results.

Funders must also clearly communicate their program goals to their grantees. Having established that funder and grantee share the same goals, funders should then insist on honest answers to the question "What will it take to deliver these outcomes consistently, or to deliver these outcomes at an even higher level of quality or quantity?"

One of our study participants, for instance, worked closely with its major funder to think through this question, and ultimately determined it needed a sizable investment in technology to support its projected growth. The funder agreed that only by making such an investment would the organization be able to track outcomes uniformly and to make program improvements quickly.

When feasible, funders should help meet grantees' identified infrastructure needs by making general operating support grants. Grantmakers and nonprofits agree that more operating support is very likely to improve an organization's ability to achieve results, finds the 2008 Grantmakers for Effective Organizations study. And a 2006 CompassPoint Nonprofit Services study of nearly 2,000 nonprofit executives in eight metropolitan areas reveals that receiving general operating support played a major role in reducing burnout and stress among executive directors.[6] Yet although 80 percent of the foundations in this study made some general operating grants, they dedicated a median of only 20 percent of their grant dollars to this kind of support.

Regardless of the type of support they provide, funders should encourage open, candid discussions with their grantees about what the latter need to be effective. Many funders' grantmaking processes are not set up to consider the full scope of what grantees do, and why. As a result, their grants are not as flexible as they need to be. Yet when funders fully understand their grantees' operations, they are more likely to meet their grantees' needs.

Although changing their expectations will have the greatest impact on the nonprofit starvation cycle, funders can also intervene in other useful ways. When making use-restricted grants, funders should commit to paying a greater share of administrative and fundraising costs. Indeed, in 2004, the board of the Independent Sector encouraged funders to pay "the fair proportion of administrative and fundraising costs necessary to manage and sustain whatever is required by the organization to run that particular project."

Likewise, rather than prescribing an indirect expense rate for all grants, government funders should allow nonprofits to define their true overhead needs in grant applications and, so long as these needs are justifiable, pay for them. For example, some federal funding contracts allow a nonprofit to justify an indirect cost rate (within guidelines), which the organization can then use for all its federal grant applications. Extending such a policy to all federal, state, and local government contracts would go a long way toward helping nonprofits deliver better programs while being able to pay for their grants' management.

Finally, to foster transparent and accurate reporting, funders should encourage the development of a standard definition of the term *overhead*. Currently, organizations have to report their overhead differently for nearly every grant that they receive. Standardization would allow funders to compare apples with apples, as well as allow grantees to understand better their own overhead investments—or lack thereof. Having a dialogue about real overhead rates could also help shift the focus to the real target: outcomes.

What Grantees Can Do

The burden of breaking the cycle of nonprofit starvation does not rest solely with funders. Nonprofit leaders also play a role. As a baseline task, they should commit to understanding their real overhead costs and their real infrastructure needs. At LGON, for instance, senior managers spent several months digging into their costs, analyzing their current systems—including the organization's subpar tracking process—and identifying gaps in capacity. After this strategic planning process, the organization could articulate a clear plan for a new tracking system and a 150 percent increase in non-program staff over three years.

Nonprofits must then speak truth to power, sharing their real numbers with their boards and then engaging their boards' support in communicating with funders. Case studies of organizations that have successfully invested in their own infrastructure have repeatedly noted the need for a shared agenda between the leadership team and the board. The executive director of LGON, for example, communicated early and often with her board members throughout the strategic planning process. She also facilitated several meetings to address infrastructure needs.

For their part, board members should ask the tough questions before funders do, namely: "What does this organization really need to succeed?" "Where are we under investing?" and "What are the risks we're taking by under investing in these areas?" Board members should encourage nonprofit leaders to develop strategies that explicitly recognize infrastructure needs. In developing plans for infrastructure, board members can help, notes Chris Brahm, chairman of the board of directors at Larkin Street Youth Services, a San Francisco nonprofit that serves homeless and runaway youth: "The people running agencies are often consumed with programs and raising money. Board members, whether businesspeople or otherwise, can bring external perspective on overhead services."

At LGON, for example, the executive director identified a handful of board members who were fervent supporters of the emerging strategic vision. These board members then communicated to their colleagues how much overhead this vision would require.

During these discussions, both board members and managers should focus on how investments in infrastructure will benefit the organization's beneficiaries, rather than reduce costs. Even within the confines of a "cost conversation," they should emphasize how infrastructure investments may actually reduce the costs of serving beneficiaries over time. One organization in our study, for instance, determined that an investment in technological infrastructure yielded $350,000 per year by freeing up staff time and consolidating "scrappy" systems.

Finally, organizations must attempt to educate their donors. "Donors don't want to pay for an organization's rent, or phone bill, or stamps," notes Paul, "but those are essential components of everyday work. You can't run a high-performing organization from your car. And there are many ways to explain these types of expenses to donors."

Both funders and grantees are feeling the sting of the current recession. But this economic downturn is no excuse to cut overhead funding. "If a nonprofit's leaders are feeling as if they cannot raise money to support overhead, I think they're confusing the issue," says Brahm. "The real issue is that they can't raise enough money, period. Either they do not have, or they have not been able to communicate, a results story that is compelling to funders."

Rather than being the reason to reduce overhead spending, the recession is an excellent opportunity to redress decades-long underinvestment in nonprofit infrastructure. "There is real potential for change if all of the major stakeholders—government, private funders, and the nonprofits themselves—take steps to acknowledge that capacity building is critical to the health of an organization," says McAuliffe. And although the forces that fuel the nonprofit starvation cycle are strong, the opportunity to achieve more for beneficiaries in the long term should compel funders and grantees alike to stop the cycle.

Former Bridgespan Group manager William Bedsworth contributed to this article.

Stanford SOCIAL INNOVATION REVIEW

This article originally appeared in the Spring 2009 issue of the Stanford Social Innovation Review.

Ten Nonprofit Funding Models

For-profit executives use business models—such as "low-cost provider" or "the razor and the razor blade"—as a shorthand way to describe and understand the way companies are built and sustained. Nonprofit executives, to their detriment, are not as explicit about their funding models and have not had an equivalent lexicon—until now.

By William Foster, Peter Kim, and Barbara Christiansen

Money is a constant topic of conversation among nonprofit leaders: How much do we need? Where can we find it? Why isn't there more of it? In tough economic times, these types of questions become more frequent and pressing.

Unfortunately, the answers are not readily available. That's because nonprofit leaders are much more sophisticated about creating programs than they are about funding their organizations, and philanthropists often struggle to understand the impact (and limitations) of their donations.

There are consequences to this financial fuzziness. When nonprofits and funding sources are not well matched, money doesn't flow to the areas where it will do the greatest good. Too often, the result is that promising programs are cut, curtailed, or never launched. And when dollars become tight, a chaotic fundraising scramble is all the more likely to ensue.[1]

In the for-profit world, by contrast, there is a much higher degree of clarity on financial issues. This is particularly true when it comes to understanding how different businesses operate, which can be encapsulated in a set of principles known as business models. Although there is no definitive list of corporate business models,[2] there is enough agreement about what they mean that investors and executives alike can engage in sophisticated conversations about any given company's strategy. When a person says that a company is a "low-cost provider" or a "fast follower," the main outlines of how that company operates are pretty clear. Similarly, stating that a company is using "the razor and the razor blade" model describes a type of ongoing customer relationship that applies far beyond shaving products.

The value of such shorthand is that it allows business leaders to articulate quickly and clearly how they will succeed in the marketplace, and it allows investors to quiz executives more easily about how they intend to make money. This back-and-forth increases the odds that businesses will succeed, investors will make money, and everyone will learn more from their experiences.

The nonprofit world rarely engages in equally clear and succinct conversations about an organization's long-term funding strategy. That is because the different types of funding that fuel nonprofits have never been clearly defined.[3] More than a poverty of language, this represents—and results in—a poverty of understanding and clear thinking.

Through our research, we have identified 10 nonprofit models that are commonly used by the largest nonprofits in the United States. Our intent is not to prescribe a single approach for a given nonprofit to pursue. (See "Ten Funding Models" on page 91.) Instead, we hope to help nonprofit leaders articulate more clearly the models that they believe could support the growth of their organizations, and use that insight to examine the potential and constraints associated with those models.

Beneficiaries Are Not Customers

One reason why the nonprofit sector has not developed its own lexicon of funding models is that running a nonprofit is generally more complicated than running a comparable size for-profit business. When a for-profit business finds a way to create value for a customer, it has generally found its source of revenue; the customer pays for the value. With rare exceptions, that is not true in the nonprofit sector. When a nonprofit finds a way to create value for a beneficiary (for example, integrating a prisoner back into society or saving an endangered species), it has not identified its economic engine. That is a separate step.

Duke University business professor J. Gregory Dees, in his work on social entrepreneurship, describes the need to understand both the donor value proposition and the recipient value proposition. Clara Miller, CEO of the Nonprofit Finance Fund, who has also written wonderfully about this dilemma, talks about all nonprofits being in two "businesses"—one related to their program activities and the other related to raising charitable "subsidies."

As a result of this distinction between beneficiary and funder, the critical aspects (and accompanying vocabulary) of nonprofit funding models need to be understood separately from those of the for-profit world. It is also why we use the term *funding model* rather than *business model* to describe the framework. A business model incorporates choices about the cost structure and value proposition to the beneficiary. A funding model, however, focuses only on the funding, not on the programs and services offered to the beneficiary.

All nonprofit executives can use our 10 funding models to improve their fundraising and management, but the usefulness of these models becomes particularly important as nonprofits get bigger. There are many ways to raise as much as $1 million a year, some of which can be improvised during the process. Once organizations try to raise $25 million to $50 million or more each year, however, there are fewer possible paths. The number of potential decision makers who can authorize spending such large amounts of money decreases (or you need to get them en masse), and the factors that motivate these decision makers to say "yes" are more established (or cannot be as thoroughly influenced by one charismatic nonprofit leader).

Our research of large nonprofits confirms this. In a recent study, we identified 144 nonprofit organizations—created since 1970—that had grown to $50 million a year or more in size.[4] We found that each of these organizations grew large by pursuing specific sources of funding—often concentrated in one particular source of funds—that were a good match to support their particular types of work. Each had also built up highly professional internal fundraising capabilities targeted at those sources. In other words, each of the largest nonprofits had a well-developed funding model.

The larger the amount of funding needed, the more important it is to follow preexisting funding markets where there are particular decision makers with established motivations. Large groups of individual donors, for example, are already joined by common concerns about various issues, such as breast cancer research. And major government funding pools, to cite another example, already have specific objectives, such as foster care. Although a nonprofit that needs a few million dollars annually may convince a handful of foundations or wealthy individuals to support an issue that they had not previously prioritized, a nonprofit trying to raise tens of millions of dollars per year can rarely do so.

This is not to say that funding markets are static; they aren't. The first Earth Day in 1970 coincided with a major expansion in giving to environmental causes; the Ethiopian famine of 1984-85 led to a dramatic increase in support for international relief; and awareness of the U.S. educational crisis in the late 1980s laid the groundwork for charter school funding. Changes cannot be foreseen, however, and, hence, cannot be depended on as a source of funding. In addition, these changes were the product or culmination of complex national and international events, not the result of a single nonprofit's work.

Earl Martin Phalen, cofounder of BELL, an after-school and summer educational organization, captured the benefits of such intentionality well, summing up his experience for a group of nonprofit leaders in 2007. "Our fundraising strategy used to be 'let's raise more money this year than last' and we always were unsure of where we'd be. Then we got serious in thinking about our model and identified an ongoing type of government funding that was a good match for our work. While it required some program changes to work, we now predictably cover 70 percent of our costs in any locality through this approach."

Ten Funding Models
Devising a framework for nonprofit funding presents challenges. To be useful, the models cannot be too general or too specific. For example, a community health clinic serving patients covered by Medicaid and a nonprofit doing development work supported by the U.S. Agency for International Development are both government funded, yet the type of funding they get, and the decision makers controlling the funding, are very different. Lumping the two together in the same model would not be useful. At the same time, designating a separate model for nonprofits that receive Title I SES funds, for example, is too narrow to be useful.

In the end, we settled on three parameters to define our funding models—the source of funds, the types of decision makers, and the motivations of the decision makers. This allowed us to identify 10 distinct funding models at a level that is broadly relevant yet defines real choices.

It is interesting to note that there were several funding models we thought we might find, but didn't. One possible model was nonprofits supported by earned-income ventures distinct and separate from their core mission-related activities. Another possible model was nonprofits that operated on a strictly fee-for-service model in either a business-to business or direct-to-consumer fashion, without important supplementary fundraising (from members or prior beneficiaries) or underlying government support. Although there are some nonprofits supporting themselves with such funding approaches, they were not present among the large nonprofits that we studied. It is our belief that these types of approaches do not lend themselves to large-scale, sustained nonprofit advantage over for-profit entities.

What follows are descriptions of the 10 funding models, along with profiles of representative nonprofits for each model. The models are ordered by the dominant type of funder. The first three models (Heartfelt Connector, Beneficiary Builder, and Member Motivator) are funded largely by many individual donations. The next model (Big Bettor) is funded largely by a single person or by a few individuals or foundations. The next three models (Public Provider, Policy Innovator, and Beneficiary Broker) are funded largely by the government. The next model (Resource Recycler) is supported largely by corporate funding. And the last two models (Market Maker and Local Nationalizer) have a mix of funders.

1. Heartfelt Connector

Some nonprofits, such as the Make-a-Wish Foundation, grow large by focusing on causes that resonate with the existing concerns of large numbers of people at all income levels, and by creating a structured way for these people to connect where none had previously existed. Nonprofits that take this approach use a funding model we call the *Heartfelt Connector.* Some of the more popular causes are in the environmental, international, and medical research areas. They are different from nonprofits that tap individuals with particular religious beliefs, political leanings, or sporting interests, who come together to form organizations in the course of expressing their interests. Heartfelt Connectors often try to build explicit connections between volunteers through special fundraising events.

The Susan G. Komen Foundation is an example of a nonprofit that uses the Heartfelt Connector model. Established in 1982, the Komen Foundation works through a network of 125 affiliates to eradicate breast cancer as a life-threatening disease by funding research grants, by supporting education, screening, and treatment projects in communities around the world, and by educating women about the importance of early detection. The foundation's mission has a deep resonance with many women, even though its work may never benefit them directly. Between 1997 and 2007 the Komen Foundation's annual fundraising grew from $47 million to $334 million. The average individual donation is small, about $33, but the foundation's fundraising efforts have been driven by its ability to reach out to an ever-widening base of support. Its major fundraising vehicle is the Susan G. Komen Race for the Cure. The foundation and its affiliates hold about 120 running races each year that draw more than 1 million participants. These events not only allow individuals to give money; they also engage volunteers to put together teams, solicit funds, and participate in the race day experience.

Nonprofit leaders considering the Heartfelt Connector funding model should ask themselves the following questions:

• Have a large cross section of people already shown that they will fund causes in this domain?

• Can we communicate what is compelling about our nonprofit in a simple and concise way?

• Does a natural avenue exist to attract and involve large numbers of volunteers?

• Do we have, or can we develop, the in-house capabilities to attempt broad outreach in even one geographic area?

2. Beneficiary Builder

Some nonprofits, such as the Cleveland Clinic, are reimbursed for services that they provide to specific individuals, but rely on people who have benefited in the past from these services for additional donations. We call the funding model that these organizations use the *Beneficiary Builder*. Two of the best examples of Beneficiary Builders are hospitals and universities. Generally, the vast majority of these nonprofits' funding comes from fees that beneficiaries pay for the services the nonprofits provide. But the total cost of delivering the benefit is not covered by the fees. As a result, the nonprofit tries to build long-term relationships with people who have benefited from the service to provide supplemental support, hence the name Beneficiary Builder. Although these donations are often small relative to fees (averaging approximately 5 percent at hospitals and 30 percent at private universities), these funds are critical sources of income for major projects such as building, research, and endowment funds. Donors are often motivated to give money because they believe that the benefit they received changed their life. Organizations using a Beneficiary Builder model tend to obtain the majority of their charitable support from major gifts.

Princeton University is an example of a nonprofit that uses the Beneficiary Builder model. The university has become very adept at tapping alumni for donations, boasting the highest alumni-giving rate among national universities—59.2 percent. In 2008, more than 33,000 undergraduate alumni donated $43.6 million to their alma mater. As a result of the school's fundraising prowess, more than 50 percent of Princeton's operating budget is paid for by donations and earnings from its endowment.

Nonprofit leaders considering the Beneficiary Builder funding model should ask themselves the following questions:

- Does our mission create an individual benefit that is also perceived as an important social good?

- Do individuals develop a deep loyalty to the organization in the course of receiving their individual benefit?

- Do we have the infrastructure to reach out to beneficiaries in a scalable fashion?

3. Member Motivator

There are some nonprofits, such as Saddleback Church, that rely on individual donations and use a funding model we call *Member Motivator*. These individuals (who are members of the nonprofit) donate money because the issue is integral to their everyday life and is something from which they draw a collective benefit. Nonprofits using the Member Motivator funding model do not create the rationale for group activity, but instead connect with members (and donors) by offering or supporting the activities that they already seek. These organizations are often involved in religion, the environment, or arts, culture, and humanities.

The National Wild Turkey Federation (NWTF), which protects and expands wild turkey habitats and promotes wild turkey hunting, is an example of a Member Motivator. It attracts turkey hunters, who collectively benefit from NWTF's work and therefore become loyal members and fundraisers. Local NWTF members host more than 2,000 fundraising banquets each year, raising about 80 percent of the organization's annual revenues. These banquets provide multiple donation opportunities: entry tickets (which cost about $50 each and include an annual membership); merchandise purchase (averaging more than $100 per attendee); and raffle tickets (generating about $16,000 per banquet). NWTF's national headquarters supplies raffle prizes and merchandise to sell at these banquets. Each banquet clears an average of $10,000 after expenses. A significant portion of the money raised is dedicated to land and turkey conservation in the community from which it was donated.

Nonprofit leaders considering the Member Motivator funding model should ask themselves the following questions:

- Will our members feel that the actions of the organization are directly benefiting them, even if the benefit is shared collectively?

- Do we have the ability to involve and manage our members in fundraising activities?

- Can we commit to staying in tune with, and faithful to, our core membership, even if it means turning down funding opportunities and not pursuing activities that fail to resonate with our members?

4. Big Bettor

There are a few nonprofits, such as the Stanley Medical Research Institute, that rely on major grants from a few individuals or foundations to fund their operations. We call their funding model the *Big Bettor*. Often, the primary donor is also a founder, who wants to tackle an issue that is deeply personal to him or her. Although Big Bettors often launch with significant financial backing already secured, allowing them to grow large quickly, there are other instances when an existing organization gets the support of a major donor who decides to fund a new and important approach to solving a problem. The nonprofits we identified as Big Bettors are focused either on medical research or on environmental issues. The primary reasons that Big Bettors can attract sizable donations are: the problem being addressed can potentially be solved with a huge influx of money (for example, a vast sum can launch a research institute to cure a specific illness); or the organization is using a unique and compelling approach to solve the problem.

Conservation International (CI), whose mission is to conserve the Earth's biodiversity and to demonstrate that humans can live harmoniously with nature, is an example of a nonprofit that uses the Big Bettor funding model. CI's ability to identify locations around the world where protecting an area of land can have a significant effect on preserving global biodiversity helps it attract donors who are willing to contribute large amounts of money so that they can have an important and lasting impact on protecting the Earth. The majority of CI's contributions come from a few large donors.

Nonprofit leaders considering the Big Bettor funding model should ask themselves the following questions:

• Can we create a tangible and lasting solution to a major problem in a foreseeable time frame?

• Can we clearly articulate how we will use large-scale funding to achieve our goals?

• Are any of the wealthiest individuals or foundations interested in our issue and approach?

5. Public Provider

Many nonprofits, such as the Success for All Foundation, work with government agencies to provide essential social services, such as housing, human services, and education, for which the government has previously defined and allocated funding. Nonprofits that provide these services use a funding model we call *Public*

Provider. In some cases, the government outsources the service delivery function but establishes specific requirements for nonprofits to receive funding, such as reimbursement formulae or a request for proposal (RFP) process. As Public Providers grow, they often seek other funding sources to augment their funding base.

TMC (formerly the Texas Migrant Council), which supports children and families in migrant and immigrant communities, is an example of an organization that uses the Public Provider funding model. At its inception in 1971, TMC tapped into the federal government's Head Start program to fund its initial work, helping children prepare for school by focusing on the bilingual and bicultural needs of families. As TMC grew, its leaders sought to reduce its dependence on this one funding source and to identify other government funds. TMC now receives funding from a variety of federal, state, and local government sources. TMC has expanded from Texas into seven additional states and is offering new programs, such as literacy, prenatal care, and consumer education.

Nonprofit leaders considering the Public Provider funding model should ask themselves the following questions:

• Is our organization a natural match with one or more large, preexisting government programs?

• Can we demonstrate that our organization will do a better job than our competitors?

• Are we willing to take the time to secure contract renewals on a regular basis?

6. Policy Innovator

Some nonprofits, such as Youth Villages, rely on government money and use a funding model we call *Policy Innovator.* These nonprofits have developed novel methods to address social issues that are not clearly compatible with existing government funding programs. They have convinced government funders to support these alternate methods, usually by presenting their solutions as more effective and less expensive than existing programs. (By contrast, Public Providers tap into existing government programs to provide funds for the services they offer.)

An example of a Policy Innovator is HELP USA. This nonprofit provides transitional housing for the homeless and develops affordable permanent housing for low-income families. Andrew Cuomo (son of former New York governor Mario Cuomo) founded HELP USA in 1986 as an alternative to New York's approach of paying hotels to house the homeless in so-called "welfare hotels." HELP USA's innovative approach to the housing crisis came about in an era when homelessness was a prominent public issue and government funders were willing to try a novel approach. Cuomo gained the initial support of government decision makers by positioning his solution as both more effective and less costly, which was critical during New York's fiscal crisis. In 2007, HELP USA's revenues were $60 million, almost 80 percent of which came from government sources, half federal and half state and local. The organization was operating in New York City, Philadelphia, Las Vegas, Houston, and Buffalo, N.Y.

Nonprofit leaders considering the Policy Innovator funding model should ask themselves the following questions:

• Do we provide an innovative approach that surpasses the status quo (in impact and cost) and is compelling enough to attract government funders, which tend to gravitate toward traditional solutions?

• Can we provide government funders with evidence that our program works?

• Are we willing and able to cultivate strong relationships with government decision makers who will advocate change?

• At this time are there sufficient pressures on government to overturn the status quo?

7. Beneficiary Broker

Some nonprofits, such as the Iowa Student Loan Liquidity Corporation, compete with one another to provide government-funded or backed services to beneficiaries. Nonprofits that do this use what we call a *Beneficiary Broker* funding model. Among the areas where Beneficiary Brokers compete are housing, employment services, health care, and student loans. What distinguishes these nonprofits from other government-funded programs is that the beneficiaries are free to choose the nonprofit from which they will get the service.

The Metropolitan Boston Housing Partnership (MBHP), a regional nonprofit administering state and federal rental assistance voucher programs in 30 Massachusetts communities, is an example of a nonprofit that uses the Beneficiary Broker funding model. Since launching the organization in 1991, MBHP has developed a reputation as a reliable provider of housing vouchers for families in need. MBHP is the largest provider of housing vouchers in the Boston area, connecting more than 7,500 families to housing at any one time. MBHP also provides related services, such as education and homelessness prevention programs. More than 90 percent of MBHP's revenue comes from the small administrative fees the state provides as part of the voucher program. The remaining funds come from corporations and foundations.

Nonprofit leaders considering the Beneficiary Broker funding model should ask themselves the following questions:

• Can we demonstrate to the government our superior ability to connect benefit or voucher holders with benefits, such as successful placement rates and customer satisfaction feedback?

• Can we develop supplemental services that maximize the value of the benefit?

• Can we master the government regulations and requirements needed to be a provider of these benefits?

• Can we find ways to raise money to supplement the fees we receive from the benefits program?

8. Resource Recycler

Some nonprofits, such as AmeriCares Foundation, have grown large by collecting in-kind donations from corporations and individuals, and then distributing these donated goods to needy recipients who could not have purchased them on the market. Nonprofits that operate these types of programs use a funding model we call *Resource Recycler.* Businesses are willing to donate goods because they would otherwise go to waste (for example, foods with an expiration date), or because the marginal cost of making the goods is low and they will not be distributed in markets that would compete with the producer (for example, medications in developing countries). In-kind donations typically account for the majority of revenues, but Resource Recyclers must raise additional funds to support their operating costs. The vast majority of Resource Recyclers are involved in food, agriculture, medical, and nutrition programs and often are internationally focused.

The Greater Boston Food Bank (TGBFB), the largest hunger relief organization in New England, is an example of a nonprofit that uses the Resource Recycler funding model. This organization distributes nearly 30 million pounds of food annually to more than 600 local organizations, including food pantries, soup kitchens, day care centers, senior centers, and homeless shelters. TGBFB acquires goods in many ways. The dominant sources of goods are retailers and manufacturers. It also receives surplus food from restaurants and hotels. In 2006, corporate in-kind support accounted for 52 percent of TGBFB's revenues. Federal and state government programs provide TGBFB with in-kind goods and money, accounting for 23 percent of its annual budget, which TGBFB uses to purchase food for distribution. Cash donations from individuals make up the remaining 25 percent of revenues, covering overhead and capital improvements.

Nonprofit leaders considering the Resource Recycler funding model should ask themselves the following questions:

• Are the products that we distribute likely to be donated on an ongoing basis?

• Can we develop the expertise to stay abreast of trends in the industries that donate products to us so that we can prepare for fluctuations in donations?

• Do we have a strategy for attracting the cash we'll need to fund operations and overhead?

9. Market Maker

Some nonprofits, such as the Trust for Public Land, provide a service that straddles an altruistic donor and a payor motivated by market forces. Even though there is money available to pay for the service, it would be unseemly or unlawful for a for-profit to do so. Nonprofits that provide these services use a funding model we call *Market Maker*. Organ donation is one example where Market Makers operate. There is a demand for human organs, but it is illegal to sell them. These nonprofits generate the majority of their revenues from fees or donations that are directly linked to their activities. Most Market Makers operate in the area of health and disease, but some also operate in the environmental protection area (for example, land conservation).

The American Kidney Fund (AKF) is an example of a nonprofit that uses the Market Maker funding model. AKF was founded in 1971 to help low-income people with kidney failure pay for dialysis. It is now the country's leading source of financial aid to kidney dialysis patients, providing (in 2006) $82 million in annual grants to 63,500 kidney patients (about 19 percent of all dialysis patients). Before 1996, health care providers were allowed to pay Medicare Part B and Medigap premiums (approximately 20 percent of total costs) for needy dialysis patients. In 1996, the federal government made it illegal for providers to do this because it might trap the patient into receiving dialysis from a particular provider. The new law left thousands of kidney patients unable to afford kidney treatment. AKF noticed this gap and established a program to fill it. AKF now pays these premiums, allowing patients to continue their treatment. AKF is funded primarily by health care providers and other corporations. AKF is now applying the same principles used in its kidney dialysis program for pharmaceuticals used to treat bone loss.

Nonprofit leaders considering the Market Maker funding model should ask themselves the following questions:

• Is there a group of funders with a financial interest in supporting our work?

- Are there legal or ethical reasons why it would be more appropriate for a nonprofit to deliver the services?

- Do we already have a trusted program and brand name?

10. Local Nationalizer

There are a number of nonprofits, such as Big Brothers Big Sisters of America, that have grown large by creating a national network of locally based operations. These nonprofits use a funding model we call *Local Nationalizers*. These organizations focus on issues, such as poor schools or children in need of adult role models that are important to local communities across the country, where government alone can't solve the problem. Most of the money for programs is raised locally, often from individual or corporate donations and special events. Very little of the money comes from government agencies or fees. Very few local operations exceed $5 million in size, but, in totality they can be quite large.

Teach for America (TFA) is an example of a nonprofit that uses a Local Nationalizer funding model. TFA recruits, trains, and places recent college graduates into teaching positions in schools across the country. TFA was founded in 1989, and by 2007 had more than $90 million in annual revenues. The organization relies on its 26 regional TFA offices to raise more than 75 percent of its funding. The reason this works is that TFA's mission—improving the quality of K-12 education—resonates with local funders. TFA developed a culture in which fundraising is considered a critical aspect of the organization at every level, and it recruited local executive directors who would take ownership of attracting regional funding growth.

Nonprofit leaders considering the Local Nationalizer funding model should ask themselves the following questions:

- Does our cause address an issue that local leaders consider a high priority, and is this issue compelling in communities across the country?

- Does expanding our organization into other communities fulfill our mission?

- Can we replicate our model in other communities?

- Are we committed to identifying and empowering high-performing leaders to run local branches of our organization in other communities?

Implications for Nonprofits

In the current economic climate it is tempting for nonprofit leaders to seek money wherever they can find it, causing some nonprofits to veer off course. That would be a mistake. During tough times it is more important than ever for nonprofit leaders to examine their funding strategy closely and to be disciplined about the way that they raise money. We hope that this article provides a framework for nonprofit leaders to do just that.

The funding paths that nonprofits take will vary, and not all will find models that support large-scale programs. The good news is that all nonprofits can benefit from greater clarity about their most effective funding model, and it is possible for some nonprofits to develop models that raise large amounts of money. As mentioned earlier, almost 150 new nonprofits (not counting universities and hospitals), surpassed $50 million in annual revenues between 1970 and 2003.

On the other side of the equation, philanthropists are becoming more disciplined about their nonprofit investing. A growing number of foundations, such as the Edna McConnell Clark Foundation and New Profit Inc., are investing in their grantees to improve both program and funding models. We hope that this article helps philanthropists become clearer about their funding strategy so that they can support their programs more effectively.

As society looks to the nonprofit sector and philanthropy to solve important problems, a realistic understanding of funding models is increasingly important to realizing those aspirations.

IDENTIFYING THE MODELS

We started by identifying a pool of nonprofits to study by combining *The Nonprofit Times'* "Top 100" list (from 2006) with our list of 144 nonprofits founded since 1970 that have reached $50 million or greater in size. Several major types of nonprofits (for example, hospitals, universities, and religious congregations) were not represented in this sample so we added them to our pool. Next, we collected revenue and funding data for each sample organization. As we categorized the data, we began to identify funding patterns. Each major funding source (for example, government) broke into a handful of sub-sources that represented distinct decision makers and motivations and linked remarkably well to the organization's missions and domains. At the end of this process, we had 10 funding models. Then, we interviewed the leaders of organizations that epitomize each model. Our goal in the interviews was to explore the challenges and trade-offs of each model, and to better understand the drivers of successful fundraising within each model. —W.F., P.K., & B.C.

Model	Characteristics	Examples	Tactical Tools
Heartfelt Connector			
Funding source: Individual **Funding decision maker:** Multitude of individuals **Funding motivation:** Altruism	• The mission has broad appeal • The benefits often touch the lives of the funder's family and friends • Nonprofit connects donors to the cause through volunteerism or other means	• Medical research (Susan G. Komen Foundation) • Environment (Natural Resources Defense Council) • International (Save the Children)	• Special events • Direct mail • Corporate sponsorship
Beneficiary Builder			
Funding source: Individual **Funding decision maker:** Multitude of individuals **Funding motivation:** Self-interest followed by altruism	• The mission initially attracts individuals pursuing, and paying for, specific individual benefits • Mission creates a strong individual connection through the delivery of the benefit (for example, spending four years on campus or having one's life saved) • Benefits created viewed as having important societal benefits	• Universities (Princeton University) • Hospitals (Cleveland Clinic)	• Fees • Major gifts
Member Motivator			
Funding source: Individual **Funding decision maker:** Multitude of individuals **Funding motivation:** Collective interest	• Most of the benefits have a group orientation (for example, religious services or hiking), creating an inherent collective community to tap into for fundraising • Uses richest mixture of tactical tools to raise money	• Religious congregations (Saddleback Church) • Arts and culture (National Public Radio) • Environment and conservation (National Wild Turkey Federation)	• Membership • Fees • Special events • Major gifts • Direct mail

Model	Characteristics	Examples	Tactical Tools
Big Bettor			
Funding source: Individual or foundation **Funding decision maker:** Few individuals **Funding motivation:** Altruism	• Builds majority of support from small number of individuals or family foundations • Mission may be fulfilled within limited number of decades (for example, finding cure to a certain disease)	• Medical research (The Stanley Medical Research Institute) • Environment (Conservation International)	• Major gifts
Public Provider			
Funding source: Government **Funding decision maker:** Administrators **Funding motivation:** Collective interest	• Provides services that are perceived as core government responsibility (for example, foster care) • Clear definitions exist of the services and processes that nonprofits must provide (for example, RFPs)	• Human services (TMC) • Education (Success for All Foundation) • International (Family Health International)	• Government contracts
Policy Innovator			
Funding source: Government **Funding decision maker:** Policymakers **Funding motivation:** Collective interest	• Secures government funds for a significant new approach to problem or to address a problem not currently viewed as a core government responsibility • Requires a high-level government "champion" • Generally succeeds when significant pressures exist on government as a result of a fiscal or media crisis	• Human Services (Youth Villages) • Education (Communities in Schools) • International (International AIDS Vaccine Initiative)	• Legislative appropriation or earmark • Executive earmark • Government pilot project

Model	Characteristics	Examples	Tactical Tools
Beneficiary Broker			
Funding source: Government **Funding decision maker**: Multitude of individuals **Funding motivation:** Self-interest	• Individual beneficiaries decide how to spend the government benefit • Must navigate and influence government decision makers for eligibility and compliance with reimbursement requirements • Requires individual marketing capability to reach and service end beneficiary	• Health (East Boston Neighborhood Health Center) • Housing (Metropolitan Boston Housing Partnership) • Employment (Peckham Vocational Industries) • Public and societal benefit (Iowa Student Loan Liquidity Corporation)	• Government reimbursement
Resource Recycler			
Funding source: Corporate **Funding decision maker:** Few individuals **Funding motivation:** Self-interest	• The nonprofit uses goods that are created in the market economy where there are inefficiencies that create a surplus (for example, food) or where the marginal costs to produce the product are low (for example, pharmaceuticals)	• Food (Oregon Food Bank) • International (AmeriCares Foundation)	• In-kind giving

Model	Characteristics	Examples	Tactical Tools
Market Maker			
Funding source: Mixed **Funding decision maker:** Mass of individuals (one side), few individuals (other side) **Funding motivation:** Altruism (one side), self-interest (other side)	• A funder with some degree of self-interest and the ability to pay exists (for example, a health system buying blood) • Often, one of the parties involved in the transaction is motivated largely by altruism (for example, a blood donor or land donor)	• Health (American Kidney Fund) • Environment or conservation (The Trust for Public Land)	• Fees • Major gifts (corporate or individual)
Local Nationalizer			
Funding source: Mixed **Funding decision maker:** Few individuals **Funding motivation:** Altruism	• The issue is one of a few top priorities for improvement or success in a locality (for example, creating a quality city school system) • The issue is common enough to exist in many localities nationwide • The level of funding available in any single geographic area is usually limited	• Education (Teach for America) • Youth development (Big Brothers Big Sisters of America)	• Major gifts • Special events

StanfordSOCIAL INNOVATION REVIEW

This article originally appeared in the Fall 2008 issue of the Stanford Social Innovation Review.

Money to Grow On

In the for-profit world, the term "investment" has clear meaning and investors have sophisticated techniques for spotting and growing the most promising companies. Yet foundations and other nonprofit donors have not developed similar clarity or approaches. As a result, the nonprofit sector's greatest gems often languish well below their full potential. By better translating for-profit concepts, donors can learn how to scout out and grow the best nonprofits. Likewise, certain nonprofits can take a page from business's playbook and learn how to attract cash for expansion.

By William Foster

Over the past decade, the nonprofit sector has been increasingly abuzz with talk of strategic philanthropy, venture philanthropy, growth capital, and other forms of nonprofit investing. Among the Web sites of the 100 largest U.S. foundations, for example, 77 tout that they are involved in some type of "investment," "leverage," or "venture activity." As entrepreneurs turn into philanthropists, they want to have the same outsized impact with their giving as they did with their business ventures. At the same time, institutional foundations want to leverage their dollars to do the most good.

Although many nonprofit donors are talking about strategic investing, few are actually putting these ideas into practice. Most make grants that are too small to have a big impact. In 2005, for example, the 100 largest U.S. foundations made (usually multiyear) grants whose average was approximately $200,000. These same foundations' assets, meanwhile, average some $2 billion.[1]

In addition, outside of gifts to universities, hospitals, and foundations, all U.S. individual donors and foundations made fewer than 150 grants of $5 million or more to the nonprofit sector in 2005. Only 25 of these went to human service organizations.[2] By contrast, in 2005, U.S. venture capitalists alone made 3,100 investments averaging $7.2 million each.[3]

What's more, most philanthropic donors restrict their gifts to specific programs, so grantees cannot use the money to grow their organizations as a whole. In 2006, only 19 percent of U.S. grants were either unrestricted or for general support.[4] The rest of the grants—81 percent—could be spent only on designated activities, such as tutoring services for youth in a particular high school or for the construction of a particular building. By contrast, most venture capital investments are not restricted to a specific product, department, or program. Instead, companies can use the money to grow—for example, opening offices in new locations, expanding the company's information technology system, and hiring sales and marketing staff.

"Only a handful of funders are making grants that function like investments to growth-oriented nonprofits," says Harvard Business School professor Allen Grossman. "I doubt that the total amount nationwide exceeds $100 million per year."

This handful is worth watching—and emulating. These funders are awarding grants that are becoming known as "growth capital"—large investments that are used to increase the size of an organization's operations and that are not needed to sustain the organization once it has gotten larger. The recipients are themselves trailblazers, using the funds to increase their impact dramatically.

Growth capital is for nonprofits that have demonstrated that their programs work and that have identified a steady source of funds that can support their ongoing efforts. It is not for small, innovative, but still untested nonprofits or for organizations that do not have a sustainable funding model. If one were to draw an analogy to venture capital funding, nonprofit growth capital would be the equivalent of later stage funding, not early stage funding.

There's great potential in nonprofit growth capital investing. To realize this potential, however, funders and nonprofit leaders alike need to understand the differences between growth capital and grants for ongoing operations—in essence, the difference between investment and revenue. They must also develop the ability to identify the limited number of nonprofits that can benefit from growth capital.

Over the last several years, the Bridgespan Group has worked with and studied both funders that provide growth capital and nonprofits that receive it. We have helped two of the most promising candidates for growth capital develop their business plans—Youth Villages, a Memphis-based organization that helps emotionally and behaviorally troubled youth and their families, and Alexandria, Va.-based Communities in Schools, which helps students stay in school. We have also helped one of the largest providers of growth capital, the Edna McConnell Clark Foundation (EMCF), develop its strategy, identify potential grantees, and assist its grantees with business planning. And we were part of the business planning for a particularly promising new growth capital intermediary, SeaChange Capital Partners, whose founding donor is the Goldman Sachs Group Inc.

Through these experiences, we have honed due diligence processes that funders can use to identify promising nonprofits that can effectively use growth capital to go to scale (and those that cannot). The common deal breaker? A sustainable funding model. Nonprofits can likewise use this process to figure out whether and how they can attract growth capital.

Growth Capital

Nonprofits and funders alike often blur the important distinction between investments that help an organization grow (growth capital) and investments that fund ongoing programs (revenue). Some of this blurring is intentional. When nonprofits ask foundations for grants, they routinely highlight onetime, growth-oriented uses for money, knowing full well that in reality the money will be needed to fund ongoing operations. Both parties talk as if they're making a deal on Wall Street when it is really a transaction on Main Street. Of course, funders are willing participants. Only a small minority of grant opportunities can really function like investments and help nonprofits grow, but that is what many foundation staff, management, and board members routinely set as objectives. This dynamic has been called "the dance of deception."

The good news is that some funders are beginning to be much more rigorous about differentiating between growth capital investments and other donations; they're also increasingly focusing on the potential impact they can have through growth capital. These philanthropists make grants large enough for nonprofits to invest in capacity-building activities, such as hiring more managers, training new staff, buying new software, and covering short-term losses as the organization expands its operations.[5] In general, these are investors with a deep commitment to organization building and an uncommon self-discipline about measuring results. Over time, they have found the need to be more selective about their grantees and to provide better forms of support. (See "Growth Capital Funders and Intermediaries" on p. 106.)

One of the leading growth capital investors is EMCF. For the past year, it has been raising $120 million from a group of institutional and individual funders to provide growth capital to three nonprofits: Youth Villages; The Nurse-Family Partnership, a Denver-based organization that helps low-income teen mothers with parenting and planning; and Citizen Schools, a Boston-based nonprofit that provides after-school programs and expanded learning time to middle school students.

EMCF committed $39 million of its own funds to this campaign and has publicly announced an additional $49 million from donors including the Picower Foundation, the Samberg Family Foundation, and the Atlantic Philanthropies. When completed, this will be the largest investment of philanthropic growth capital to date.[6]

"To help disadvantaged youth on a national scale, we must raise much more capital and direct it more effectively," says Nancy Roob, president of EMCF. "Each of these grantees has proven its program, is poised for growth, and has a business plan with an increased emphasis on financial strategies that will lead to sustainability. Ultimately, this infusion of growth capital from the private sector will leverage significant public investment, aligning philanthropic and government resources to provide truly effective remedies to serious social ills facing our nation's youth today."

On the other side of the checkbook, several additional nonprofits are using such investments to pursue their growth. In 2005, for example, Washington, D.C.-based College Summit, an organization that helps schools and districts increase the number of students enrolling in college, raised $15 million from 10 investors and is using the money to quintuple its size.

Similarly, in 2006, New York-based Teach for America, a nonprofit that trains outstanding recent college graduates and places them in teaching positions in urban and rural schools, raised $60 million in growth capital. It is using this funding to more than double the size of its teacher corps and to increase their impact.

And in 2007, Boston-based Year Up, a national nonprofit that trains urban young adults and helps them secure living-wage jobs, closed an $18 million growth capital campaign and plans to use this money to build the infrastructure needed to serve four times as many young adults.

The increase in growth capital investments is a positive trend, but it will pay off only if grantees are able to sustain their new size and scope. And therein lies the challenge: How can a philanthropist tell if an organization has what it takes not only to get bigger, but also to stay effective? More than unraveling an accounting dilemma (although it is that too), the key to making a successful growth capital investment lies in finding the few nonprofits that can use the funds to achieve important and lasting social impact.

Spotting Potential

Before venture capitalists invest in a company, they conduct a thorough review of the company's management team, business model, and strategic plan, along with an analysis of the company's competition and market. More often than not, they walk away from deals that are in many respects attractive. Few nonprofit donors undertake such rigorous due diligence. But they should.

We have identified seven criteria that nonprofit donors should use to choose recipients of their growth capital investments. To be sure, there is no magic in the number seven. We could condense these criteria into six or expand them into eight. The important point is that nonprofit donors need a due diligence process to guide their investments.

The first three characteristics are important for many kinds of funding and can be found in a wide range of nonprofits. The next three characteristics relate to the readiness of an organization for growth and narrow the pool of candidates considerably. The seventh and last characteristic is the most difficult to find, but also the most important, because it identifies those nonprofits that can sustain growth and are therefore ready for growth capital.

First Round of Due Diligence

1. The organization addresses a critical need. No investment can succeed in a big way if the nonprofit is tackling a small or unimportant problem. Of course, determining this is a matter of opinion and values. Philanthropists should fund the issues that they themselves view as critical. If the philanthropist believes that the nonprofit will need to attract funding from other donors, however, she should assess whether broader society views the problem as a critical unmet need. Some issues (for example, failures in the education system) are more widely viewed as such than others (for example, increasing youth soccer skills[7]).

Citizen Schools, College Summit, and Teach for America all focus on educational inequities—a top priority of most local governments, politicians, and many philanthropists.

2. The organization has strong leadership. Philanthropists need to look beyond charisma to the management strength of both the executive director and the overall leadership team, including managers and board members. As with any successful venture capital investment, nonprofit growth capital investments succeed because of the leadership more than the specifics of a plan. Circumstances and conditions will change, and the team will need to react. In the nonprofit world, moreover, boards of directors often play a significant role in helping executive directors and management teams adapt. Although part of a growth plan may include augmenting the team, the core members should be in place.

It is worth noting that the leadership of the organizations that have raised or are raising growth capital are widely acclaimed. For example, Patrick Lawler, the CEO of Youth Villages, was named one of America's best leaders by *U.S. News & World Report* in 2006. Bill Milliken and Dan Cardinali of Communities in Schools are recognized for having created an exemplary pairing of an inspirational founder and results-oriented CEO. And the leaders of Year Up, College Summit, Citizen Schools, and Teach for America have all been recognized by *Fast Company* among the social entrepreneurs of the year.

3. The organization has strategic clarity. The management team must be able to state clearly what it wants to accomplish. Its approach for accomplishing these goals must be compelling and credible, and must logically lay out the sequence of steps necessary. Before initiating growth capital campaigns, all of the organizations mentioned above had completed rigorous business plans that laid out the objectives and steps that they would take. Most secured outside consulting assistance to test and refine their plans.

Second Round of Due Diligence
4. The organization's programs are demonstrated successes. Many nonprofits have a compelling vision but little proof that what they are doing is actually working. Because the return on the investment into a nonprofit's growth is increased social impact, investors need some evidence that the nonprofit is having an impact in the first place. Different investors have different standards of evidence, but all should require some substantial proof.

Consider two examples: Communities in Schools is trying to keep students from dropping out of school. Before exploring a growth capital campaign, Communities in Schools' leaders invested in a rigorous, multiyear study of the organization's impact, the first phase of which showed that the promotion and graduation rates of entire schools improve where the program was implemented with fidelity.[8]

The Nurse-Family Partnership conducted three randomized controlled trials that showed that, even 15 years later, mothers in the program earned more money than did ones in a control group who did not participate in the program; they were also less likely to be involved in criminal behavior. Children in the program have greater school readiness and fewer adjudications, even when they reach their teenage years.

5. The organization's programs are cost-effective. Not only must organizations prove that their programs are successful, they must also show that they get the most value out of their funding. Youth Villages is a good example of a cost-effective organization. It is difficult to make a sweeping generalization, but as a general rule, for $8 million, the national child welfare system, which relies heavily on residential institutions, can serve 100 youths, only 40 percent of whom are likely to be successful (defined as being in school or working and not back in state custody) two years after being discharged. For the same $8 million, Youth Villages can serve 550 youths, 80 percent of whom are likely to achieve long-term success. Youth Villages achieves these results with a research-based, in-home support service it calls "intercept." Each of the organization's counselors focuses on supporting four or five children and their families in a highly structured environment, 24 hours a day, seven days a week. Intensive? Yes. But it is much less costly and more successful than institutionalization.

6. The organization has grown successfully. Growth can strain every aspect of a nonprofit organization. Its cultural fabric can fray as the number of employees grows. Tensions can arise between program-oriented founders and outsiders brought in for functional expertise. The demands on a leader's time increase dramatically and require new skills. And so investors should look for a track record of successfully adapting to the demands of growth—even modest growth—before making large investments in further growth.

Consider the example of Year Up. Before beginning its campaign to raise growth capital in 2007, Year Up pursued a very deliberate strategy of phased growth. First, the organization honed its Boston program in a proof-of-concept phase, and then it demonstrated that the program could work elsewhere by expanding to Providence, R.I., Washington, D.C., and New York. In each of these sites, its program, operations, and partnerships were up and running, helping Year Up to make the case to growth capital investors that its model was truly replicable.

The Deal Breaker
7. The organization has a sustainable funding model. Conventional wisdom says that nonprofits do not have sustainable funding models—that is, they cannot develop predictable, ongoing financial support that covers core operating expenses. The common image of nonprofits is that they are often led by an executive director

who is not sure how he will find enough money to meet the year's budget and is perpetually pulling rabbits out of his hat to do so.

Yet sustainable nonprofits do exist, and there are more of them each year. In fact, almost every nonprofit that has grown large in recent decades has cultivated sustainable funding. And the larger a nonprofit becomes, the more it needs a well-developed funding model. Large amounts of dollars cannot be consistently raised without identifying and building expertise in highly aligned sources of funding.

Unfortunately, not all causes have equal opportunities for securing ongoing financial support. For example, advocacy groups—those giving voice to the voiceless—have a notoriously hard time attracting significant amounts of ongoing funding. Yet many types of nonprofits are able to raise substantial amounts of money, and their sources are familiar. (For these sources, see "How Nonprofits Get Really Big" in the spring 2007 issue of the *Stanford Social Innovation Review.*)

Youth Villages, for instance, has secured a steady stream of funding from the government. Because state governments view taking care of emotionally and behaviorally troubled children as a core responsibility, and Youth Villages has partnered closely with government, 95 percent of Youth Villages' ongoing costs are covered through government reimbursement. The organization currently has more than 15 contracts across multiple states. Still, most government agencies won't pay for nonprofits' expansion, so Youth Villages has sought and secured foundation grants to expand into new states.

Many educational nonprofits likewise rely on government funding. For example, the fees that College Summit charges schools and districts for its services nearly cover the organization's variable costs. Teach for America has shown across many cities that it can secure funding from a mix of local sources—individual donors, foundations, and corporations—to cover the vast majority of a location's ongoing expenses.

Ironically, an organization with a solid fundraising base often looks unattractive to funders, who wonder whether the organization is already too rich and well established. Yet this kind of financial health is what a philanthropist must demand if a grant is truly going to fuel substantive and sustainable impact.

Impact on Funder

Having examined the finer details of good growth capital candidates, funders must then turn the lens on themselves. Nonprofit growth investors need a set of processes and skills different from other types of philanthropists.

Growth capital funders must devote more time and attention to finding the right nonprofits to invest in, and less time to current grantees' board meetings, annual galas, and site visits. Like private equity investors, who spend as much as two years looking at companies before investing in them, nonprofit growth investors must be careful and choosy. In this way, they can assess whether potential grantees meet all seven criteria. They must also be willing to say "no" much more often than they do now, even turning down existing grantees that are doing fine work.

Donors will also need to co-invest with other donors—something done too rarely. Co-investing differs from simply giving a grant to a nonprofit that already receives grants from other philanthropists. In co-investing, a group of funders invest at the same time, on the same terms, using the same reporting, and share credit for the impact. Donors need to co-invest because the amount of funding many growth capital candidates need often exceeds what any one funder is able to provide. To date, the most notable growth capital campaigns have raised more than $10 million, some have raised more than $50 million, and all have been backed by groups of multiple funders.

Once funders identify and invest in a suitable nonprofit, they need to make sure that the influx of money does not distort the organization's ongoing funding model. Large amounts of money can do so a number of different ways. The unaccustomed influx of large amounts of money can weaken an organization's financial discipline and undermine part of what made the nonprofit attractive in the first place. Even with a well-developed funding model, core ongoing support may be able to grow only at a certain rate. If the growth capital plan calls for unrealistic levels of growth, nonprofit executives may fail to meet their goals. And even compelling nonprofits may find it takes longer than expected to attract growth capital. If anchor funders encourage a nonprofit leader to set too large a goal for their growth capital, the time it takes to secure the philanthropic investment could undercut the time they need to do their work.

At the same time, nonprofit growth investors have to be less restrictive with the terms of their grants than are other kinds of philanthropists. They must eschew many common practices, such as restricting dollars (explicitly or implicitly), giving only short-term funding, or demanding specialized reporting, as these undermine the long-term success of a growth capital investment. The whole point of growth capital is to support the leaders of the highest-potential nonprofits—leaders and nonprofits who are chosen precisely because they can be trusted. These organizations need to spend their time and resources growing, not fundraising. The philanthropist's source of satisfaction needs to be in the results.

Only a few pioneering donors are currently pursuing growth capital investments. And only a few nonprofits have the funding models and other characteristics to use these funds successfully. The art is in matching these funders and nonprofits, and in increasing the numbers in both groups.

Nevertheless, these matches are possible because remarkable nonprofits do exist. Equivalent organizations in the for-profit world would attract large amounts of money from great investors. Why, in the nonprofit world, shouldn't these organizations attract large sums from the greatest philanthropic investors? If these organizations did attract growth capital, the most vulnerable people and places in our country would be the big winners. Perhaps one day soon, a $5 million philanthropic donation won't be notable simply because of its rarity, but rather because it enables the nonprofit to be more effective in tackling one of society's big problems.

This article has benefited from the thoughtful and ongoing insights of my fellow Bridgespan partners, especially Alan Tuck and Kelly Campbell.

WHEN SHOULD A NONPROFIT SEEK GROWTH CAPITAL?

The idea of raising lots of money gets most nonprofit leaders excited. But growth capital is not for everyone. In fact, it is not for most organizations. To determine whether your nonprofit might be a good candidate for growth capital, first answer these questions:

1. Does our organization address a critical need?

2. Do we have a strong leadership team?

3. Do we have a credible approach to the problem we are trying to solve?

4. Can we demonstrate our results?

5. Is our solution cost-effective?

6. Have we grown successfully in the past?

If you can answer "yes" to these six questions, then ponder the deal breaker:

7. Do we have a clear and logical funding model that provides core ongoing funding?

Then ask two very pragmatic questions:

Is there a likely anchor funder who can provide a substantial percentage of the desired funding?

Do our board members and senior executives have the personal relationships needed to connect with promising additional funders?

GROWTH CAPITAL FUNDERS AND INTERMEDIARIES

A small but growing number of organizations are involved in providing growth capital. They can be divided into funders that provide growth capital and intermediaries that help secure it. —*The Editors*

Funders

Edna McConnell Clark Foundation, New York. A foundation that advances opportunities for low-income youth ages 9 to 24 in the United States.

The Jenesis Group, Irving, Texas. A family foundation that supports nonprofits focused on youth development, education, and social entrepreneurship.

The Kresge Foundation, Troy, Mich. A foundation that supports nonprofits around the world in the areas of health, the environment, arts and culture, education, human services, and community development.

New Profit Inc., Cambridge, Mass. An organization that provides financial and strategic support to social entrepreneurs and their organizations.

NewSchools Venture Fund, San Francisco. A venture philanthropy firm that seeks to transform public education.

REDF, San Francisco. A venture philanthropy firm that invests in organizations that employ people who would otherwise remain in long-term poverty.

Robertson Foundation, New York. A foundation that makes grants in the areas of the environment, education, medical research, and religion and spirituality.

Surdna Foundation, New York. A family foundation that makes grants in the areas of the environment, arts, community revitalization, effective citizenry, and the nonprofit sector.

Venture Philanthropy Partners, Washington, D.C. A philanthropic organization that invests in nonprofits that improve the lives and opportunities of low-income youth in the Washington, D.C., area.

Intermediaries

Bridgespan Group, Boston. A nonprofit consultancy that advises nonprofits and foundations on growth capital.

Nonprofit Finance Fund Capital Partners, New York. A broker that helps nonprofits raise equity-like capital.

SeaChange Capital Partners, South Norwalk, Conn. An organization that creates connections between wealthy donors and high-performing nonprofits.

StanfordSOCIAL
INNOVATION REVIEW

This article originally appeared in the Spring 2007 issue of the Stanford Social Innovation Review.

How Nonprofits Get Really Big

Since 1970, more than 200,000 nonprofits have opened in the U.S., but only 144 of them have reached $50 million in annual revenue. Most of the members of this elite group got big by doing two things. They raised the bulk of their money from a single type of funder such as corporations or government—and not, as conventional wisdom would recommend, by going after diverse sources of funding. Just as importantly, these nonprofits created professional organizations that were tailored to the needs of their primary funding sources.

By William Foster and Gail Fine [Perreault]

Squeezed around a conference table designed for eight people, 12 leaders of a highly regarded nonprofit discuss how to fund the organization's growth. With the support of a large national foundation, several family foundations, a few major individual donors and many smaller ones, a handful of government agencies and corporations, and even an earned-income venture, the organization has grown significantly, if erratically, to reach about $3 million in annual revenues.

The group's programs bring young people from the inner city together with their peers from the suburbs to engage in leadership activities. Now, a decade after the organization's founding, the board and staff are eager to grow. The problem is, some board and staff members fear, that their funders are nearing the limits of what they can or will contribute. And without increased funding, the organization will not be able to expand. Has the organization hit a funding wall? Where should it turn for additional money?

One board member makes the case for additional government funding. Another sees enormous potential in a direct mail campaign. The executive director and staff maintain that the organization can secure funding from one more large national foundation.

Without any clear path, no idea is a bad one. As the conversation winds down, the leaders identify the most promising funding sources, divide responsibilities, and put the next steps into motion. They do not know the odds of success, but their hopes are high.[1]

Funding Growth is Difficult

As the number of nonprofits and the scope of their ambitions explode, conversations such as this one have become commonplace in nonprofit board meetings across the U.S. Almost to a person, all of the nonprofit leaders with whom the Bridgespan Group has worked want to increase their organization's reach.[2] In a recent study of the most dynamic, midsized youth-serving nonprofits in the country, the people we talked to repeatedly asked, "How do we get really big?"[3]

The answers to this question are anything but obvious. And examples of nonprofits to imitate do not readily come to mind. The average founding year of the 10 largest U.S. nonprofits is 1903.[4] What can younger nonprofits learn from organizations that began before the First World War?

Moreover, figuring out how dollars flow within the nonprofit sector is infamously difficult. The nonprofit "capital markets" are often irrational. Some donors strictly limit the number of years that they will provide support, and they often meet increased efficiencies with decreased funding.[5] Many of the most successful nonprofit leaders have their hands full simply keeping existing funders engaged, let alone planning for major growth. When funding breakthroughs do occur, they seem idiosyncratic—due more to luck or personal charisma than to planning.

To discover whether there is logic hidden in the haze, Bridgespan identified and studied nonprofit organizations and networks founded in the U.S. in or since 1970 that had achieved $50 million or more in annual revenue by 2003. (Hospitals and colleges, where sources of major funding are well understood, were not included in the study.) Our hope was that we might discover some rules of the road for nonprofits that want to jump to the next level and get really big.

Our findings contradict some of the conventional wisdom about nonprofit growth. First and foremost, although it may be hard to get really big in today's environment, it is not impossible—nor is it simply luck and connections that help a nonprofit make the jump. Greater numbers of nonprofits achieve substantial growth than is generally perceived.

Bridgespan identified 144 nonprofits that have gone from founding to at least $50 million in revenue since 1970. Some of these organizations, like Habitat for Humanity International, America's Second Harvest, and the Make-a-Wish Foundation of America, are household names. Most, like Youth Villages, Communities in Schools, and the National Wild Turkey Federation (NWTF), are not—at least not yet.

Further, the way funding flows to organizations this large is neither completely random nor illogical. On the contrary, we identified three important practices common among nonprofits that succeeded in building large-scale funding models: (1) They developed funding in one concentrated source rather than across diverse sources; (2) they found a funding source that was a natural match to their mission and beneficiaries; and (3) they built a professional organization and structure around this funding model.

Getting big is not the right choice for every nonprofit, of course. Securing large-scale funding generally involves some programmatic trade-offs. And large sources of funding appear to be more readily available for—and appropriate to—some missions than others.

Admittedly, using revenue as the metric for growth has its limitations. It does not necessarily capture all the elements of an organization's "scale" (for example, volunteer hours). But revenue does allow comparison across organizations, and it is the central constraint that prevents many nonprofits from growing. For those nonprofits that do want to grow their revenues, understanding the paths that others have blazed over the past three decades will increase their odds of success.

The Myth of Diversification

Many leaders of aspiring nonprofits state that their No. 1 funding objective is diversification. It seems sensible. When government funding stalls, why not try to raise money from individual donations? When corporate money dries up, why not try to replace it with foundation grants? And isn't having a wide array of funding sources a good way to mitigate the risk of losing any single source of money?

Diversification may seem like a good idea, but in practice most of the organizations that have gotten really big over the past three decades did so by concentrating on one type of funding source, not by diversifying across several sources of funding. Bridgespan obtained solid financial data for 110 of the 144 high-growth nonprofits we identified. Of the 110, roughly 90 percent had a single dominant source of funding—such as government, individual donations, or corporate gifts. And on average, that dominant funding source accounted for just over 90 percent of the organization's total funding.

To better understand this finding, we conducted in-depth interviews with leaders of 21 of these 110 organizations. We found that more than two-thirds of them had not only a dominant source of funding, but also a specialization within that area:

for example, not just government funding but also state government funding; not just individual donations but also small individual donations; and not just corporate donations but also in-kind corporate donations.

Only a few of the 21 interviewees knew from the start where they would find their most promising funding sources. Often, they were uncertain about which source was most promising. But as these organizations pursued their growth, they realized which sources of funding seemed most promising and were willing to concentrate their efforts on that source, recruiting people and creating organizations that could best pursue that funding source.

Consider the example of the American Kidney Fund (AKF), which helps low-income people with kidney disease. From its founding in 1971 until the mid-1990s, the AKF was a relatively small organization, never surpassing $6 million in revenue and relying on a mix of funding including a large number of small individual donations. In 1996, changes in federal law made it illegal for medical providers to assist low-income patients by subsidizing the roughly 20 percent of dialysis expenses that Medicare did not cover—effectively cutting patients off from treatment. To cover these expenses and restore care to low-income patients, the AKF set up a major initiative to raise donations from corporations. The AKF became highly skilled at this work and the organization grew rapidly, passing the $20 million mark in 2000 and reaching nearly $70 million in 2004. "Switching our emphasis to corporate partners was the real turning point in our organization," says Chief Financial Officer Don Roy.

Previous Bridgespan research suggests that the AKF's experience is not idiosyncratic.[6] In multiple nonprofit domains (such as environmental advocacy and youth services) there are distinct breakpoints at which the number of nonprofits decreases dramatically from one revenue category to the next. After each of these breakpoints, both the average level of diversification and the mix of funding change.

Take the examples of youth services and environmental advocacy. When nonprofits in these domains are small, they typically have a diverse set of funding sources, with a large percentage of the money coming from foundations. As these organizations grow to $3 million and $10 million in size, respectively, they diversify their funding sources even more. But as they get larger these organizations increasingly rely on a single funding source—in these cases, government and individual support, respectively. As they reach $50 million or more in size, the concentration of funding from one source increases even more.

This concentration by funding source does not replace the need for diversification and risk management. The leaders we interviewed were quite focused on minimizing funding risk. Although most relied on a single source for the bulk of their funding, they did not rely on a single payer. Organizations achieved diversification and mitigated their funding risk by securing multiple payers of the same type to support their work. Youth Villages, for example, receives more than 90 percent of its funding from state government contracts, but it has minimized its risk by tapping a number of government departments in a number of states. Similarly, when Population Services International (PSI) had roughly $4 million in revenues, it received more than 90 percent of its funding from the U.S. Agency for International Development. Now, with revenues in excess of $200 million, PSI still receives the large majority of its funding from government agencies focused on international development—but its supporters include the governments of Germany, the United Kingdom, and the Netherlands, as well as the United Nations.

Although dominant funding sources fuel nonprofit expansion, secondary sources are still important. Of the 101 organizations that have a dominant funding source, more than 20 percent have a secondary source that accounted for 10 percent or more of their revenue. Even when secondary funding sources account for a smaller percentage of total revenue, they can be quite valuable for furthering the mission. The Metropolitan Boston Housing Partnership, for example, receives less than 1 percent of its funding from unrestricted foundation and corporate donations. But according to Executive Director Julia Kehoe, those funds "allow us to do critical prevention work that is not currently funded by government programs."

Finding the Right Match

When nonprofits are small, they often raise money from a wide variety of sources. That's because there are many potential donors who are able to give small amounts of money, and because a particularly inspiring executive director can stand out from the crowd and convince these small donors to give. But when very large sums of money are involved, the picture changes. Sizable funding sources are fewer, and their goals are more developed. As a result, the funders' interests matter more than does the executive director's charisma.

The NWTF is one organization that found a funding source—hunters—aligned with its mission. The NWTF aims to preserve and expand wild turkey habitats. Since its founding in 1973, the NWTF has helped increase the U.S. wild turkey population from 1.3 million to more than 7 million birds. The NWTF is also a financial success: Its revenues in 2003 totaled some $87 million, with the lion's share coming from

2,000 local chapters made up of more than 500,000 members. Hunters, who tend to make a sharp distinction between conservation and environmentalism, are the primary donors. The organization raises about 80 percent of its annual revenues by sponsoring more than 2,000 fundraisers each year, generating large numbers of individual contributions and event-related purchases. Local chapters run the fundraisers with assistance from national headquarters, and then funnel the proceeds back to the national organization.

Many nonprofits never find a dominant funding source, while others hesitantly drift toward it. This need not be the case. There are natural matches between many organizations and particular funding sources. Nonprofit leaders need to identify and target those funding sources that are most likely to be a natural match with their organizations. Far from being random, large funders' interests often fall into distinct categories. Corporations almost always offer in-kind support focused on hunger or health issues. And individuals tend to give to issues that cross socioeconomic boundaries—like environmental advocacy—and to organizations that have clear, compelling, and simple messages.[7] We have broken funding sources into five categories—government, service fees, corporate, individuals, and foundations—and describe what we have learned about their general areas of interest. (See the table at the end of this article for a list of all 144 organizations and their principal funding source, and visit www.bridgespan.org for profiles of 21 of the organizations.)

Government. Government is by far the most important source of funding for the high-growth nonprofits in our study. It provided most of the money for 40 percent of the organizations. In most cases, government-funded nonprofits address needs that easily fall within a particular government agency's set of responsibilities. Federal agencies, for example, are most likely to support organizations in medical research, food, and foreign affairs. State and local governments are most likely to support human services, employment development, and education organizations. Government also provides most of the financial support for nonprofits that address the needs of low-income Americans. The major exceptions are food banks, which receive large amounts of in-kind corporate contributions, and Habitat for Humanity, which relies for the most part on individual donations.

Most of the organizations that have gotten really big over the past three decades did so by concentrating on one type of funding source.

Many people talk about the government getting out of the social sector, but available data tell a different story. Not only our findings, but also national data show that government funding of the nonprofit sector is growing faster than the nation's GDP.[8]

People may perceive reduced government funding because of the devastating and often public impacts of reductions in particular services, or because of increases in what nonprofits are expected to accomplish with each dollar. The perception of reduced government funding is not accurate, however, and could be harmful if it leads nonprofits to forgo government funding, or if it reduces the public's attention to government's role as the primary funder of social services.

Service fees. Program service fees are the second most important source of funding for high-growth nonprofits, providing most of the money for 33 percent of the organizations in our study. Service fees are also the second most important source of funding in the nonprofit sector as a whole.[9] Community health clinics, student loan providers, and employment agencies for the disabled are likely to depend on program service fees as their dominant source of funding.

Many of the human services organizations (such as Vinfen Corporation, which serves people with mental illness, mental retardation, or behavioral health disabilities) contract with the government to provide services. In healthcare, several large community health clinics earn a large portion of their fees from Medicaid reimbursements. The 12 student and housing loan organizations in our study likewise rely on fees and interest income.

Analyzing service fees is notoriously difficult because nonprofits have wide latitude in what they report as program service fees. Funding from the same source could be treated as government support by one nonprofit and as program service fees by another nonprofit. Adding to the confusion is the fact that program service fees are often equated with earned-income and social enterprise ventures. Contrary to the current buzz over social enterprises, free-market commercial ventures are not the major generators of program service fees for nonprofits in this study.[10] Instead, in 90 percent of the cases for which we have detailed information, the fees had some government connection (for example, government guarantees of student loans or favorable contracting rules for those employing the disabled), further emphasizing the important role of government in the nonprofit sector.

Corporate. Corporate giving represents a relatively small share of total charitable giving in the nonprofit sector, but it is a prominent source of funding among these high-growth nonprofits. Corporations are the primary funders of 19 percent of the nonprofits we surveyed. The vast majority of corporate support is in-kind donations, not cash. Every food bank and about half of the international development nonprofits, for example, rely on in-kind corporate gifts of food and medical supplies.

In the small number of cases when corporate cash fuels a nonprofit's growth, the corporation usually has both an altruistic and a financial motive for the support. Nonprofits often garner corporate cash when a real market exists for their products or service, but laws or public opinion prevent corporations from entering the market. For example, there is a real market for blood, bone marrow, and other human body parts, but by and large, corporations do not enter this market, and instead fund the nonprofit organizations that handle these transactions.

Individuals. Individuals are the primary funders of only 6 percent of the high-growth nonprofits in our study. Interestingly, small gifts power all of the surveyed high-growth nonprofits in this category, even though major gifts account for a large majority of individual giving in the U.S.[11], [12] Although some organizations develop major donors as a significant secondary source of funds, small donations seem to fuel the broadest expansions. This may be because major gifts require greater personal involvement or because the kinds of techniques that generate smaller donations (direct mail and special events, for example) are easier to scale up.

Issues that directly touch middle-class Americans, such as the environment and health, tend to secure broad individual support. In some cases, as with the Juvenile Diabetes Research Foundation, they involve a benefit that will accrue to society in the future. In others, the benefit is more personal and immediate, as with the NWTF. Organizations that receive strong support from individual donors typically have a clear and basic message. Paul Velaski, vice president and chief financial officer of the Make-a-Wish Foundation of America, states that the top reason for their growth is "the purity and simplicity of our message. We cannot muddy it up." A clear message also helps build a strong brand that resonates with individual donors, as in the case of Habitat for Humanity.

Foundations. The least frequent source of funding for high-growth nonprofits is foundations, which are the primary funders for only two of the organizations in our study, or 2 percent of the high-growth nonprofits. These two organizations are both in healthcare: Program for Appropriate Technology in Health; and the Stowers Institute for Medical Research, which employs nearly 300 people and researches ways to prevent and cure genetic diseases. The only other organization that comes close to this level of foundation funding is Conservation International, which aims to protect the 2.3 percent of land that contains over half of the Earth's biodiversity. In the case of the Stowers Institute and Conservation International, the pathways to solving their target issues are relatively clear, though very expensive. (This is in contrast to other issues, like education reform, where the pathway itself is still a matter of debate.)

Though it is impossible to draw conclusions from so few examples, it seems plausible that foundations become dominant funders only when sufficient funding seems to be the major missing ingredient from solving an enormous problem. In general, foundations seem to be more focused on their traditional role of starting new programs rather than supporting them at scale. This may make sense, because foundations represent only 5 percent of nonprofit funding for the domains that we studied.[13]

The organizations that grew the most brought in talent and built organizations that support a high-growth strategy.

Unlocking Growth

Finding the right funding source to scale an organization is important, but it's only the first step. The high-growth nonprofits in our study also invested significant amounts of time and money to develop their ability to attract and solicit the right kinds of funding. The organizations that grew the most brought in talent and built organizations that support a high-growth strategy. As Catherine D'Amato, chief executive officer of the Greater Boston Food Bank, states, "We started as a charity and became a charitable business."

For example, Help USA, a housing organization, created a finance staff of more than 30 people to apply for and manage complicated government contracts. The Oregon Food Bank built a $10 million distribution center that can handle both fresh and frozen food, which greatly expanded the range of food donations it can accept. And Opportunity International cultivated a sophisticated fundraising group that is on par with those of the best universities and medical centers.

Many leaders of high-growth nonprofits experienced a pivotal point when they needed to bring in new talent. Typically, there was a strong tension between promoting internal, often program-oriented employees and hiring external candidates with deep experience in areas like marketing or logistics. Introducing new blood into critical roles, though vital, is usually trying. Similar tensions often arise when someone with a greater focus on management takes over from a visionary leader.

Bill Milliken, founder and vice chairman of Communities in Schools, recently elevated a new president within the organization. "The '60s saw a lot of great movements that died," he says. "They were led by great frontier people who couldn't relate to the settlers. They wanted new ideas but didn't build organizations. Passion and professionalism keep them in balance."

Many high-growth leaders also concluded that "virtuous and poor" was not the best way to fulfill their missions. For organizations built on the passion of committed program people, this represented a real cultural shift. Focusing on dollars and cents was not what brought them into the sector. And with so many problems to address, the idea of reserving money to create financial stability or to fund future capacity was often deeply, even morally, uncomfortable. But they realized that to fulfill their missions they needed to spend as much time, or more, on margins.

When Patrick Lawler arrived at Youth Villages in 1980 as the new chief executive officer, he was just 24 years old. "I'd been a probation officer," recalls Lawler. "I'd never seen a budget. I didn't know anything about management. What I knew about was how to take care of tough kids. For my first two or three years, I acted like we were a charity and we had to take in just enough money to pay the bills. Around 1982, one of our board members told me how we had to have margins or we couldn't run our business. Not a charity, a business. We were running on extremely limited resources and raising money via yard sales, car washes, and garage sales. That board member opened my eyes to a broader future."

In 1984, Youth Villages began focusing on its financial margins and launched its first capital campaign. The money raised was used to acquire land in the middle of Tennessee for a residential facility. This helped Youth Villages grow from a western Tennessee service provider to one that served the entire state. Having identified the state as its dominant funding source, Youth Villages proposed a contract structure that reduced the state's financial burden during a time of financial crisis. "We convinced the state that they shouldn't be buying beds. They should buy outcomes, successful outcomes." Youth Villages made sure it was in the business of providing those outcomes—adding services, such as family-based, in-home counseling, to do so. Today, Youth Villages has over $70 million in revenue and has had an annual growth rate of more than 20 percent since 1990.

Focusing on margins is not just about growing revenues. It is also about controlling costs. Core to the success of the NWTF's special events is supplying auction items and gifts—what it calls "banquet-in-a-box"—to each chapter that is having a fundraising banquet. Originally, the national office had multiple retailers ship their wares to each local event. Then they centralized purchasing, built a warehouse, and shipped just one package to each location. Now the organization orders many of its banquet supplies (such as diamond bracelets, guns, and gas grills) directly from the manufacturers, including some in China. "We had been running it like a small business, but then we realized we had grown far beyond that," says Chief Financial Officer James Sparks. These moves have reduced costs by more than 70 percent. As Sparks notes, "To save a dollar is as good as to earn a dollar."

Limits to Growth

Growth is not always the right choice, or even a possible choice, for an organization. Some missions simply do not have many (or any) natural large-scale funders. And when money is available, it often comes with restrictions that can drive an organization off course. Above all, it is important to remember just how rare it is for a nonprofit to get big. These 144 high-growth organizations, although greater in number than one might expect, represent less than one-tenth of 1 percent of the nonprofits founded since 1970. Knowing when not to pursue growth is as important as knowing what may improve the odds of success when you do try to grow.

Timing can have a major influence over a nonprofit's ability to raise money and to grow. Some nonprofits have the good fortune of being founded during a period of heightened interest in their mission. Take environmental and international aid groups, for example. About 70 percent of all U.S. environmental groups over $50 million in size were founded in or after 1970. And about 40 percent of all U.S. international aid groups were founded since 1970. By contrast, only 15 percent of all educational groups and 16 percent of all arts and culture organizations of that size were founded during that period.[14]

Before 1970, the environmental movement was still in its infancy. Many experts point to the first Earth Day on April 22, 1970, as the real awakening of the movement. Hence, it isn't surprising that environmental groups starting in or after 1970 had a better chance of growing rapidly during a period in which public concern about the issue was also growing rapidly. Judith Keefer of the Natural Resources Defense Council, which was established in 1970, explains: "The issues took off. It's the macro stuff." International aid organizations seem to have experienced similar growth after the Ethiopian famine of 1984.

Growth can also be limited by nonprofits' missions and activities. For instance, funding for services—be it from government, individuals, or corporations—is more readily available than funding for advocacy. Less than 5 percent of the organizations in this study cite advocacy as their central activity. The Oregon Food Bank provides a good illustration. Its mission is to "eliminate hunger and its root causes, because no one should be hungry." In 2003, the organization was approximately $55 million in size, with more than two-thirds of that support coming from in-kind corporate contributions of food. Although the Oregon Food Bank cares deeply about policy issues and willingly takes controversial stands on such issues as the minimum wage, its primary program, the one that has received the most funding, is providing food to people who need it.

Most of the nonprofits that we studied also report that their programs or operations were restricted as a result of their dominant funding source. Some organizations choose to give up funding in order to avoid having to change their missions, whereas others choose to make adjustments. In housing, for example, government funding now favors giving housing directly to individuals rather than developing facilities, and so Help USA has had to modify its programs to accommodate that shift. Likewise, federal testing objectives have narrowed schools' focus to very specific reading objectives, forcing Success for All to modify its programs.

PSI has developed a creative way to manage these tensions. PSI receives funding from a wide range of federal and international bodies, each of which carries some restrictions. PSI has developed terms to identify activities that are off-mission (the "mush") and those that are on-mission but inefficient (the "yuck"). At times PSI must conduct activities that are mush or yuck to satisfy the interests of important funders. Nevertheless, its leadership is always cognizant of the percentage of its work that falls into these two categories.

Finding the Right Path

The fact that so many nonprofits have gotten big in recent decades is encouraging. It demonstrates that organizations tackling solutions to social problems can grow to large scale. But not all paths and practices are equal. As is the case in business, nonprofit leaders must consider the best long-term path for their organizations, whether that is choosing to stay small or trying to grow.

The good news is that nonprofit executives and board members pursuing expansion do not have to resort to guessing or hoping. With large-scale funding, there are rules to the game, even if at times they may seem unfair or opaque. If nonprofit leaders become more systematic in evaluating how (and whether) to pursue large-scale growth, boardroom conversations could become more productive, greater numbers of those in need could receive help, and scarce social resources could be better deployed.

HIGH-GROWTH NONPROFITS

These 144 nonprofits, all founded after 1969, were earning at least $50 million per year by 2003

Rank	Name	State	Year Founded	Revenue (Millions)*	Domain	Dominant Source of Funding
1	AmeriCares Foundation	Conn.	1982	$697.9	International & Foreign Affairs	Corporate
2	Feed the Children	Okla.	1979	$568.4	International & Foreign Affairs	Unknown
3	Habitat for Humanity International	Ga.	1976	$478.6	International & Foreign Affairs	Individuals
4	America's Second Harvest	Ill.	1979	$467.9	Food, Agriculture, & Nutrition	Corporate
5	Food for the Poor	Fla.	1982	$465.2	International & Foreign Affairs	Corporate
6	Gifts in Kind International	Va.	1983	$438.6	International & Foreign Affairs	Corporate
7	King Benevolent Fund	Va.	1993	$432.4	International & Foreign Affairs	Corporate
8	Brazos Group	Texas	1975	$359.4	Education	Service Fees
9	American Legacy Foundation	D.C.	1999	$288.8	Healthcare	Government
10	Electric Power Research Institute	Calif.	1973	$268.4	Public & Societal Benefit	Corporate
11	Fred Hutchinson Institute	Wash.	1975	$240.2	Medical Research	Government
12	Musculoskeletal Transplant Foundation	N.J.	1987	$229.4	Healthcare	Service Fees
13	Population Services International	N.Y.	1970	$204.2	International & Foreign Affairs	Government
14	Samaritan's Purse	N.C.	1970	$200.6	International & Foreign Affairs	Unknown
15	Chela Education Financing	Calif.	1979	$181.5	Public & Societal Benefit	Service Fees
16	Concurrent Technologies Corporation	Pa.	1988	$180.5	Public & Societal Benefit	Government

Rank	Name	State	Year Founded	Revenue (Millions)*	Domain	Dominant Source of Funding
17	Crystal Stairs	Calif.	1980	$178.9	Food, Agriculture, & Nutrition	Government
18	Elderhostel	Mass.	1975	$177.0	Human Services	Service Fees
19	Macomb-Oakland Regional Center	Mich.	1972	$173.7	Human Services	Unknown
20	Trinity Broadcasting Network	Calif.	1973	$171.2	Arts, Culture, & Humanities	Unknown
21	Christian Aid Ministries	Ohio	1981	$168.5	International & Foreign Affairs	Unknown
22	Communities in Schools	Va.	1980	$168.1	Education	Government
23	Nehemiah Corporation of America	Calif.	1997	$163.3	Housing & Shelter	Service Fees
24	Polish-American Freedom Foundation	Pa.	2000	$158.8	International & Foreign Affairs	Unknown
25	Buyers Fund	Utah	1999	$152.7	Housing & Shelter	Service Fees
26	AmeriDream	Md.	1999	$152.1	Housing & Shelter	Service Fees
27	The Trust for Public Land	Calif.	1971	$147.7	Environment	Service Fees
28	National Associations for the Exchange of Industrial Resources	Ill.	1977	$144.0	Public & Societal Benefit	Corporate
29	Texas Guaranteed Student Loan Corp.	Texas	1980	$139.4	Public & Societal Benefit	Service Fees
30	North Los Angeles Co. Regional Center	Calif.	1974	$138.3	Public & Societal Benefit	Government
31	Family Health International	N.C.	1971	$137.0	International & Foreign Affairs	Government
32	Make-a-Wish Foundation	Ariz.	1980	$136.9	Healthcare	Individuals
33	Juvenile Diabetes Research Foundation International	N.Y.	1970	$136.7	Healthcare	Individuals
34	Skirball Cultural Center	Calif.	1995	$129.9	Arts, Culture, & Humanities	Unknown

Rank	Name	State	Year Founded	Revenue (Millions)*	Domain	Dominant Source of Funding
35	Educational Funding of the South	Tenn.	1987	$129.1	Public & Societal Benefit	Service Fees
36	Focus on the Family	Colo.	1977	$128.0	Arts, Culture, & Humanities	Individuals
37	The Carter Center	Ga.	1982	$127.1	International & Foreign Affairs	Corporate
38	Educational Credit Management Corp.	Minn.	1995	$126.8	Public & Societal Benefit	Service Fees
39	Philadelphia Workforce Development Corp.	Pa.	1982	$126.1	Employment	Government
40	National Marrow Donor Program	Minn.	1987	$120.2	Healthcare	None
41	National Public Radio	D.C.	1970	$120.0	Arts, Culture, & Humanities	None
42	Texas Migrant Council	Texas	1971	$117.3	Education	Government
43	Neighborhood Reinvestment Corp.	D.C.	1980	$117.3	Public & Societal Benefit	Government
44	Mercy Corps	Ore.	1979	$116.5	International & Foreign Affairs	Government
45	Southeastern Universities Research Assoc.	D.C.	1980	$115.8	Public & Societal Benefit	Government
46	National Center for Employment of the Disabled	Texas	1977	$115.5	Employment	Unknown
47	Access Group	Del.	1993	$115.4	Public & Societal Benefit	Service Fees
48	Hope for the City	Minn.	1999	$108.3	Food, Agriculture, & Nutrition	Corporate
49	The Conservation Fund	Va.	1985	$106.0	Environment	Unknown
50	New York State Industries for the Disabled	N.Y.	1975	$105.4	Human Services	Service Fees
51	Whitehead Institute for Biomedical Research	Mass.	1982	$104.7	Medical Research	Government

Rank	Name	State	Year Founded	Revenue (Millions)*	Domain	Dominant Source of Funding
52	LifeNet	Va.	1982	$102.2	Healthcare	Service Fees
53	Metropolitan Boston Housing Partnership	Mass.	1974	$100.4	Housing & Shelter	Government
54	S. Carolina Student Loan Corporation	S.C.	1974	$100.1	Public & Societal Benefit	Service Fees
55	Family Central	Fla.	1971	$99.3	Human Services	Government
56	Child Action	Calif.	1976	$97.3	Human Services	Government
57	Child Care Resources Center	Calif.	1975	$97.0	Human Services	Unknown
58	Resources for Human Development	Pa.	1970	$95.4	Human Services	Unknown
59	Program for Appropriate Technology in Health	Wash.	1977	$93.4	International & Foreign Affairs	Foundations
60	Conservation International	Va.	1987	$92.2	Environment	None
61	Iowa Student Loan Liquidity Corp.	Iowa	1979	$92.1	Education	Service Fees
62	The Vaccine Fund	D.C.	1999	$91.4	International & Foreign Affairs	Government
63	Ludwig Institute for Cancer Research	N.Y.	1971	$90.7	Medical Research	Unknown
64	EDFUND	Calif.	1997	$89.4	Public & Societal Benefit	Service Fees
65	The Education Resources Institute	Mass.	1985	$89.0	Public & Societal Benefit	Service Fees
66	Local Initiatives Support Corporation	N.Y.	1979	$87.5	Public & Societal Benefit	None
67	Philadelphia Corporation for Aging	Pa.	1973	$85.2	Human Services	Government
68	American Nicaraguan Foundation	Fla.	1992	$81.6	International & Foreign Affairs	Corporate
69	The Stanley Medical Research Institute	Md.	1989	$80.7	Medical Research	Unknown

Rank	Name	State	Year Founded	Revenue (Millions)*	Domain	Dominant Source of Funding
70	Northwest Medical Teams	Ore.	1979	$80.2	International & Foreign Affairs	Corporate
71	Opportunity International	Ill.	1971	$80.0	International & Foreign Affairs	None
72	Management Sciences for Health	Mass.	1971	$77.0	International & Foreign Affairs	Service Fees
73	Food for the Hungry	Ariz.	1971	$77.0	International & Foreign Affairs	Unknown
74	Alamo Workforce Development	Texas	1994	$76.6	Employment	Government
75	Stowers Institute for Medical Research	Mo.	1994	$76.5	Medical Research	Foundations
76	Dallas Co. Local Workforce Dev. Board	Texas	1984	$76.3	Human Services	Government
77	Coastal Dev. Services Foundation	Calif.	1983	$76.2	Human Services	Unknown
78	Heart to Heart International	Kan.	1992	$75.0	International & Foreign Affairs	Corporate
79	Tides Center	Calif.	1976	$71.2	Environment	Unknown
80	YouthBuild USA	Mass.	1990	$70.3	Human Services	Unknown
81	Consortium for Worker Education	N.Y.	1985	$69.5	Employment	Government
82	Western Reserve Area Agency on Aging	Ohio	1976	$69.1	Human Services	Government
83	Christian Foundation for Children and Aging	Kan.	1981	$68.0	Human Services	Individuals
84	Vinfen Corporation	Mass.	1977	$67.5	Human Services	Service Fees
85	Options: A Child Care and Human Services Agency	Calif.	1981	$67.4	Human Services	Service Fees
86	International Relief & Development	Va.	1998	$66.9	International & Foreign Affairs	Government
87	United States Holocaust Memorial Council	D.C.	1980	$66.6	Arts, Culture, & Humanities	None

Rank	Name	State	Year Founded	Revenue (Millions)*	Domain	Dominant Source of Funding
88	Family Health Center of Marshfield	Wis.	1982	$66.5	Healthcare	Service Fees
89	Warren Clinic	Okla.	1988	$65.7	Healthcare	Service Fees
90	Concepts of Independence	N.Y.	1979	$65.4	Human Services	Unknown
91	Operation Blessing	Va.	1978	$64.9	International & Foreign Affairs	Corporate
92	Gulf Coast Regional Blood Center	Texas	1975	$64.2	Healthcare	Service Fees
93	National Fish and Wildlife Foundation	D.C.	1984	$63.9	Environment	Unknown
94	Peckham Vocational Industries	Mich.	1976	$63.6	Employment	Service Fees
95	E. Boston Neighborhood Health Center	Mass.	1970	$63.5	Healthcare	Service Fees
96	Florida Blood Services	Fla.	1992	$63.1	Healthcare	Service Fees
97	International Medical Corps	Calif.	1984	$62.9	International & Foreign Affairs	None
98	Harvest Foundation of the Piedmont	Va.	2002	$62.5	Religious	Unknown
99	LifeSource	Ill.	1987	$62.1	Healthcare	Unknown
100	Stavros Center for Independent Living	Mass.	1974	$61.5	Human Services	Unknown
101	Center for Creative Leadership	N.C.	1970	$61.1	Public & Societal Benefit	Service Fees
102	Institute of Nuclear Power Operations	Ga.	1979	$61.1	Public & Societal Benefit	Corporate
103	Council on Aging of SW Ohio	Ohio	1970	$60.8	Human Services	Government
104	Youth Villages	Tenn.	1986	$60.4	Human Services	Government
105	Education & Health Centers of America	N.J.	1983	$60.3	Healthcare	Unknown
106	Christian Relief Services Charities	Va.	1985	$60.3	International & Foreign Affairs	None
107	Natural Resources Defense Council	N.Y.	1970	$59.8	Environment	Individuals

Rank	Name	State	Year Founded	Revenue (Millions)*	Domain	Dominant Source of Funding
108	In Touch Ministries	Ga.	1972	$59.3	Religious	Unknown
109	Futures Home Assistance Programs	Ga.	1998	$59.2	Housing & Shelter	Unknown
110	Child Care Resources	N.C.	1981	$59.2	Human Services	Government
111	Self-Help Ventures Fund	N.C.	1980	$59.1	Public & Societal Benefit	Unknown
112	National Constitution Center	Pa.	1988	$59.0	Arts, Culture, & Humanities	Unknown
113	International AIDS Vaccine Initiative	N.Y.	1996	$57.9	International & Foreign Affairs	Government
114	AIDS Healthcare Foundation	Calif.	1987	$57.9	Healthcare	Unknown
115	Help USA	N.Y.	1975	$56.8	Public & Societal Benefit	Government
116	Maniilaq Association	Alaska	1975	$56.7	Human Services	Government
117	Orange County Performing Arts Center	Calif.	1974	$56.2	Arts, Culture, & Humanities	None
118	Rocky Mountain Elk Foundation	Mont.	1984	$56.1	Environment	Unknown
119	Ronald McDonald House Charities	Ill.	1974	$55.1	Healthcare	Unknown
120	National Endowment for Democracy	D.C.	1983	$55.1	Public & Societal Benefit	Government
121	Youth Advocate Programs	Pa.	1975	$55.1	Human Services	Government
122	Nat. Board for Prof. Teaching Standards	Va.	1987	$54.9	Education	Service Fees
123	Services for the Underserved – Mental Health Programs	N.Y.	1978	$54.6	Housing & Shelter	Unknown
124	Oregon Food Bank	Ore.	1982	$54.5	Food, Agriculture, & Nutrition	Corporate
125	Los Angeles Regional Foodbank	Calif.	1973	$54.4	Food, Agriculture, & Nutrition	Corporate

Rank	Name	State	Year Founded	Revenue (Millions)*	Domain	Dominant Source of Funding
126	American Kidney Fund	Md.	1971	$54.3	Healthcare	Corporate
127	North American Family Institute	Mass.	1974	$54.0	Human Services	Government
128	Cambridge Credit Counseling Corp.	Mass.	1996	$53.8	Human Services	Unknown
129	Burnham Institute	Calif.	1976	$53.6	Medical Research	Government
130	Cabs Home Attendant Services	N.Y.	1980	$53.5	Human Services	Government
131	Centerstone Community Mental Health Centers	Tenn.	1997	$53.4	Healthcare	Unknown
132	Joint Oceanographic Institutions	D.C.	1976	$53.0	Public & Societal Benefit	Government
133	Hope Worldwide	Pa.	1991	$52.4	International & Foreign Affairs	Corporate
134	National Wild Turkey Federation	S.C.	1973	$52.2	Environment	Individuals
135	The Greater Boston Food Bank	Mass.	1981	$51.9	Food, Agriculture, & Nutrition	Corporate
136	NISH	Va.	1971	$51.7	Employment	Service Fees
137	Safe Horizon	N.Y.	1978	$51.5	Human Services	Government
138	Westside Food Bank	Calif.	1973	$51.4	Food, Agriculture, & Nutrition	Corporate
139	JSI Research & Training Institute	Mass.	1978	$51.3	Healthcare	Government
140	The Institute for Genomic Research	Md.	1992	$51.1	Public & Societal Benefit	Government
141	FamiliesFirst	Calif.	1974	$50.8	Human Services	Government
142	Success for All Foundation	Md.	1987	$50.6	Education	Service Fees
143	Community Day Care Center of Lawrence	Mass.	1973	$50.3	Human Services	Government
144	Parent/Child Inc. of San Antonio & Bexar County	Texas	1979	$50.2	Education	Government

*Revenue is from fiscal year 2002, 2003, or 2004. Gross receipts instead of revenue is used in some cases. Revenues of networks are estimated by summing the revenues of organizations within those networks.

HIGH-GROWTH NONPROFITS: A CLOSER LOOK

Less than one-tenth of 1 percent of U.S. nonprofits founded in or after 1970 reached $50 million in annual revenues by 2003. Below, we take a closer look at this elite group.

Which Domains Were Represented?

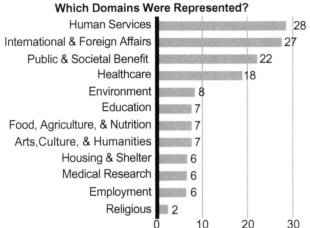

Domain	Value
Human Services	28
International & Foreign Affairs	27
Public & Societal Benefit	22
Healthcare	18
Environment	8
Education	7
Food, Agriculture, & Nutrition	7
Arts,Culture, & Humanities	7
Housing & Shelter	6
Medical Research	6
Employment	6
Religious	2

More than one-third of these high-growth nonprofits were human services or international and foreign affairs organizations.

Who Were the Dominant Funders?

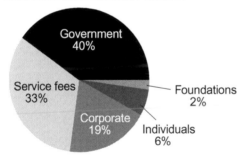

Government 40%
Service fees 33%
Corporate 19%
Foundations 2%
Individuals 6%

Nearly all of the nonprofits received the bulk of their money from a single dominant source. The biggest source was government, which funded nearly half of the high-growth organizations. Foundations and individuals were the dominant funding source for only a few organizations.

Where Were They Founded?

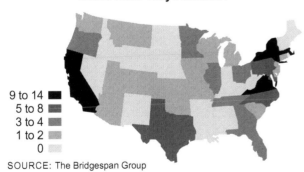

9 to 14
5 to 8
3 to 4
1 to 2
0

California, Massachusetts, New York, and the Virginia/Washington, D.C., area spawned the most high-growth nonprofits – 61 altogether – whereas 17 other states, including Indiana, Louisiana, and Nevada, created none.

SOURCE: The Bridgespan Group

This article originally appeared in the February 2005 issue of the Harvard Business Review.

Should Nonprofits Seek Profits?

Eager to reduce their dependence on fund-raising, more and more nonprofits are launching earned-income ventures—with disappointing results.

By William Foster and Jeffrey L. Bradach

Twenty years ago, it would have been shocking for the Chicago Children's Choir to run a singing telegram business and a Ben & Jerry's Scoop Shop or for Shelter, Inc., of Contra Costa County, a California organization dedicated to serving the homeless, to launch a property management firm. Today, it seems routine. Promoted in books and articles, conferences and courses, earned-income initiatives are becoming accepted—even expected—throughout the nonprofit world. In a 2003 Bridgespan Group survey of U.S. nonprofits' executives, half of the respondents said they believed earned income would play an important or extremely important role in bolstering their organizations' revenue in the future.

What's driving nonprofits to pursue profits? The phenomenon is as much social as economic. The general enthusiasm for business, which reached a fever pitch during the booming 1990s, has had a profound impact on nonprofits and the institutions that support them. Like their counterparts in the commercial world, managers of nonprofits want to be viewed as active entrepreneurs rather than as passive bureaucrats, and launching a successful commercial venture is one direct route to that goal. Board members, many of whom are accomplished business leaders, often encourage and reinforce that desire. At the same time, many philanthropic foundations and other funders have been zealously urging nonprofits to become financially self-sufficient and have aggressively promoted earned income as a means to "sustainability." As a result, nonprofits increasingly feel compelled to launch earned-income ventures, if only to appear more disciplined, innovative, and businesslike to their stakeholders. (The sidebar "The Pressure from Funders" at the end of this article takes a closer look at such forces.)

But while the case for earned income may seem persuasive at first glance, a closer look reveals reasons for skepticism. Despite the hype, earned income accounts for only a small share of funding in most nonprofit domains, and few of the ventures that have been launched actually make money. Moreover, when we examined how nonprofits evaluate possible ventures, we discovered a pattern of unwarranted optimism. The potential financial returns are often exaggerated, and the challenges of running a successful business are routinely discounted. Most important, commercial ventures can distract nonprofits' managers from their core social missions and, in some cases, even subvert those missions. We're not saying that earned-income ventures have no role in the nonprofit sector, but we believe that unrealistic expectations are distorting managers' decisions, ultimately wasting precious resources and leaving important social needs unmet.

Rhetoric and Reality

Earned-income ventures are nothing new in the nonprofit sector, of course. Universities, hospitals, and theater groups, for example, have long been run by charitable organizations. What is new is the breadth of interest. No longer relegated to education, health care, and the arts, revenue-generating initiatives are being launched or considered in virtually every nonprofit domain, from human services to housing to the environment. Some of the new ventures derive income from products or services within existing programs; others are completely separate from the nonprofits' core programs. But almost every venture takes the nonprofit into unfamiliar commercial waters.

Burgeoning interest in earned income has generated a flood of publications, events, and experts. How-to books with titles like *Venture Forth! The Essential Guide to Starting a Moneymaking Business in Your Nonprofit Organization* and *Selling Social Change (Without Selling Out)* have recently appeared. The Yale School of Management–The Goldman Sachs Foundation Partnership on Nonprofit Ventures sponsors a celebrated and rigorously judged business-plan competition for nonprofits; in 2004, it garnered more than 500 entries. Even organizations that promote the broader topic of social entrepreneurship, such as the Social Enterprise Alliance, are often primarily focused on earned income. At that group's 2004 National Gathering for Social Entrepreneurs, attendance "flew past 600, a 50% growth rate that dramatically illustrated surging interest in the field of social enterprise," organizers reported. And Nonprofit Business Solutions advertises that it can help "discover the earned-income opportunity you may have missed, for only $100." Indeed, the widespread enthusiasm for earned-income ventures has drowned out the handful of people, such as Greg Dees of Duke and Jed Emerson, a cofounder and former executive director of the Roberts Enterprise Development Fund, who have sounded cautionary notes.

It is clear that there has been a significant increase in the number of nonprofits considering, investing in, and launching ventures, and the press has helped create the impression that these enterprises are contributing substantial profits. In late 2001, for example, the *Chronicle of Philanthropy* ran the headline "The Business of Charity: Nonprofit Groups Reap Billions in Tax-Free Income Annually." The wide circulation of selected data reinforces the notion of a boom in earned income. From the impressive body of work published by Johns Hopkins' Lester Salamon, one statistic is mentioned with particular frequency: "Fees and charges accounted for nearly half of the growth in nonprofit revenue between 1977 and 1997—more than any other source."

But out of context, such statistics can be misleading. Fees and charges grew no faster in that 20-year period than other sources of revenue; they represented nearly half of the sector's total revenue in 1997, just as they had in 1977 (see "No Outsized Surge in Earned Income," page 132). And the reason the fraction is so high is that educational and health care institutions, which extensively use fee-for-service income, account for nearly 70% of total nonprofit revenue and thus dominate the data.

To more clearly document the prevalence of earned income in the nonprofit sector, Bridgespan analyzed revenue trends from 1991 to 2001. We drew our data from the IRS 990 forms that nonprofits prepare annually to report their finances. While these filings don't list "earned income" per se, they do include a category for "program service revenue," which includes government fees for service as well as private payments and fees. This is far from a perfect proxy, but it is a decent one and, in any case, it is the best available. Our analysis revealed that the relative contribution of program service revenue had actually declined by three percentage points over the ten-year period and that such revenue remains heavily concentrated in health care and education. Outside those domains, earned income's contribution grew substantially only among employment and community improvement organizations. In environment and youth development, it showed a marginal gain, while in arts, education, housing, recreation, and human services, it declined slightly.

If the growth in the revenue contribution of earned-income ventures seems overstated, so does the financial success of the projects. In discussions of the topic, a handful of success stories are told again and again—cases like those of Pioneer Human Services, the Seattle-based nonprofit that offers job training and counseling to former inmates and others on the margins of society, and Juma Ventures, the Bay Area organization that gives employment opportunities to local youth. These organizations certainly deserve accolades for their income-earning endeavors, but they appear to be the exception, not the rule. At Bridgespan, we are frequently asked to assist nonprofits that have had trouble making their earned-income ventures profitable, and as part of our research we routinely hunt for similar ventures that have been profitable and might thus serve as benchmarks. We almost never find them. We have had no trouble, however, finding money-losing ventures.

Two widely circulated surveys of earned-income ventures seem to suggest that our experience is anomalous. "Enterprising Nonprofits: Revenue Generation in the Nonprofit Sector" by the Yale School of Management–The Goldman Sachs Foundation Partnership on Nonprofit Ventures and "Powering Social Change: Lessons on Community Wealth Generation for Nonprofit Sustainability" by Community Wealth Ventures (CWV) report that between half and two-thirds of the ventures these organizations examined were either profitable or breaking even. Given the challenges of accurately gauging the returns of earned-income ventures, however, we think it is important to keep in mind two caveats about these findings.

The first concerns the composition of the samples. Are they truly representative, or are they biased toward successful (and surviving) initiatives? The Yale–Goldman Sachs Foundation survey solicited research participants by highly publicizing the study through postings and advertisements. Such announcements are an efficient way to attract participants, but they amass a self-selected pool of research subjects, virtually guaranteeing a positive bias. Failing organizations are less likely to volunteer than successful ones—and ventures that have already closed their doors never do. The CWV study drew its initial sample from experts' suggestions and the researchers' personal contacts; this sample was then expanded through referrals from the initial group of nonprofits. Here again, the probability of a positive bias is high, because successful ventures tend to have a much higher public profile than unsuccessful ones.

The second caveat involves the definition of "profitable." Are the financial claims accurate? The results were self-reported, and our experience with nonprofits reveals a tendency to overlook or undercount commercial ventures' operating costs (including management time, facilities costs, and other overhead expenses). In addition, the reported "profitability" may not adequately account for hefty start-up costs. This question is difficult to assess in the Yale–Goldman Sachs Foundation study, because the calculation of financial returns is not documented in detail. There is more detail in the CWV calculations, however, and here we find that the reported financial results are probably overly optimistic.

In the CWV study's sample of 72 organizations, only four—just 5%—earned more than $50,000 in annual profit. In addition, the average time to profitability for most organizations was 2.5 years, and the average initial investment for all ventures was $200,000. Assuming a $200,000 start-up cost, two years of zero profit, and $25,000 in annual profit thereafter, a venture would take ten years to repay the initial investment, even without discounting the future profit for inflation. The venture's intangible returns may be real, but from a purely economic perspective, the same return could be generated simply by hiding $200,000 under a mattress for ten years.

NO OUTSIZED SURGE IN EARNED INCOME

Revenues for the nonprofit sector have jumped from $109 billion to $632 billion in a 20-year time span. But the percentage generated by earned income (fees and charges) has stayed nearly the same.

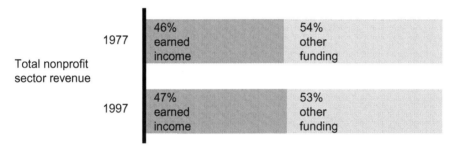

Fees and charges include return on investments. Other funding indicates private contributions and government payments. Based on data from *The New Nonprofit Almanac and Desk Reference*.

To better understand the odds of success, Bridgespan selected a random sample of nonprofits that had received philanthropic funding for an earned-income venture in 2000 or 2001. (We drew the sample from a database of nonprofits maintained by the Foundation Center, a leading nonprofit research organization.) This approach limited the pool to organizations of interest to philanthropy, but it tempered the likelihood of either a positive or negative sample bias. To determine profitability, we conducted interviews with executives of 41 of these organizations—a diverse group of agencies representing the youth services, arts and culture, employment, and community improvement domains and having annual budgets ranging from $200,000 to $15 million. The ventures included both separate enterprises and core programs that had been commercialized. We excluded health and educational institutions from our sample. We also excluded basic co-branding relationships that some nonprofit organizations enter into with for-profit corporations. (The National Wildlife

Federation, for instance, endorses environmentally friendly outdoor products like birdbaths sold by Home Depot and receives a percentage of the product sales.) The results were not encouraging: Seventy-one percent of the ventures reported that they were unprofitable, 24% believed that they were profitable, and 5% stated that they were breaking even. Of those that claimed they were profitable, half did not fully account for indirect costs such as allocations of general overhead or senior management time. Simply put, there is every reason to believe that the lion's share of earned-income ventures do not succeed at generating revenues beyond their costs.

The Disadvantages of Nonprofits

Why is there such a gap between the rhetoric and the reality of earned income in the nonprofit sector? One important factor is a lack of realism in evaluating the challenges of running a business. Launching an enterprise is difficult under the best of circumstances. According to the National Federation of Independent Business's Education Foundation, only 39% of small businesses are profitable, and half fail in the first five years. The odds are stacked even higher against nonprofits, for several reasons.

Conflicting Priorities. Unlike purely commercial enterprises, nonprofits focus on both financial and nonfinancial concerns. They may, for instance, feel obliged to pay what they consider a "living wage" or to hire employees from some disadvantaged pool of people. They may price products to be more affordable to low-income groups or offer products that are deemed "better" or "healthier" than market norms. And they may reach out to customers in locations or in groups that have not had access to certain products or services.

Those are all appropriate social objectives. But they can put nonprofits at a distinct disadvantage in the intensely competitive commercial marketplace, dramatically reducing the likelihood that profitability will be achieved. Even if a nonprofit's managers and staff are as talented as its competitors', such secondary considerations can doom a venture by dampening revenues or increasing costs or both. They can also keep a nonprofit from building the kind of highly competitive, profit-focused culture that is essential to the success of many commercial enterprises.

Despite the hype, earned income accounts for only a small share of funding in most nonprofit domains, and few of the ventures actually make money.

Lack of Business Perspective. Because philanthropic contributions typically do not have significant operating costs associated with them, nonprofits can easily misjudge the actual financial contribution that a venture will deliver. In particular, they tend to overlook the distinction between revenue and profit. If a nonprofit receives an unrestricted charitable donation of $100,000, all $100,000 (except for the comparatively small fund-raising costs) can be put to work in pursuit of the organization's mission. In this case, revenue is essentially the same as profit. However, if a nonprofit generates $100,000 from a venture, such as a catering business, some of the funds must be used to cover expenses. Typically, what's left over is at best a small portion of total sales. An examination of standard for-profit business margins shows, for example, that retail eating and clothing businesses with less than $1 million in annual revenues have profit margins of just 2.5%, while the margins of similarly sized employment agencies (we cite these examples because many nonprofits operate ventures in these areas) run at only 2%. Even if we assume that the margin on a nonprofit's earned-income activity is 10%—an extremely optimistic assumption—a $100,000 business would generate only $10,000 of unrestricted funds in a year. In this regard, the widespread use of the term "earned income" to mean the revenues of nonprofit ventures has not been helpful. It has made the distinction between revenue and profit less clear.

As an example of how widely off the mark financial perspectives can be, consider the experience of a nonprofit we'll call Midwestern Youth Services, or MYS. The organization received philanthropic funding to outfit a commercial kitchen and launch a food products enterprise. It pursued the venture with gusto and hired local youths as staff. One year after its launch, the venture began selling its first product, MYS Salad Dressing, to local supermarkets. MYS prided itself on this initial success and began gearing up to increase its investment in the venture. Fueling its optimism was a sense that the business was already breaking even. The organization believed it spent $3.15 to produce a bottle of salad dressing, which it then sold for $3.50, yielding a 35-cent profit. MYS was confident that even if some costs were unaccounted for, the venture was covering its expenses and profitability was in sight.

But an analysis completed by Bridgespan revealed that the relevant expenses were far higher. MYS counted direct labor expenses as well as the cost of ingredients, but it considered only the ingredients going into the bottles and the time employees spent working on the product. In reality, the time spent preparing the dressing was a small percentage of the hours for which employees were paid. The workers' downtime was not being allocated to the product. Similarly, a significant amount of the purchased ingredients was being used for product development or was going unused. With these factors added in, the direct cost per bottle was $10.33.

Yet even that figure was an understatement. The nonprofit had also neglected to account for major indirect expenses, including the kitchen manager's salary, the facilities cost (rent for the kitchen and equipment depreciation), and the venture's share of the nonprofit's overhead (executive salaries and the like). When a modest allocation to cover these expenses was included, the cost per bottle reached a staggering $90. Far from breaking even, the venture was losing nearly $86.50 on every item it sold.

Granted, the cost per unit would shrink with increasing volume. But to break even, MYS would have to increase sales 150-fold, well beyond the kitchen's capacity. Given the philanthropic funding for the start-up costs, the absence of investors clamoring for returns, and some genuinely mission-related objectives, it is easy to see how the nonprofit ended up in this situation. But if an enterprise is designed to make a nonprofit more disciplined, as is often the case, or if it is intended to form the groundwork for greater financial self-sufficiency, such miscalculations can provide false comfort.

Reliance on Indirect Customers. In many earned-income ventures, the intended users can't afford the products or services. That's hardly surprising—many nonprofits work with society's most disadvantaged citizens. But it means that ventures must often rely on indirect customers for their revenues, making for complex and sometimes convoluted business models.

For example, one human services nonprofit recently developed an impressive Internet-based tool to help disadvantaged citizens search for government benefits they might be eligible for. The tool would bring these individuals a direct financial benefit, but it's unlikely they would be able to afford the necessary fees. Would corporations that also serve these people pay for the tool? It's easy to see how the nonprofit could have persuaded itself that the answer is yes—utility companies would surely rather help customers get a government credit for electricity than shut off their power. But the answer is probably no.

That's because third parties cannot calculate with any precision the financial benefit they would receive, so structuring a deal that's attractive to them would be difficult, if not impossible. The utility companies, to continue with the example, would be unable to determine how many of their customers would use the tool or receive the government benefits. And sharing customer data with third parties is never straightforward. Additionally, nonprofit organizations generally know far less about potential indirect customers than they do about their own beneficiaries, and in business, there is no substitute for a deep understanding of customer needs. In many cases, a nonprofit would be better off targeting third parties for grant requests rather than for sales pitches.

Philanthropic Capital and the Escalation of Commitment. Even when nonprofit managers realize that their ventures are facing financial problems, they rarely pull the plug. Instead, as is sometimes the case in the for-profit sector, they tend to throw good money after bad, hoping to turn the ventures around and avoid the embarrassment of failure. One nonprofit, for example, had a mission to offer teenagers a safe after-school environment with Internet access. It found a historic building with more space than the program needed. With government funds, the organization rehabilitated the building and rented out the upper floors. But the rental income didn't cover the lease and maintenance costs, so the nonprofit launched an additional earned-income activity—an after-school café selling cappuccinos and baked goods to the teenagers—to fill the gap. Unfortunately, the teenagers were not interested in, or couldn't afford, its offerings, so the café lost money too.

Rather than abandoning its money-losing ventures, the nonprofit expanded its earned-income program by extending the café's hours, broadening the menu, and opening the doors to adults. The results are not yet known, but the likelihood of success seems low. What remains is the picture of a well-intentioned nonprofit, which had simply intended to offer Internet access to teenagers, on its way to building a large, money-losing conglomerate encompassing property management and food service.

The slope for weakly performing businesses is always slippery, regardless of which sector they belong to. But the problem of commitment escalation is made even more acute when philanthropic contributions provide the funding for an earned-income venture during its first few years. Because expenses during this period are covered, the risk of losing money seems less pressing to the nonprofit. If (or, more likely, when) the philanthropic funding stops a few years later, what began as a well-funded earned-income venture may become an unfortunate legacy.

A nonprofit that had simply intended to offer Internet access to teenagers was building a money-losing conglomerate encompassing property management and food service.

A Question of Mission

Nonprofits that take a cold look at the disadvantages of launching a commercial business will probably conclude that the odds of it generating real financial returns are extremely low. That does not mean that all potential ventures should be abandoned. Rather, it means that executives of nonprofits must ask a critical question: "Does this venture contribute to our organization's core mission?" If a venture furthers a nonprofit's mission while allowing it to recoup some portion of the costs, the venture could well be attractive even if it never breaks even.

We have found examples of earned-income ventures that do support nonprofits' missions, particularly in the area of job training. Rubicon Bakery, in Richmond, California, employs adults from a wide range of disadvantaged communities to produce premium cakes and tarts that it sells to retailers. Pedal Revolution, in San Francisco, employs homeless youths to repair and sell bicycles. These businesses operate primarily to fulfill the social goal of providing training to the poor; any money they earn in the process is a side benefit that helps them supplement their philanthropic funding.

Such success stories, however, are rare. Our research reveals that many earned-income ventures fail the mission test as well as the financial test. Our survey of nonprofits' executives asked about their motivations for starting their ventures. Thirty-two percent said they had entered into the endeavors predominantly for mission reasons, whereas 58% cited a mix of financial and mission reasons. Only 10% reported launching ventures purely for the money. But as we probed more deeply into the mission-focused ventures in this survey—and into the endeavors we encountered through our case work—we found that the meaning of "mission focused" often became blurred. In some cases, the ventures were truly central to the missions (for example, a job-training organization creating employment opportunities); others were only loosely related (a children's theater renting out costumes); for still others, there was a vague mission-related element on top of the operation (a children's choir starting an ice cream venture whose employees sing while scooping). The lure of potential "profits" not only distorts financial analysis but also thwarts an impartial evaluation of a venture's mission contribution.

Sometimes, the pursuit of profit directly conflicts with the pursuit of social good. Take the case of one environmental organization that had a unique database of statistics on important environmental issues. The broad dissemination of the information helped support the organization's causes, but the database was expensive to maintain. The organization decided, therefore, to begin charging users for access. But as soon as fees were imposed, the number of users plummeted and dissemination of the information was severely curtailed. The organization had reduced its environmental impact in its effort to generate revenue. That may be a trade-off worth making, but it highlights the complex interplay—and the managerial challenge—of balancing mission and income.

Even without such a direct conflict, an earned-income venture can impede a nonprofit's pursuit of its mission. Launching and running a venture consumes scarce management resources, diluting an organization's focus on its social programs. Consider what happened to an agency we worked with that provides training and support to the disabled. It opened a medical supplies store that proved to be chronically unprofitable—direct costs were routinely more than two times revenue. The store took up more and more of the agency's time and energy as the nonprofit's management team made "figuring out this issue" one of its highest priorities. Yet the store was doing little to fulfill the organization's mission. Only a small percentage of the agency's targeted beneficiaries shopped there. It drew only about 25 customers a week and was competing with at least ten other large stores. After ten difficult years, the agency shut down the venture.

In cases where a clear mission fit is identified, fulfilling the mission's goals through the earned-income venture may be more difficult than envisioned. One job-training organization that focused on serving the homeless wanted to expand the types of training it provided. A major soft drink company offered it the opportunity to run a distribution venture. Enthusiastic about training its beneficiaries in truck driving and enchanted by a partnership with a major corporation, the nonprofit jumped in with both feet. Unfortunately, few of its homeless clients had or could get driver's licenses. To this day, the organization has trouble hiring its target beneficiaries into the venture.

Putting Mission First

Given the low likelihood that earned-income ventures will contribute significant funds and the substantial likelihood that they will hamper the pursuit of a social mission, we urge nonprofits to ask themselves the following questions. Rather than start with the venture's financial potential, begin with its mission contribution. Ask:

1) What set of mission-focused activities should be our highest priorities?

2) If we had additional, unrestricted philanthropic dollars, would these activities still be our top priorities? In other words, have we made an impartial assessment of our mission priorities?

3) Do any of these activities have the potential to generate earned income? If so, which ones do and how would they do it?

4) Would generating earned income in this manner materially compromise our mission, perhaps by excluding some of our target beneficiaries from the goods or services we sell? How much management time and other resources would the

venture probably consume? What's the worst-case scenario for the venture, and what would that scenario mean for our mission and finances?

If, after these questions have been answered, the opportunity still seems promising, then ask:

5) Taking into account any constraints or disadvantages we would have in running a commercial enterprise, what is a preliminary but reasonable estimate of the financial potential for each activity (for example, "The venture might be able to cover half its costs")? Have we fully accounted for all direct and indirect costs in estimating profit (management salaries, facility costs, other overhead)?

6) What additional amount of philanthropic funding would be needed to fully finance the activity?

7) Given the estimated philanthropic requirements of each activity (full cost minus realistic earned-income contribution), which activities deliver the most mission-related impact per philanthropic dollar? (A mission-promoting activity that covers half its costs through earned income could have more impact per philanthropic dollar than a less mission-focused activity that covers three-quarters of its costs.)

8) Would other new or existing activities that don't earn income bring a greater impact per philanthropic dollar contributed?

Such a mission-first approach might lead nonprofits' executives to overlook an enormously attractive business opportunity that isn't mission related. But our experience suggests that such opportunities are few and far between and that the overenthusiastic pursuit of doomed ventures is much more common. The kind of analysis we are proposing can help nonprofits avoid such missteps by imposing rigorous discipline on the evaluation of opportunities. The risk of mission drift and wasted funds will be considerably reduced.

A mission-first assessment of earned-income opportunities also returns the nonprofit sector to its fundamental principles. The reason nonprofits are nonprofits is that the marketplace does not take adequate care of the needs they address. If the most promising mission-based programs are able to generate some earned income, of course they should. For the vast majority of nonprofits, however, that is not a pathway to financial health or to mission accomplishment.

The allure of earned income is understandable, considering the way philanthropy is often practiced today. In many cases, the impulse that leads nonprofits' leaders to search for earned income is their passionate commitment to their organizations' missions; they want to help the organizations escape the challenge—and often the enormous frustration—of attracting the necessary philanthropic support. Most grants are small, short-lived, and restricted to specific uses. Earned income is precious because it comes with no strings attached. It can be used for whatever purpose the nonprofit's leaders deem most important, including operating support for programs that have proven their worth and "overhead" such as managerial talent and development that philanthropic and government funding typically do not cover.

Nevertheless, executives of nonprofit organizations should not be encouraged to search for a holy grail of earned income in the marketplace. Sending social service agencies down that path jeopardizes those who benefit from their programs—and it harms society itself, which depends for its well-being on a vibrant and mission-driven nonprofit sector.

THE PRESSURE FROM FUNDERS

To further its mission of preparing students for jobs in the culinary arts, a nonprofit job-training agency that we recently worked with raised funds to build a full-scale industrial kitchen. Hoping to earn income as well as advance the agency's social goals, managers used the kitchen to launch a café, a catering operation, and a wholesale food business. They found that by making the nonprofit seem more entrepreneurial, innovative, and disciplined, the commercial endeavors generated enthusiasm among philanthropic foundations. Funders were happy to help bankroll initiatives that seemed likely to push the agency toward sustainability.

But the results of the three enterprises were dismal. Unable to achieve high volumes, the kitchen operations lost more than $250,000 a year. Even from a mission standpoint, the ventures failed. Only ten students a year were being placed in jobs, and only a couple of them were actually going into the culinary arts. Nevertheless, the agency continued to operate the kitchen and the three businesses. Why? Because they had become an integral part of the pitch used to solicit funds. "It was," says one of the agency's leaders, "the part of our story that most excited donors about our operations."

It's understandable that the nonprofit organization would be reluctant to end a program that was generating donations. At the same time, it's problematic that the part of the agency's story that funders so wanted to hear would lead a nonprofit to continue operating a money-losing program that did little to fulfill its mission.

Leadership

How will we build effective
organizations and recruit the
right people to lead them?

The Bridgespan Group

Leadership Priorities: What Facets of Management Shouldn't You Delegate?

There aren't enough hours in a day for a nonprofit leader to effectively address all of the issues vying for his or her attention. Delegating some of the responsibilities, and the attendant decision-making authority, can help. However, there are two critical areas of responsibility that should not be assigned to anyone but the top manager: aligning staff and stakeholders around priorities, and developing the organization's leaders.

By Jeffrey L. Bradach and Kirk Kramer

As a nonprofit leader, you know in your bones that there aren't enough hours in the day to invest equally—and effectively—in all the issues vying for your attention. To make your job doable, you have to delegate some of your responsibilities as well as, whenever possible, the attendant decision-making authority. But which ones cannot be assigned to anyone but you? Bridgespan research points to two critical areas that uniquely require the top manager's attention: *aligning staff and other stakeholders around a common set of priorities* and *developing the organization's leaders.*

Why goal alignment and leadership development? There are three key reasons. First, these are the areas most often in need of reinforcement according to the leaders and staff of more than 200 nonprofits who have taken Bridgespan's organizational diagnostic survey. Leadership development and succession is far and away the number one organizational weakness cited by survey respondents, while setting priorities and communicating them, internally and externally, are both among the top five.

Second, it is very difficult to delegate responsibility for these areas effectively (although you can certainly get assistance). Setting priorities requires *you* to synthesize multiple valid and important points of view and ultimately articulate how the organization's vision connects to impact. Getting the organization to agree requires *you* to engage with board members, management team members, other staff, and volunteers. And by definition, *you* are the only one with an overview of the senior management team, and the only one who knows whether team members collectively have the capabilities required to achieve the organization's goals. You are the only one who can assess these managers, help them determine what it will take to develop, and identify gaps in expertise that cannot realistically be filled internally.

Finally, many other management tasks flow from these two areas, including resource allocation, assigning people to priorities, role definition, project initiatives, and process improvements. Ultimately, the success of the organization—its ability to deliver consistent results and increase its impact over time—rests with having thoughtful and well-understood goals and the right senior leadership team making decisions about how the organization can best deliver on those goals.

This brief article offers advice on these two very important areas of focus. It is based on Bridgespan's experience with clients, results from our organizational diagnostic survey, and interviews with nonprofit chief executive officers (CEOs) and executive directors (EDs) who have purposefully worked to define clear organizational goals and build their organizations' managerial "bench strength."

The Power of Aligned Priorities

Your organization should be a function of your strategy, not the other way around; that's why we're starting with this area of focus. With shared goals, priorities become clear. When priorities are clear, it's easier to make a compelling case for funding. It's also easier for members of the senior management team to agree on the most effective way to allocate people's time and the organization's financial resources. It's easier to see where you might be able to delegate certain elements of your job with confidence—maybe to someone who is actually better suited to take on those challenges, or maybe to someone with leadership potential. "Holes"—in terms of roles and skills—are more readily revealed, as are vague or misleading reporting structures. Last but definitely not least, it's easier to say "No" to any proposals, programs, or other activities that are not core to your organization.

The experience of James O'S Morton, CEO of the YMCA of Greater Springfield (MA), offers a good example. Morton was fortunate in that he became CEO shortly after a new, five-year strategic plan was completed and approved by the board (Morton, in fact, had participated on the strategic development committee as a community member). As he explained, "[For] everything we do, my job is to make sure that it rings true with and is connected with one of the strategies set out in our plan. If it isn't a part of the strategic plan then I don't do it and I don't move forward with it.

"Someone called me [recently] and said, 'Is your Y interested in teaching English as a second language?' Well that's what I did before I came here. It would be a perfect fit in many ways with what our mission is here at the Y. But that's not something that we should be doing. So what I said to that person is, 'If you are interested in leasing space from us, and you want to come in and run that kind of program, then let's talk. But if you're looking to the Y to actually operate an English-as-a-second language program, we're not the organization that can do that right now.' I'm trying to be very intentional in the work that we do so that we don't try to do too much."

Establishing a Common Frame of Reference and Understanding

The first step in fostering alignment around priorities is determining whether such alignment already exists and, if so, to what extent. One way to find out quickly is to conduct a simple experiment: At the next meeting of your top team, ask everyone to write down the organization's top priorities for the next one to two years—no conversations, just write them down. If there's significant convergence in the answers, that's good news. Unfortunately, for most nonprofits, universal agreement is rare. (Even among highly focused organizations, it's possible for priorities to change for certain constituencies without the rest of the organization's knowledge, because of budget pressures, funder's desires, shifting beneficiary needs, or other influences.)

Another way to assess alignment is to ask each member of the senior team to reflect on the events of the past 12 months. Before that period began, how did they think they were going to spend their time? How did they want to? What actually happened and why? The answers can paint a vivid picture of real-time concerns and illuminate key gaps between intention and practice.

Does divergence on priorities amongst your management team mean that you need to engage in strategic planning? Maybe, but probably not. In our experience, you are likely to be facing one of three situations, each of which requires a different approach. First, you might have a strategic plan with well-defined priorities, but those priorities might not be clear to everyone in the organization. Perhaps once the plan was completed, they weren't shared regularly along with updates on progress. Or maybe you've had turnover in the management team and the newer members need to understand prior thinking. To get everyone on the same page, size the effort to the challenge. You might need to work with a few individuals to get them up to speed. Perhaps a management team offsite would help refresh and refine the team's understanding of the strategy and key priorities, and set in motion a communication process to reach others in the organization. (As previously mentioned, this is a common organizational weakness.)

Second, you may have a good strategy, but with changing times (e.g. an economic downturn) you may need to clarify the goals and specific priorities for the next few years. This scenario is likely to require more effort, most likely a series of off-site meetings involving the management team and possibly key board members or other stakeholders. You may also need some analysis of the current situation to confirm that the fundamental strategy is sound and to help guide the setting of goals and priorities for the next few years.

Finally, if it has been some time since you've developed a strategic plan, and the environment has changed, then it might well be time to update your strategy and set new priorities. That was the catalyst for Dan Cardinali, the executive director of the youth-serving organization Communities In Schools (CIS), to engage the organization in a strategic planning effort in 2004. While it might have been more expedient to set new goals for CIS by himself, or with feedback from a small group of people, Cardinali felt that an inclusive strategic planning process would both encourage an earlier and deeper level of understanding and engagement throughout the organization, and result in a plan that reflected a true synthesis of top-down and bottom-up points of view. To that end, he solicited input from the management team and full staff at the CIS national office, state and regional office directors, directors of local affiliates, and CIS board members. As Cardinali reflected in February 2010, "Looking back at what we've accomplished since 2004, it's clear that the complexity of the process was worth the effort. Our strategy is stronger because it reflects knowledge from all parts of this organization about the way things get done on the ground. Plus, the process now serves as a powerful tool validating our network-wide direction and encouraging us to continue forward despite internal and external resistance. Our organization as a whole is stronger because our constituencies understand why we have the priorities we do, and that they accurately reflect the needs of the people we serve."

Importantly, establishing clarity and alignment on priorities is not a one-off proposition. Monitoring performance against priorities is also necessary: to maintain alignment by keeping the organization's priorities front and center (thereby addressing the communications issues highlighted in Bridgespan survey results); and to help you determine if they need to be revised because of changing circumstances.

Developing Today's Leaders and Tomorrow's

Investing in your organization's current leaders and its potential leaders can feel like a luxury. But the capabilities and capacity of your top team determine the organization's future. Most organizations simply can't scale their impact faster than they grow their people—individually and collectively.

It may be helpful to think about this task as a three-step process (even if, in practice, the experience won't be linear): 1) Look at your organization's strategy and priorities through the lens of the capabilities they require, and assess your management team against those requirements; 2) Identify ways to develop current team members and consider development opportunities for promising staff at lower levels in your organization; 3) Determine where gaps exist and hire in to fill them.

Step 1: *Translate your organization's strategy and priorities into the leadership and management capabilities that will be required to execute on them, and then assess your current management team against those requirements.* Ask: What capabilities will require fortification if this organization is to act effectively on the priorities we have identified? To illustrate, consider the experience of Father Steven Boes, the national executive director of Boys Town. When Boes developed a growth strategy premised on scaling local sites, he recognized he would also need general managers to run them. Historically, Boys Town's site managers were selected because of their strong program management skills. But as Boes considered the site manager role against the organization's future needs, he realized that they would need strong fundraising, financial, advocacy, and team leadership skills as well.

Step 2: *Based on that assessment, identify ways to develop the capabilities of your current management team (considering the possible turnover your organization might reasonably expect to have in the next few years as well). Apply the same thought process to the potential replacements for your current management team—the rising stars from the next level down in your organization.* These individuals are a good source of bench strength. In fact, in a Bridgespan study published in 2009, "Finding Leaders for America's Nonprofits," responding nonprofit leaders indicated that from June 2007 to December 2008, 25 percent of all senior management positions were filled via internal promotions.

With your current senior team, focus your development thinking two to three years out, and ask: What capabilities will these individuals need? In our experience, most nonprofits provide few development opportunities for their current managers. And much of what is provided is reactive: for example, sending a person to a conference or possibly a course that he or she has asked to attend. These experiences can be helpful, but they are seldom enough to build the skills he will need to take on additional responsibility or move into a higher level position. To do that, it's likely you will need a development plan that spans several years. For example, suppose you have a fantastic program leader whom you see as a potential successor for your position. She is very strong on internal management skills, but lacks both the externally-facing skills and the financial acumen needed to excel as an executive director. In this case, the best development plan would include systematically involving her in a series of relevant activities. You could have her: attend meetings with funders and potential funders, and, over time, take the lead with presentations and follow-up; ask her to play a larger role in board meetings, including helping you structure the agenda for meetings; manage groups of volunteers; and/or participate in financial reviews and eventually take the lead to develop the organization's overall budget. Courses and conferences that directly reinforce such skill-building activities are certainly worth considering as well, but they must complement rather than substitute for hands-on experience.

The process for developing rising stars from lower levels of management is roughly similar, although it will necessarily involve more people, since they will not be your direct reports, and developing them will necessitate building their growth into the organization's overall human resources system and performance evaluation practices. The first step is identifying the two or three things the person needs to develop to qualify to take on another role. Then look for natural leadership-building opportunities within your organization that dovetail well with those development objectives. Conventional wisdom to the contrary, opportunities to exercise leadership (and test leadership potential) do exist—and even the smallest organizations have an amazing repertoire. Natural candidates include: leading an IT project; developing a grant proposal; and organizing an annual staff retreat.

The way in which Year Up, a nonprofit that serves urban young adults, structures regional ED roles provides a good example of effective internal talent development. Regional EDs have budget and operational responsibility for their local sites. They also spend 10 to 15 percent of their time on "corporate" projects, which provide them with broad organizational perspective and experience. In some cases, the regional EDs gain experience leading their peers; in others, they work as project team members, learning about their peers' interests, strengths, weaknesses, and work styles. This approach helps Year Up develop well-rounded leaders who are steeped in the organization's culture; an added benefit is that it keeps Year Up's national office well connected with the field.

While developing people slowly and deliberately is not easy, in our experience, sourcing talent internally has many benefits. These individuals tend to be a strong cultural fit, having lived the organization's values for an extended period of time. What's more, they will have developed their managerial skill set in a way that's tailored to the organization's specific needs. As Kathleen Yazbak, a Bridgespan partner who has led dozens of executive searches in the sector, notes, "If an internal candidate brings at least 70 percent of the skills needed to do the job, and you know that this person has the cultural fit to be successful, there's less risk involved than with an external hire. Of course the biggest challenge is figuring out what the 100 percent should be, and thus whether someone hits 40 percent, 60 percent, or 70 percent."

Step 3: *Determine where gaps in roles and/or expertise will persist despite internal development, and engage in external hiring at the appropriate time.* Despite the advantages of promoting internally, hiring from the outside is often necessary and can bring distinct benefits, such as much-needed specialized expertise, an infusion of fresh thinking, or an enhanced ability to understand the policy or funding landscape or the communities or regions in which the organization operates.

Several factors can complicate external hiring, however. One is an internal bias (however subtle) against senior-level hires from the "outside." Current members of the management team may worry about cultural fit, particularly if the new hire is coming from the corporate world. Referring back to the organization's priorities can help build the case for external hires in this situation. Tailoring your recruiting process to ensure that you're identifying and attracting the best outside candidates can smooth the eventual transition. And there are numerous "onboarding" methods to help new and existing staff begin to work together effectively as quickly as possible. Funding may be another complicating factor, but again, having solid goals and priorities should help you bring a compelling business case to funders.

The experience of Self Enhancement, Inc. (SEI), a nonprofit agency supporting at-risk youth on the northeast side of Portland, OR, shows the value of facing up to this challenge sooner rather than later. In 2006, SEI's board approved a three-year growth-oriented strategic plan, which was subsequently funded by several foundations, including the Edna McConnell Clark Foundation (Clark). SEI, led by president and CEO Tony Hopson Sr., then swung into implementation mode. During the planning process, SEI's leaders had been encouraged by Clark and outside advisors to add management capacity, but they had demurred. They believed that they could grow successfully with their existing staff, and they were worried about diluting the organization's close-knit culture. Soon, however, team members realized that SEI's new plan required specialized expertise that they did not possess, as well as additional senior staff. To cite two examples: The IT area needed additional expertise to develop a performance management data system, a key supporting feature of the growth strategy; and the existing HR function simply did not have the capacity to hire the youth coordinators required by the plan while concurrently making dramatic improvements to SEI's internal training programs.

There was no provision in SEI's budget to address these needs; however, Hopson and his colleagues had become convinced that the additional staff and expertise in HR, IT, and other areas were essential if SEI were to execute successfully on its plan. They made the call to go ahead and hire the additional staff, even though it meant additional fundraising to secure the money to do so. Looking back on this decision, they saw it as a turning point in their implementation—the point at which they fully came to terms with the requirements of their growth aspirations and determined to follow through on them.

One of Your Organization's Most Valuable Resources: You

Building your organization's management potential is critical. But beware of getting so caught up in running your organization that you neglect to pay sufficient attention to one of its most valuable resources: yourself. It's not just your team members who need to keep getting better at what they do. You do, too—and for the same reason that flight attendants tell airline passengers to put their own oxygen masks on before helping others. If your capabilities fall short of potential, you won't be able to lead your organization as effectively.

A big part of paying attention to yourself means getting meaningful feedback on how you're doing from the multiple constituencies you serve and acting on that feedback appropriately. This feedback is critical because, as our surveys have consistently shown, the top manager's view of how his or her organization is doing is often distorted. More to the point, your organization's managerial weaknesses may well be greater than you perceive them to be. Our organizational diagnostic research has shown that leaders systematically rate their organization's performance on key dimensions of management more highly than their broader management teams do. (For more on this topic, see the article "Beware Your Leadership Blind Spots," in the Winter 2009 issue of *The Nonprofit Quarterly*.)

Getting this feedback can be painful, as shortcomings in your leadership approach will likely surface. But these feedback loops will also show you your strengths. And they'll provide another data point that you can use to inform your thinking as you consider the responsibilities of your job against your organization's priorities, and against what you can reasonably hope to accomplish as an individual.

The **Bridgespan** Group

Finding Leaders for America's Nonprofits

The Bridgespan Group polled 433 executive directors of nonprofit organizations in the first quarter of 2009. The study, commissioned by the American Express Foundation, sought to determine the nature and dimensions of the evolving nonprofit leadership deficit and to look at the extent to which leadership development can fill the gap as well as the potential for transitioning talent from for-profits to nonprofit leadership roles. All respondents came from organizations with revenues greater than $1 million.

By David Simms and Carol Trager

Foreword
By Kenneth I. Chenault, Chairman and Chief Executive Officer, American Express

The definition of leadership I've found most helpful over the years is that good leaders define reality and give hope. This is true regardless of an organization's for-profit or nonprofit status. The reality today is that many organizations are facing tough challenges, including intense competition for talented employees. If the strength of an organization is in its people, then the need to find, attract, and retain talented leaders is even more critical.

In 2006, the Bridgespan Group published a study that revealed the reality of a looming leadership deficit in the nonprofit sector. "The Nonprofit Sector's Leadership Deficit" concluded that the sector would need to attract and develop a leadership population 2.4 times the size of the total number currently employed.

This updated study confirms that the leadership deficit has become more pronounced in the past few years. Impending retirement of baby boomers is still an important factor, but today the main driver of the demand for leaders is the new roles created as a result of organizational growth and complexity.

In the face of this environment, our hope for success lies in building a cadre of strong leaders poised to be at the helm of the nonprofit sector. One possible solution to this leadership deficit is enticing talented managers from the for-profit sector. Another solution might be to expend more resources to develop and support emerging leaders currently in the sector.

American Express established our efforts to develop emerging leaders for the nonprofit sector in 2007. Through our grants and volunteer efforts, we support nonprofit organizations that prepare promising nonprofit leaders for the sector's demanding leadership roles.

Our most ambitious project to date is the American Express Nonprofit Leadership Academy ("Academy"). The Academy is a week-long program created by American Express in partnership with the Center for Creative Leadership (CCL) to develop the sector's highest potential, emerging leaders.

The important work Bridgespan is conducting to highlight the leadership needs in this area is key to fostering collaboration between the nonprofit and for-profit sectors. Together, I believe we can bridge the leadership gap with dedicated, passionate, and well-prepared individuals, thereby strengthening our communities and expanding the impact of the nonprofit community.

Introduction

The Bridgespan Group's Bridgestar initiative, which helps individuals pursue management-level careers at nonprofits and foundations, polled 433 executive directors (EDs) of nonprofit organizations in the first quarter of 2009. The study, commissioned by the American Express Foundation, sought to determine the nature and dimensions of the evolving nonprofit leadership deficit and to look at the extent to which leadership development can fill the gap as well as the potential for "bridging" talent from for-profits to nonprofit leadership roles. All respondents came from organizations with revenues of $1 million or more.

This report summarizes the results of the survey in four key messages; it is also informed by Bridgespan Group strategy consulting and executive search experience. The data show that now, more than ever, nonprofits are looking for talented individuals with critical functional skills, and that they are open to finding these people in the for-profit workforce. The challenge for would-be "bridgers"—managers moving from the for-profit to the nonprofit sector—is figuring out cultural fit, being clear about one's values, and understanding the trade-offs that must be made when transitioning from one sector to the other. The challenge for organizations is to fully develop their own leadership talent as well as to cast their nets more broadly, including outside the sector, to find rightly skilled leaders who can ensure effective operations and also, particularly in these lean times, foster much-needed innovation. In all cases, what is needed are processes that effectively attract, develop, and retain high-potential candidates, helping those new to the sector to adapt culturally. Report author David Simms, head of Bridgespan's Bridgestar initiative, directed the survey. Co-author and consultant Carol Trager worked with City Square Associates to conduct and analyze the poll.

Message No. 1: The leadership deficit in nonprofit organizations remains large, and the gap includes "new–to-the-organization" positions as well as vacancies due to baby boomer retirements (a trend that may have slowed with the downturn, but certainly not abated).

During the 18 months from June 2007 to December 2008, nonprofit organizations with revenues of $1 million or more hired, on average, 1.1 senior managers. With 68,500 such organizations in the U.S., this translates into an annualized 49,000 senior management openings per year.

Importantly, 22 percent of the positions filled in 2008 were newly created, largely based on growth in prior years and increasing organizational complexity. And as of January 2009, respondents projected that their need for senior talent to join their organizations would continue in the next 12 months, anticipating job openings for 24,000 more senior managers.

This is potentially good news for people hoping to transition from a for-profit management role into the nonprofit sector. Studies show that about half of trailing-edge boomers—today's 44 to 50 year-olds—are interested in moving into the social sector. But, as survey respondents confirmed, it also signals strong competition among nonprofits for the same in-sector talent pool. Survey findings also revealed a lack of resources to find or cultivate new leaders from within nonprofit organizations.

Of note: From June 2007 to December 2008, 25 percent of nonprofit leadership vacancies were filled through internal career progression, 41 percent through in-sector hiring, and 21 percent via bridging talent from the corporate sector.

Two key questions: Are there ways to enable more private sector talent to effectively bridge into the social sector and help fill critical needs? And what avenues are available for nonprofits seeking to develop new leaders from within?

DEVELOPING LEADERS WITHIN THE NONPROFIT SECTOR

Survey respondents report that resources are scarce for developing leaders from within an organization. However, grant money can be pursued for this purpose, and the opportunities for leadership development targeted at nonprofit managers are increasing. In a 2009 survey of 10 top MBA programs, for example, Bridgespan found that nonprofit management course offerings had more than doubled in the last five years. In addition, some corporations have launched initiatives to support nonprofit management development. One program that is helping to feed the pipeline by training emerging leaders is the American Express Nonprofit Leadership Academy, created in partnership with the Center for Creative Leadership (CCL). Those nominated to attend the Academy—individuals who are dedicated to a career in the nonprofit sectors, and who hold management-level positions in a nonprofit organization—work with government officials, trainers, and American Express executives to hone the personal, business, and leadership skills needed to run a successful nonprofit. As part of the training, they set goals and action plans; subsequently, they have access to follow-up support from CCL in the form of online networking tools, telephone coaching sessions, leadership goal checkpoints, and a one-year review.

The Annie E. Casey Foundation (AECF) provides another approach. AECF offers a leadership development opportunity in the form of an 18-month fellowship program designed specifically to help nonprofit and public sector leaders in the field of child and family services broaden their visions, expand their knowledge, and enhance their capabilities and confidence. Broadly, the AECF Children and Family Fellowship program is designed to increase the pool of leaders with the vision and ability to frame and sustain major system reforms and community capacity-building initiatives that benefit large numbers of children and families. While balancing the demands of their current positions, Fellows participate in a series of leadership opportunities, including executive seminars, site visits to observe innovations in the field, and work on custom-crafted projects to provide real-time application and learning.

Message No. 2: Functional skills matter (and are transferable across sectors or domains)

Specific functional experience is the most highly rated criteria for hiring, with 79 percent of respondents rating it as "very important." This builds on prior Bridgespan experience in executive recruiting that pointed to multidisciplinary project management skills, experience of doing more with fewer resources, and flexibility/adaptability as skills and attributes especially transferable to the nonprofit sector.

Some leadership roles, such as the heads of development and program, tend to require deep functional expertise developed in the sector. For individuals seeking career advancement within the sector, moving to another nonprofit is, in many instances, the way to move up. Other leadership roles involve skills that can be transferred across sectors. The experience of John Smart at NPower (see "Transitioning Corporate Talent"), for example, illustrates how functional skills can transfer from for-profits to nonprofits.

TRANSITIONING CORPORATE TALENT

John Smart, the former global director of financial planning and analysis for Deloitte's network of member firms around the world, is a good example of a "bridger." Smart recently moved into the new position of chief administrative officer (CAO) at NPower, a national network of nonprofits with 10 regional offices that provides technology support to other nonprofits. Smart was able to tap into NPower's need to broaden its senior finance role, to engage in more complex legal and contractual issues, and to identify and recruit talent with experience in managing multiple, independent subsidiaries—experience often honed in the for-profit world. In his new role, Smart is responsible for managing the business processes and administrative operations of NPower's New York office, as well as developing and tracking the national network's strategic business plan.

According to respondents, 50 to 75 percent of the roles they will need to fill in the near future look to require traditional business skills (finance, general management, marketing/communications, planning, evaluation, operations, technology, and human resources).

Nonprofit organizations clearly recognize the power of for-profit experience. Seventy-three percent of the survey's 433 respondents affirmed they value private sector skills. A full 42 percent of nonprofit chief executive officers (CEOs) surveyed reported that they, themselves, had significant for-profit management experience. And 53 percent of organizations surveyed had other senior leaders with significant for-profit management experience. At the same time, 60 percent believe they will face a paucity of qualified candidates. It's a wake-up call: Even as the rolls of unemployed executives swell, nonprofits are struggling to fill key positions. There is an overwhelming perception that these roles will be difficult to fill due to the need for specialized skills, compensation and funding challenges, competition for the best candidates, and lack of career development opportunities.

HISTORICALLY, NPOS CREATING NEW ROLES AND LEADERS DEPARTING FOR OTHER ORGANIZATIONS CAUSED KEY VACANCIES. PROSPECTIVELY, RETIREMENT TOPS THE LIST

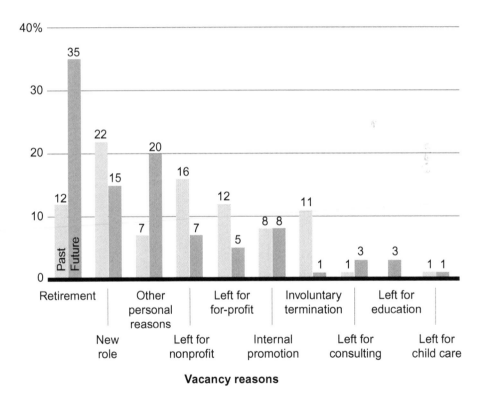

Vacancy reasons

BRIDGING IN EXPERTISE

MicroEnsure (formerly Micro Insurance Agency), an organization that report co-author David Simms has come to know well via board membership, provides a good example of a nonprofit that has tapped the corporate sector for specific functional expertise. As a provider of affordable life, credit, health, and crop insurance to poor families in Africa and Asia, MicroEnsure needs senior managers with deep expertise in the area of insurance as well as deep functional expertise. The organization found exactly this combination in Keith Weaver, a corporate veteran with 30 years' experience in the insurance industry.

Weaver had recently retired as senior vice president and chief financial officer for Manulife Financial in Asia when he joined the MicroEnsure board in 2007. At that time, the nonprofit was small and struggling financially. But it had just gotten word that it was being considered for a major grant from the Bill & Melinda Gates Foundation. Because of his multinational insurance experience, Weaver became a key participant in special board sessions held to review the Gates proposal and to develop the nonprofit's growth strategy. As time passed and the Gates grant became a certainty, Weaver said he felt "called" to play a more direct, formal role in MicroEnsure's future. "I felt like a consultant who helps a client with a project, but then isn't asked to see it through or asked to follow up," he said. "I kept thinking, 'I could help more here.'"

Weaver said that prior to joining the MicroEnsure board, he had never considered working full-time for a nonprofit, but he was captivated by the organization, its Christian mission, and the growth challenges it faced. "[MicroEnsure] was on the cusp of a major ramp-up with a pretty slim management team," Weaver said. "It was really starting from scratch. They were going to need significant management experience to make it work. I felt quite aligned with the objectives of [the organization], and I wanted it to succeed."

Weaver said he and the organization's leaders came to the realization that he would be a valuable addition to the senior staff at virtually the same time. He became chief financial and administrative officer in September 2007, just two months before the organization was formally awarded the $24.2 million Gates Foundation grant. "No question, this was the right thing for me to do," Weaver said. "To see the effect this work has is very gratifying."

DEVELOPING EXPERTISE ON THE JOB

Boston-based Citizen Schools provides an example of a nonprofit that has developed leaders from within, as well as drawing on corporate expertise. Citizen Schools is a national after-school education initiative that improves student achievement through real-world learning projects and rigorous academic support. Its senior leadership team includes people who have developed expertise while working at the organization and also at other nonprofits, as well as in the for-profit sector. Take Emily McCann, who joined the organization in 2003 as the chief financial officer (CFO) and is now chief operating officer (COO), responsible for developing and overseeing top-level financial, technology, human resources, and administrative support services for the organization. Before coming to Citizen Schools, Emily worked in business planning and development for The Walt Disney Company. She wanted to get into nonprofit work, however, and when she heard that Citizen Schools was looking for a CFO, she threw her hat in the ring even though she thought it was an unlikely fit because she wasn't an accountant. Despite her doubts, she went to meet with President and Chief Executive Officer Eric Schwarz about the position. "I was an outside-the-box candidate, but he said he liked my energy and the fact that I was an 'athlete'—a high performer eager to learn about the nonprofit engine. He said, 'You have a complementary set of skills and a similar vision for what this organization can be, and you have worked at places with the scale and size we want to have in the next 30 years.'" McCann joined Citizen Schools as CFO in January 2004.

Less than two years later, she became the organization's first COO. Creating the position was a result of the organization's business-planning process. After the basic outlines of the plan were in place, the management team came together to determine the organizational structure that would enable them to operationalize it. They talked about needing a COO to coordinate the various functions across the organization and create the capacity necessary for growth and ultimately designed a COO position that was a peer of the other members of the senior management team rather than being second in command.

Schwarz considered searching for someone who had experience as a COO in an organization of the scale Citizen Schools intended to achieve, but in the end, he told McCann that he felt she had the personality, the skills, *(Continued)* and the respect from the organization to make it work. The move has been an exciting one for McCann: "Finance had been my pet passion, but it was never the only thing I wanted to do. This role gives me the chance to work with a lot more people and really build a system of support delivery for the sites. And it's a great opportunity to play a role in building the organization, which had been my dream from the beginning."

FUNCTIONAL EXPERIENCE AND CULTURAL FIT WERE BOTH "VERY IMPORTANT" IN HIRING THE FINALIST FOR THE ROLE

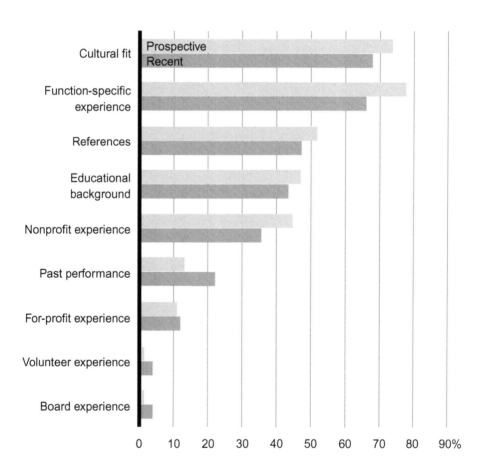

LEADERS WITH FOR-PROFIT EXPERIENCE ARE PERCEIVED TO BRING BEST PRACTICE KNOWLEDGE, BROADER PERSPECTIVES, AND A BOTTOM-LINE ORIENTATION

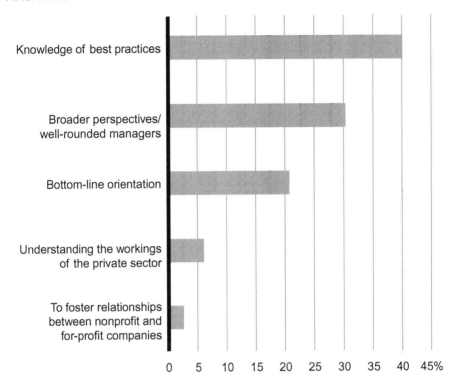

Message No. 3: Cultural fit is the deal breaker

A nonprofit organization's appetite for new roles and its recognition of relevant functional expertise can put a prospective bridger on the short list. But Bridgespan's study indicates that only cultural fit can get him the job, or make her successful once hired. While 79 percent of respondents cited functional experience as very important, just a hair fewer, 75 percent, gave "fit with the culture of our organization" the same high priority. (Trailing far below this, in third and fourth places, were professional references and recommendations.)

In our experience, cultural fit cuts both ways. Individuals seeking to move from the corporate to the nonprofit sector need to be thoughtful about their own values and management styles, and about how they will integrate into a nonprofit culture. Job seekers often make the mistake of assuming that figuring out fit is largely the responsibility of their potential employers. As a bridger, particularly at the senior leadership level, one needs to make it easy for employers to see the fit, during the hiring process and on the job. To do so, requires learning about yourself, not just the organization you hope to join. Nonprofit organizations, for their part, need to think more broadly about their candidate pools, and the skills their organizations truly need; when hiring from outside the sector, they also need to design a thoughtful "onboarding plan" to acculturate bridging employees.

The starting point for an individual is to clarify what he or she is looking for in a job, beyond the specific responsibilities and tasks listed in the job description. It's important to think about everything desirable in the next job, up to and including things like how leadership decisions are arrived at, and where and how strategic initiatives percolate. And it's important to think about which of those things are must-haves, which are negotiable, and which could be trade-offs. It's also useful to review prior experiences and itemize what worked in the past and what didn't.

Nonprofit organizations, in preparing to bring on new managers, may find it useful to review past cases where the fit worked: how talent developed inside or imported from outside the sector rooted and grew, and where it failed to take root. Organizations that have actively recruited in the past three years report that filling roles with suitable leaders is more difficult than it was three years ago, most frequently citing hurdles of compensation issues, the lack of meaningful career growth opportunities, and the need for specialized knowledge and experience. In fact, slightly more than half (53 percent) of the organizations surveyed have made trade-offs themselves in their efforts to fill leadership roles. Trade-offs around flexible work arrangements and increased compensation led the list.

CULTURAL FIT AT THE READ FOUNDATION

When the READ Foundation of New York City was looking for a leader who could bring it to the next level, cultural fit was clearly an important factor. READ is a fairly young, high-growth organization that recruits, trains, and employs teens to teach young children who are struggling with learning to read. READ and its board knew they needed someone who could develop the organization's capacity for growth, including building functions like finance and human resources as well as growing funding partnerships and community relationships. At the same time, the right candidate would need to be passionate about READ's mission and have the ability to work with a variety of internal and external stakeholders, from volunteers and board members to grantees. In short, the Board wanted a hybrid—a corporate skill set combined with a nonprofit leader's cultural bent for building consensus around decisions and harnessing passion to problem-solving. They needed to find someone who embodied the best of both worlds: a candidate steeped in a culture of collaboration and able to engage stakeholders, who also was able to set clear priorities, define roles and responsibilities, and establish effective processes for growth.

Yvonne Petrasovits became president of READ in the fall of 2008, after pursuing her own transition for six months. She had developed an understanding of nonprofit culture during 10-plus years as a board member at Communities In Schools (the nation's largest dropout prevention network) and service on the Advisory Board of the Allwin Initiative for Corporate Citizenship at the Tuck School of Business at Dartmouth College. But in her day job, Petrasovits had been managing director at investment firm Aetos Capital, where she created the internal structure and team to grow the organization from two to 275-plus employees and $10 billion in assets. Her demonstrated management expertise made her an ideal candidate, and her social sector sensibilities sealed the deal.

HOW ORGANIZATIONS CAN FOSTER CULTURAL FIT

When assessing candidates:

• Take a look at where the candidate has spent his/her discretionary time in the past. How have they invested of themselves in organizations and circumstances that matter culturally to you?

• During the interviewing/getting acquainted process, invite them to participate in a small project and have them actually interface with a group of peers in the organization. See how things go. This might very well be the best 'surrogate' for what it will be like to work together.

• Make sure to spend some time with the candidate outside the office just to see how they conduct themselves in different settings. A great opportunity to consider is to have the candidate attend a management retreat or a company picnic if such events are already on the docket.

• Emphasize actual behavioral examples for the candidate to talk through with you both during interviewing and, importantly, during referencing.

To ease the transition:

• Encourage the new hire to "make the rounds" with all of the people he/she will interface with in the new role. Give them the chance to listen and learn from others in the organization before they get too deeply exposed to "live fire."

• Don't simply assign a mentor to the new hire; after the exercise above, let the new hire choose a mentor on the basis of chemistry and shared interests. Such a mentoring role will be far more effective and purposeful, not just another set of duties to conduct.

• As the new hire's boss, schedule regular check-ins not so much to make demands, rather to see how the situation is developing, where information or experience gaps are surfacing, and how best to address them.

COMPENSATION LEADS THE LIST OF OBSTACLES TO FINDING SUITABLE LEADERS*

The inability of our organization to offer the level of compensation necessary to attract the right person	3.5
Difficulty finding executives with the specialized skills we need	3.3
Our inability to offer prospective managers meaningful career development opportunities	2.8
Growing competition from other nonprofit organizations recruiting from the same talent pool	2.8
The lack of resources necessary to find or cultivate new leaders	2.7
Not having ready access to networks of the best leaders	2.4
The fact that many in the talent pool have gone to or returned to the for-profit sector	2.3
The fact that many in the talent pool have reached retirement age	2.2
Not having a clear idea personally of how exactly to go about finding qualified management candidates	1.9

* Mean rating on a 4-point scale

Message 4: Job boards, networks, and search professionals most effectively connect talent to jobs

For nonprofit job candidates with relevant skills who have assessed their cultural fit, the study found that getting started means getting out there. And "there" is as much in the ether as in person: Surprisingly, for a sector that is notorious for relying on personal relationships, job boards surpassed external networking for first place as a way to reach candidates, with 49 percent of organizations using job boards versus 44 percent using external networking to identify their candidates. Thirty-eight percent of respondents also used general print advertising, but it was found to be among the least effective tools. Only 13 percent used executive search firms, but found them highly effective. Clearly job seekers are wise to review job boards like Bridgestar.org, Idealist.org, and Opportunityknocks.org, and post resumes and cover letters that are job-board friendly.

JOB BOARD USE

Consider the case of Ruth Passo, who found her way back into the nonprofit sector via researching job board postings. Passo had begun her working life as a Spanish teacher, before her foreign-language skills landed her a for-profit banking job underwriting loans in Latin America. After 25 years and numerous management roles in the banking industry, Passo felt her greatest professional strength lay in relationship building. When she began searching job boards, her first thought was to focus on nonprofit roles that centered on fundraising, possibly an executive director position. But as she pursued her research—including looking at sample job descriptions and resume formats—she discovered a role that was a better fit for her talents and interests: chief operating officer (COO). A COO role would require internal relationship building, but also draw on mentoring skills from her teaching days and the managerial oversight skills she'd acquired in banking, most recently managing the foreign currency advisory sales desk at a financial services institution. "The more I started reading about the positions [on job boards], the more I saw that the COO role fit me, and the more sense it made to look at a COO position," Passo said.

Passo restructured her resume to highlight her skills in operational management and relationship building. Then, she began applying for COO-type positions. In interviews, she played up her abilities as a team leader. Her job search ended successfully when she was hired in the COO-equivalent position of deputy director of Food Export Northeast USA, a nonprofit organization that promotes the region's food and agricultural products around the world.

Passo's advice to other nonprofit job seekers is to do their homework via both networking and job boards before they start applying and to be open to all the possibilities that the nonprofit sector has to offer. "I recommend research, research, research," she said. "Read postings. Do informational interviews and talk to a lot of people. One thing people told me in interviews was that I was very focused. I knew where I wanted to be."

And what are nonprofit organizations looking for when they scan job board applicants? In Bridgespan's experience, they want to see nonprofit board and volunteer positions on a resume, as well as in any correspondence with the hiring organization, as one way to communicate readiness to bridge. Those entries communicate a candidate's alignment with the values and/or mission of the nonprofit. It's also important for candidates from in or outside the sector to map their experience to the needs of a target job and provide context, such as examples of how they've influenced teams and stakeholders toward action, or managed people in resource-constrained environments. Showing proficiency in such areas will allow a recruiter or hiring manager to visualize the value a job applicant can generate in his or her environment, even if the applicant doesn't have strong knowledge of the employer or domain.

Conclusion

Survey respondents reported that they believe it will be more difficult to fill nonprofit leadership jobs in 2009 and beyond than it has been in the past, even given the current economic conditions. The number of job candidates may increase as people are laid off, as tough times trigger career reevaluations, and as baby boomer retirees throw their hats in the ring. But respondents still reported concerns, based on the reasons outlined earlier in this report, including: a lack of qualified candidates given the specialized needs and complexity of larger nonprofit organizations; salary constraints and funding issues that plague many nonprofits; and the difficulty of finding people who are also good cultural fits and passionate about the mission of the organization.

Additionally, some respondents expressed wariness of job seekers who are looking for "any port in a storm" in the current economy. Further, they expressed concern that competition from within the sector for leaders possessing deep nonprofit expertise and critical skills will be increasingly fierce.

Bridgespan asserted in the 2006 Leadership Deficit study that: "nonprofits increasingly do the work required to fulfill our desire for a civil, compassionate, and well-functioning society...[and]...their ability to consistently deliver results depends more on the quality of their people than on any other single variable."

As the downturn puts even more pressure on the social sector to care for those in need, the talents of in-sector leaders and "bridgers" are bringing sought-after skills to the task.

ANTICIPATED DIFFICULTY OF FILLING VACANCIES

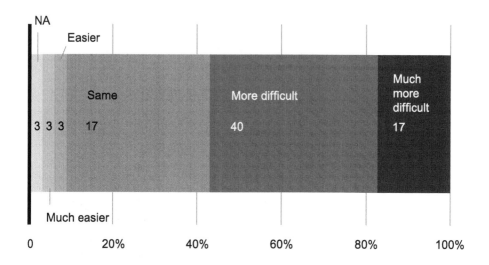

Where Do We Go from Here?

Bridgespan's 2006 study, "The Nonprofit Sector's Leadership Deficit," emphasized the importance of investing in infrastructure to support the recruiting, hiring, and retention of qualified leaders. In its aftermath, a number of readers pointed to obstacles to finding qualified candidates for nonprofit leadership roles, such as inadequate compensation. As our 2009 results show, such obstacles are unlikely to go away soon. But we can also use the results of this survey to think more expansively about what sector leaders *can do now* to increase the candidate pool.

Some thoughts

Sell the vision of how your organization is changing the world. In these challenging economic times, one might expect (and some of the respondents confirm this) that the available talent pool will only grow. We should not be so complacent. Great people are inspired by great opportunity. If an organization can't lay out a compelling case for potential managers, then it is not likely to attract the best. Every organization must be able to articulate not only its mission, but also its vision for change in the world and the role it seeks to play in achieving those ends.

Cultivate an expanded view of "cultural fit" at the interview stage to increase the size of the candidate pool. In the survey, functional experience emerged as critical, but "cultural fit" emerged as the deal-breaker. For some organizations certain criteria, like religious background, are must-haves. But in the experience of Bridgespan executive search consultants, "fit" tends to be an intangible, more associated with "like" or, more to the point, "like us." It may be challenging to associate a candidate from another domain, or with a different background, with the cultural characteristics of any particular organization. In addition, nonprofits' expectations around specialized experience and skills may be unrealistic. Existing leadership teams may need to cultivate greater willingness to hire for aptitude and transferable experience. "Fit" could just as easily mean "ability to establish credibility, alignment, and trust." In order to get the best candidates, they may also want to place greater emphasis on the capacity to understand and respect the mission and passion of the organization, and to grow into a full understanding once on board, rather than to have actively shared it before coming on board.

Invest time now to expand your network. In a Bridgestar article Bridgespan Partner Wayne Luke notes that the majority of senior executive changes are facilitated by someone affiliated with the organization who already knows the successful candidate, and this is borne out by the survey data. If personal and organizational networks are narrow—confined to a domain, to a city, or to a college or alumni network—the contact pools are also likely to be narrow. While understanding that domains within our sector have unique characteristics and challenges, it's important to facilitate greater cross-domain and cross-sector germination as a way to expand both the talent pool and our own thinking.

Invest in the people you hire, to increase the likelihood of impact and retention. By the time most senior people are hired they have inherited a backlog of work and a line of staff eager for their time and attention. Organizations must find ways to manage their entry, or onboarding, so that they acclimate quickly and effectively. Onboarding must include not only support for the new role, but also introductions within the organization's network, visibility with the organization's board of directors and key lay leadership committees as appropriate, and training in concepts and topics close to the organization's mission.

At the same time, nonprofits must be careful not to wholly immerse new leaders in the organization's "way" of doing things. New perspectives, especially from across the sectors and domains, have the potential to open our eyes to the possibilities for our organizations—and, most importantly, to the possibilities for those we serve.

Over the long-term: Foster ways to develop leaders internally. There's no question that the private sector is a valuable source of management talent. But if nonprofits are able to design strong, internal leadership development programs, they should do so. In addition, we as a sector need to make such development opportunities more widely available, and ensure that funding is in place to allow individuals to take advantage of them. Further, leadership development needs to be built into the "regular work" of nonprofit managers—as a requirement, and as a goal. In the morass of keeping up with day-to-day operational demands, it is too easy for highly important but non-urgent activities to get lost if they are not formalized in this manner.

We believe the upside is worth the effort. When managers are developed from within, they are able to hone their skills and tailor them to the real-time needs of the organization. Once in leadership roles, this home-grown talent then can help develop the skills of other high-potential staff members. Ultimately this type of internal re-seeding will maximize the organization's ability to deliver on its mission. The organization will be led by people who have lived its values over a long period of time.

Methodology

The survey was conducted in two phases. Five thousand organizations with revenues of $1 million or more were contacted by telephone. To be considered for our random sample, organizations had to have a National Taxonomy of Exempt Entities (NTEE) classification, with a small number of NTEE categories and sub-categories excluded. Additionally, selection was made only from the list with three or more years of 990 data on file, at least one of which was from 2006 or more recent. (Full details of the criteria are available upon request.) An effort was made to reach the senior executive of the organization in the best position "to answer questions about recent and future hiring of senior management." Once this individual was reached, the recruiter explained the nature and purpose of the survey and invited the individual to participate. Prospects were promised that, in exchange for participation, they would receive an executive summary of the survey results.

Those who agreed to participate (1140) were asked to provide email addresses and direct contact telephone numbers. The names and contact information for those who accepted the invitation were then transmitted to City Square Associates, who sent links to the online survey out to prospective respondents by email. The questionnaire consisted of a total of 70 individual questions, although, depending on the situation of an individual organization (e.g., no new management hires in the past 18 months, no new management hires expected in the coming year), a completed survey could have consisted of as few as 40 items.

In addition to the initial invitation, each respondent received two email reminders at one-week intervals and a phone reminder if he/she did not respond to the email reminder. Telephone recruiting took place between Friday, November 14, 2008, and Monday, January 5, 2009. Online surveys were completed between Tuesday, November 17, 2008, and Friday, January 30, 2009. A total of 433 nonprofit leaders completed surveys.

DISTRIBUTION OF SAMPLE AND COMPLETES BY REGION

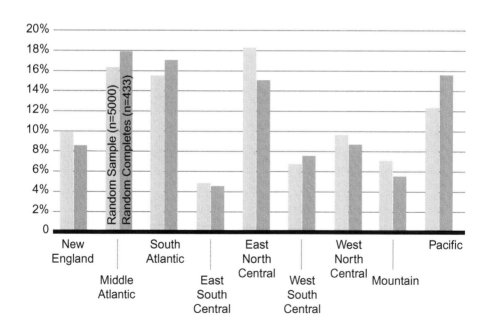

DISTRIBUTION OF SAMPLE AND COMPLETES BY NTEE CODE

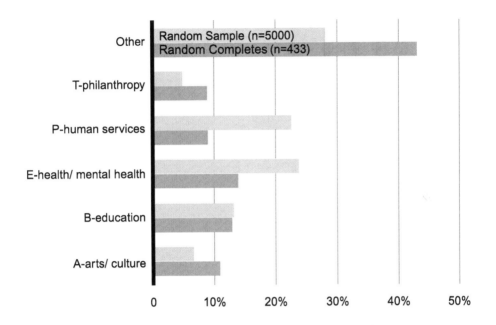

We wish to thank Sarah Hershey, Regina Maruca, Carole Matthews, Rebecca Menges, Katie Smith Milway, and Ken Weinstein for their assistance with this project.

Strongly Led, Under-managed

How can visionary nonprofits make the critical transition to stronger management?

By Daniel Stid and Jeffrey L. Bradach

Editor's Note: *This article also appears as "How Visionary Nonprofit Leaders are Learning to Enhance Management Capabilities" in the January 2009 issue of* Strategy & Leadership.

Without sound management practices, even the most successful nonprofit will be unable to sustain, let alone increase, its impact over time. And yet, when Bridgespan consulting teams surveyed senior staff members at 30 nonprofits, the respondents consistently rated their organizations much higher on leadership dimensions like developing an overall vision than on management dimensions like making trade-offs and setting priorities in order to realize that vision. Many nonprofits appear to be strongly led, but under-managed.

Why is this so? In our work with the leaders of more than 100 nonprofits, we've heard the same answer time and again: The environment in which they operate often reinforces visionary leadership at the expense of management disciplines. Passion, coupled with the ability to make a compelling case for a cause, drives fundraising and helps leaders attract and motivate staff and volunteers. But nonprofit leaders generally are not recognized or rewarded for their managerial qualities.

The signs of inadequate management are easy to spot: Staff members are confused about their roles and responsibilities. Out-of-control finances, arising from an inability to set and operate within a sustainable budget and/or inadequate financial systems, threaten to overwhelm the organization's focus on impact. But while it's not difficult to recognize the problems—and to see that more effective management practices are needed—getting the job done is no small feat.

What can be done? We recently discussed this topic in depth with a select group of leaders whose nonprofits are purposefully navigating the path towards stronger management. Our goal was to better understand this apparent rift between leadership and management, and to learn how these leaders have been working to overcome it.

As the conversations progressed, it became clear that these leaders had each used essentially the same three levers to ensure that their organizations appreciate, build, and sustain strong management practices. They each worked hard to clarify their organization's strategy, they established meaningful metrics with which to assess progress, and they made it a priority to assemble a balanced team at the top. They also made a point of engaging the organization to adapt these changes in ways that were consistent with—and animated by—the overall vision.

Taken at face value, the three levers sound straightforward—even obvious. And in a theoretical sense, they are. But applying them in the context of nonprofit leadership is difficult. This article will explore how the leaders of a small group of nonprofits— Teach For America (TFA), Communities In Schools (CIS), the Partnership for Public Service, the Corporation for Supportive Housing (CSH), and Jumpstart—have used these levers to strengthen their organizations.

Understanding the Tension between Leadership and Management

Before exploring the three levers in more detail, it is important to be clear about the differences between leadership and management, and the inherent tension between the two roles. The sidebar "Leadership and Management: What's the Difference?" (found at the end of this article) provides a brief explanation of the differences between the two; Rob Waldron's early experiences as chief executive officer (CEO) of the youth-serving Jumpstart organization illuminate the tension.

Upon joining Jumpstart, a national network focused on mobilizing college students to provide tutoring to young children in Head Start programs, Waldron quickly realized that the fast-growing organization was losing its most precious resource— talented, committed people—through turnover. As he put it, "People were working so hard to muscle everything. They were quitting because it was so tiring to keep up with the complexity." Waldron knew that Jumpstart needed to bolster its management practices. Simultaneously, however, he was learning firsthand about the tension between leadership and management in the sector. "[I told funders,] 'I want to be the best manager of a nonprofit in Boston, and I want us to be the best managed nonprofit in America,'" he said. "Based on my for-profit experience, I thought that strong management was what people would seek and want to invest in. But no one gives a &$#@. They don't make the decision that way. It's not the thing that drives the emotion to give."

As Waldron came to realize, the qualities that make for strong leadership are critical to an organization's ability to attract money and talent. The capacity to share the mission in compelling ways is absolutely vital to success in these dimensions. The challenge, then, is to not only deepen management capabilities, but to do so without diminishing the mission-based leadership aspects of the organization.

Getting to strategic clarity. The first and most important lever utilized by the nonprofit executives we interviewed is achieving strategic clarity. We say "most important" because the other two levers depend upon this one; in practice, however, any one lever without the other two is not effective.

Achieving strategic clarity means answering, in very concrete terms, two questions that are core to a nonprofit's mission: "What impact are we prepared to be held accountable for?" and "What do we need to do—and not do—in order to achieve this impact?"

Developing this clarity is a critical step in aligning the organization's systems and structures around a common objective. It also enables the distribution of decision-making authority beyond the executive director, as decisions that once required judgment calls by the leader can be made by a broader group aiming towards an agreed-upon set of outcomes.

Getting to strategic clarity is *not* synonymous with developing yet another strategic plan; too many nonprofit leaders have had the experience of developing strategic plans that consumed large amounts of their senior teams' time, only to see them end up on a shelf because they couldn't be implemented or were quickly outpaced by events. As Wendy Kopp, founder and CEO of TFA, remembers concluding at one point in a strategic planning exercise, "I am not going to read another overly detailed plan that tries to lay out what every part of the organization is going to do for several years. This makes no sense. We are going to forget all this planning, and we are going to come up with a few priorities and very clear goals."

At TFA, the question about accountability came down to: 1) attracting a new source of teachers to underserved public schools who will have a meaningful impact on their students' achievement (with one measure being having children make one and a half years of progress in one year of school) and 2) providing an ever-expanding force of leaders who continue working—inside and outside the education system—to ensure educational opportunity for all (which links tightly to measures such as alumni assuming leadership roles in schools, government, and other nonprofits). The fact that everyone at TFA aligned around these answers not only provides stability for the organization's strategy but also makes it easier to answer the question of how to achieve the desired impact by setting priorities, establishing performance measures, and making trade-offs.

TFA, like many successful nonprofits, has often been urged to expand its scope and take on new tasks, such as opening and running charter schools. But the organization increasingly has focused on what it considers "core," thereby holding to the theory of change that has helped it achieve its impact thus far. "I'm so clear about it," Wendy Kopp notes, "and part of my role is to make sure everyone else is clear about it. It's hard to describe how many times, even in a day, I end up saying, 'But that wouldn't make sense given our theory of change.'"

Importantly, getting to strategic clarity is not about dumbing down what you are trying to do and how you are trying to do it, so that you can convey it to funders in the proverbial elevator speech. CSH, which has helped catalyze a seachange in the way that federal, state, and local funders and providers think about serving the homeless, especially the hardest-to-serve chronically homeless, provides a compelling example on this point.

CSH has operated for some time on three distinct levels: conducting advocacy at the state and federal levels to bring about policy change; building capacity among organizations in the field, so that they become more effective developers and operators of supportive housing; and providing financing and technical assistance on a project-by-project basis. As Carla Javits, the former CEO, recounts, at one point in CSH's development, "Several members of the board really pushed us on the question of which of the three lines of business would be most important. Which one is the most critical, the most central to our work? And we went back and really talked that through." Eventually, they concluded that they really couldn't prioritize one above the other. "The beauty of CSH was the interaction among the three," Javits recalls. "But that forced us to think about it…[and] to better articulate our theory of change." The point is to get to what Oliver Wendell Holmes called "simplicity on the far side of complexity," or the simplicity that reflects deep and sustained thinking about the focus of the organization's work, so that it hangs together on its own and in the broader context in which it is operating.

Anchoring strategic clarity in a few key metrics. Once a nonprofit has achieved strategic clarity, homing in on a small number of key metrics can be a powerful way to keep everyone in the organization focused. In effect the metrics become the shorthand to measure both the fidelity of the implementation and the ultimate outcomes.

At Jumpstart, Rob Waldron zeroed in on three metrics: the number of kids served, the gain per child, and the cost per tutor hour. Once those three measures were in place, the organization was able to flag unproductive variations across sites, drive increased growth and effectiveness, and lower unit costs. As a result, when it became apparent that one site was consuming twice as many resources as another to serve the same number of children with the same results, few people questioned the need for change—or the desirability of spreading best demonstrated practices throughout the network.

As the Jumpstart example illustrates, the key to establishing effective performance measures is to focus on ones that will be highly motivating because they are so clearly aligned with the organization's mission. Unfortunately, external pressure for transparency, accountability, and demonstrated results does not always result in the establishment of meaningful performance measures. Instead, the tracking and reporting become an exercise in process, make-work that the organization has to do to satisfy its external stakeholders.

Sadly, nonprofits that do not push beyond this thin way of thinking about metrics are missing a powerful tool for managing—and improving—performance. At TFA for example, accountability and measures were central to instilling a results-oriented culture. As Wendy Kopp observes, "Our people are so focused on what it is that we're trying to accomplish from a social impact perspective, that it leads them to be really open to the idea that this is not about us—it's about getting to the goals more quickly."

For all their appreciation of the power of metrics, however, nonprofit leaders we have worked with and spoken to also confess to being ambivalent about them. The ambivalence stems in part from the ongoing challenge of finding meaningful measures to track and reflect the full scope of what their ambitious organizations are trying to do. The Partnership for Public Service, for example, is dedicated to improving the effectiveness of the federal government, and yet the government agencies themselves typically have no clear and compelling benchmarks to assess their own effectiveness. One of the Partnership's goals is to help the government create and refine these indices. But in the interim, its own commitment to measuring its performance is hard to make operational. Max Stier, the executive director, observes: "We certainly don't have a single metric that everything can be boiled down to, like there is in the for-profit sector." At the same time, however, the effort to define the right metrics is an ongoing topic for the group. "[Although we haven't yet gotten to closure,] every conversation we have talks about metrics in some form or fashion."

Building and aligning a team. Augmenting the experience and capabilities of the senior leadership team is often the most visible sign of change in organizations that are becoming more strongly managed. While there are a variety of ways of going about this, one of the most common is naming someone with managerial experience and a mindset oriented around systems and processes as the organization's second-in-command. At CIS, for example, Bill Milliken, the visionary founder, long-time CEO, and current vice chair, elevated a protégé with an aptitude for management concerns—Dan Cardinali—to become president of the organization. The two now work in tandem, with each exercising both leadership and management. When one of the organization's state directors pushed back on some of the changes that the top leadership team had determined were necessary, for example, it was Milliken, not Cardinali, who weighed in, saying, "This is where we need to go. This is what is going to make us effective to serve more kids and leverage more resources."

At TFA, Wendy Kopp initially took a different tack. After TFA's tumultuous but successful start-up phase, she initially considered handing things off to a new leader, "because what did I know about how to manage this, really?" But then she decided that TFA would be best served by her staying on—and shoring up her own weak points as a manager. "I just thought I'd better learn how to do this stuff. I think it is just so learnable." However, she is also quick to acknowledge that she has hastened her education by bringing in colleagues with private-sector experience who have established and help drive best practices on multiple management fronts. "Everyone's always asking me 'Who are your mentors?' and 'What is the board's role?' The honest truth is I've learned so much from the people who've worked here and pushed us in various ways…And that's really what's driven our evolution."

More recently, Kopp has brought in a chief operating officer (COO) to whom she has turned over much of the operational responsibility for TFA. She observed that, "The reality is that while I became decent at management and got things headed in the right direction, the new COO is better. Beyond his natural abilities, he also brings an experience base that I simply don't have. At this point in our development—given our size and complexity—that has made a huge difference."

The flip side of augmenting the team with individuals who possess needed skills is letting go of employees who may be passionately dedicated to the organization, but who are not able to contribute to the level they should. Here the dynamics of the nonprofit sector can make decisive and often necessary action especially difficult.[1] As one leader told us, "There is a woman on the staff right now whom I am struggling with. She will say, 'I just want to dedicate my life to this organization.' And when she throws that at you, she's basically saying, 'You are going to jeopardize my happiness and my sense of meaning if you change my employment status.'" That said, this leader, like many others with whom we have spoken, went on to say that if he were to do things over again, he would move much sooner to complete both the hiring and the firing for his senior team.

While creating new roles and/or elevating certain positions can reinforce a new emphasis on management, many leaders point to a necessary complement: explicitly connecting these individuals with the mission-related work of the firm. After Carla Javits became CEO at CSH, for example, she created a chief financial and administrative officer (CFAO) position to oversee augmented finance, IT, HR, and business-support functions. "Each of those departments got a little more beefed up under the leadership of one person, who then brought all four functions together and really raised their profile." At the same time, Javits also made a point of having her CFAO operate at the same level as the COO, who oversaw all the programmatic work, thereby ensuring that "the business leadership became part of the senior leadership team of the organization."

Similarly, Max Stier established a trusted colleague in a COO-like position shortly after founding the Partnership for Public Service, and relies on him to manage the administration, finance, and HR functions—freeing Stier up to focus on the board, the press, funders, and other external stakeholders. Importantly, however, over the years, Stier and his colleague have made a point of not making a clean "Mr. Outside/Mr. Inside" split. "It's a bad idea to have a full distinction," Stier believes, in part because the person in the operations role has relevant programmatic expertise, and in part because he feels it's important for him to stay in touch with some of the key internal issues.

Managing the Change Process in Ways that Reflect the Vision

The changes discussed above—achieving strategic clarity, anchoring it in a few key metrics, and building and aligning the team—are critical. But at times, they can also appear to be at odds with the vision that animates the organization. That's why actively managing the change process—reinforcing not only why change is necessary, but also how it will strengthen the organization's ability to sustain its impact and live into its mission over time—is an ongoing leadership challenge.

Engaging the line staff in the work of change by soliciting their perspectives is an important piece of the puzzle. In part, this is common sense, since their work often gives them the clearest view of what the issues and opportunities facing the organization actually are. Getting them involved also helps to foster the commitment and support that will be needed to sustain the changes and energize people. When CIS was establishing its new direction, for example, the senior team solicited input from all three levels of the network (local, state, and national) about the new roles and responsibilities. "We ran this very iterative process," Dan Cardinali remembers, so that we could "create some transparency around the fact that this was a new day, and we were going to make some changes." The Partnership for Public Service, a much smaller organization that operates in one office, generated buy-in by creating a Strategic Planning and Review Committee, consisting mostly of junior staff. The group ramps up or down as needed depending on the issues facing the organization—a development Stier views as "very, very beneficial."

Helping people see the upside of more rigorous management practices is another critical piece of the process, not only because the pain and disruption of new ways of working always precede the benefits, but also because personal commitment to the organization's mission is what tends to keep the best people on board. Carla Javits found this especially important when CSH moved to establish more effective and detailed accounting and data-reporting systems in its local offices. While the initiative was essential for the overall health of the organization, it placed a greater administrative burden on the local office leaders. Javits observes: "The questions then become, 'Is this going to be worth it? ...What are we going to get out of it?' [You need to] really drill down on what the payoff is, why it needs to be done—especially in a mission-driven organization."

Initially, she emphasized the fact that better financial information would not only give the local leaders a better view into what was going on, but also help them "make [the state of play] more transparent to the people in the organization who need to know." It wasn't long, however, before she was in a position to share information from the new systems that could help CSH have greater impact, because "we thought X, but actually it's Y."

Javits also created a powerful institutional bridge between the programmatic and management sides of the organization by having the CFAO and head of finance join the regional program leaders for their recurring leadership team meetings. "In some ways it annoyed people," Javits said of the change in process, "because the program leaders didn't necessarily want to be spending that much time on business issues, and the business leadership wasn't necessarily prone to spend so much time listening to program issues. But doing that made an immense difference in the organization [by fostering] mutual respect and understanding."

Wendy Kopp noted the value of continually communicating the idea that stepped-up management practices aren't distractions from the work—they are the work. But, at the same time, she said, recognizing and encouraging the passion that drives nonprofit work is crucial: "You need all of the systems, but you just can't afford to lose the spirit. We have to sell our people on the idea of using data….[by] getting them to realize that focusing on their kids' academic achievement is the greatest form of social activism, and that measuring their progress is critical if they are going to do that. [Along the way], you also need to make sure you're not inadvertently doing things that meet the measures but don't maximize your ultimate impact…Getting all of that right is very hard."

Even as new practices take hold, the tension between leadership and management considerations will persist. And so it is important to be continually on the alert for symptoms that might indicate a need to adjust or renew efforts to strengthen management. As we have observed—and as our conversations with nonprofit leaders have confirmed—unforeseen challenges always accompany growth. So even if the leadership team is doing the organizational equivalent of changing its oil and filter every 3,000 miles and rotating its tires regularly, the "check engine" light is bound to come on as the odometer spins upward. Long-term success lies not in anticipating and pre-empting every single challenge, but in being receptive and prepared to take action when a new warning light flickers on.

LEADERSHIP AND MANAGEMENT: WHAT'S THE DIFFERENCE?

In a nutshell:

- **Leadership** is the set of activities required to articulate an organization's vision and ensure that all of its stakeholders will support that vision. These activities include: setting the organization's direction and envisioning its future; communicating with and aligning the stakeholders whose efforts and contributions are necessary for success; and motivating, inspiring, and energizing people throughout the organization.

- **Management** is the set of activities required to ensure that an organization will reliably produce results, especially as it grows larger and/or becomes more complex. Management's core activities include: goal setting and budgeting; establishing systems, organizational structures, and processes; and monitoring performance and problem-solving.

If leadership is—in John Kotter's apt phrase—"a force for change," then management is geared to reliably delivering the product or service of the organization amid complexity. The framework on the following page illustrates the shift that many nonprofits need to work through in order to become a high-performing organization.

Leadership and management need to be understood in terms of the collective capacity of an organization and not as characteristics of individual people. Although individuals may gravitate toward one or the other, all of these activities are essential if an organization is to deliver great results over time.

We are indebted to the pioneering work of John Kotter for these definitions and the framework. See John Kotter, *A Force for Change* (New York: Free Press, 1990), especially pp. 3-8.

KEY CHALLENGE FOR GROWING NONPROFITS: BECOMING STRONGLY LED AND STRONGLY MANAGED

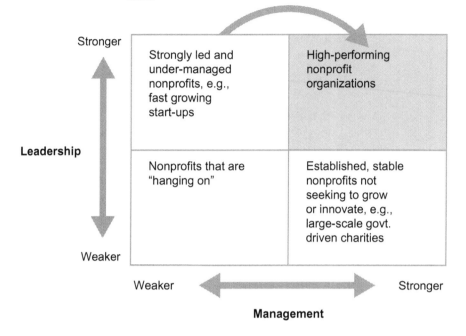

This article originally appeared in the Fall 2008 issue of The Nonprofit Quarterly.

Who Decides? Mapping Power and Decision Making in Nonprofits

Even if your organization determines that a particular decision-making tool isn't the right choice, the process of making that determination helps clarify how your organization functions.

By Jon Huggett and Caitrin Moran [Wright]

Editors' note: This article discusses tools to improve organizational decision making. These tools can identify who should make critical decisions and how participants should make them. The authors explain these tools and offer a case study in how these methods helped diagnose a decision-making challenge, clarify zones of responsibility, and streamline decision making. Decision-making tools of the type discussed here have been in use from at least the 1970's (an early approach to this can be seen in Vroom and Yetton's 1973 piece entitled "Decision Making and the Leadership Process"). The tool discussed in this article, RAPID [developed by Bain and Company],[1] is one of several models currently available to help organizations formalize and make conscious choices about how decisions are made.

How decisions are made can reveal a lot about how an organization performs. Consider some of these decision-making scenarios:

• Without consulting any of those who will actually do the work, an executive director promises an old friend that his organization will take on a complex project, leaving his staff feeling out of the loop and disgruntled.

• Twelve busy staff members spend numerous hours discussing whether their organization should hire a summer intern, but no one knows who has the final say, and every meeting ends without resolution.

• Several organizations work together to support a single initiative, but none of the participants understand where their responsibilities begin and end. When they disagree, no one has overall authority to decide. In addition, there's overlap in the work done.

Do these situations resonate? If so, you are far from alone. Decision making is difficult for many reasons, including vague reporting structures and the inherent complexities of a growing organization that suddenly has to accommodate new stakeholders sitting at the leadership table.

The result is often wasted time, confusion, and frustration. Individually, everyone's intentions are good, yet the whole performs poorly. And in the worst case, decision-making problems create a climate of mistrust and undermine an organization's mission.

What can be done? One way to address the issue is to diagnose the source of the problem by mapping out how difficult decisions are now made. Another is to map how future decisions can be made. Several tools can facilitate these processes and help people become more thoughtful about how decisions *should* be made.

The Benefits of Decision-Making Tools

The core purpose of most decision-making tools is to untangle the decision-making process by identifying all activities that must take place for a decision to be made well and within an appropriate time frame. At their best, these tools give real accountability to the right people, enabling power to be shared but also setting useful boundaries. Involving the right people, while minimizing the involvement of tangential players, saves time and creates better decisions.

What's more, by simply providing greater clarity about who is and isn't involved, such tools can generate greater buy-in for decisions; nonprofit leaders who have experience with these tools can attest to this. "Even though there are people who aren't involved, they're ecstatic just to know who is involved and what the decision-making process entails," says Joyce McGee, the executive director of the Justice Project, an advocacy nonprofit. "They feel more engaged just from understanding something that had been opaque to them before."

This clarity can also generate additional indirect benefits. "We were able to hire higher-quality people for key senior management positions as a result of being transparent about how decisions are made," says John Fitzpatrick, the executive director of the Texas High School Project. "I was able to sit down with top-tier candidates and demonstrate the clear lines of authority and responsibility they would have, and it allayed concerns about the chain of command and their scope of decision making."

While most organizations can benefit from decision-making tools, they first need to look hard at how a decision-making tool can address their needs; they also need to understand how the tool they select works and assess whether the timing is right to introduce it.

"We were able to hire higher-quality people for key senior management positions as a result of being transparent about how decisions are made."
—John Fitzpatrick, executive director, the Texas High School Project

Finding the Right Time and Place

Is your organization ready for a decision-making tool? To answer this question, you need to ask the following questions. (Even if your organization determines that a particular tool isn't the right choice, the processes of making that determination helps clarify how your organization functions.)

Is there is a shared sense of frustration with decision making across the organization? If many staffers believe that their organization's current decision-making process is flawed, tools can add great value. If this concern isn't shared, however, introducing these tools can generate more heat than light. Those who believe that the decision-making process is fine will be resistant.

Is decision making the problem? If the leadership and management teams are strong but frustrated with how decisions are made, mapping tools can help. But if the real problem is a lack of leadership alignment on mission or values, decision-making tools won't solve the problem. If an organization is in flux, it may also be the wrong time to introduce a new tool.

In the case of one organization with which we've worked, for example, the management team was in the midst of a massive overhaul. Suddenly, new teams were developed that hadn't worked together previously, and team members were unclear about their roles and authority. Initially, they thought that mapping decision making would help them gain clarity. But once they began the actual process, they realized that they would need a better understanding of the organization's new structure first.

Is the organization's leadership ready for a tool that reveals how decisions are made? If those in power are uncomfortable about making power and roles explicit, they should not use a tool that makes these dynamics public. Many organizations function with the original founder and a familial set of relationships. Mapping the flow of power in this "family" formalizes informal relationships. If the organization isn't ready for these kinds of changes, using a tool may be counterproductive.

Can you allow enough time to decide how to decide? Changing the decision-making process strikes at the heart of how an organization does things. As noted, outlining the decision-making process means making power explicit, which is unsettling. It may mean empowering some and taking others out of the loop. Working through various stakeholder views to get to the right solution takes time.

The recommender is the go-to person who participates in the process from start to finish, ensures that others understand what they need to do, and keeps things moving until a decision has been made.

The RAPID Method

Organizations and teams of various sizes confronting various situations have effectively used the tool RAPID (which stands for recommend, agree, perform, input, and decide); we'll profile that tool here.

RAPID is an acronym for the roles or activities that participants can take on in the decision-making process. Each letter stands for a specific role or activity; but participants can have more than one role assigned to them, depending on the context of the decision and the size of the group. The order of the letters is not important, but, the acronym "R-A-P-I-D" is a device to remember these roles. In fact, the reality is iterative, although the roles and activities are likely to appear in the following order during any decision-making process.

• **R stands for *recommend*.** A recommender initiates the decision-making process. A recommender is the go-to person who participates in the process from start to finish, ensures that others understand what they need to do, and keeps things moving until a decision has been made.

• **I stands for *input*.** An I stakeholder must be consulted before a decision can be made. Although an I has the right to be heard, he has no vote or veto power. Including someone as an I says that an organization values her or his opinion.

• **A stands for *agree*.** An A stakeholder must agree to or approve a decision. An A stakeholder is essentially an I, but with vote and veto power (such as a CFO, who needs to approve financial decisions). Generally, the more As who are involved in a decision, the more time a decision takes.

- **D stands for *decide*.** A D stakeholder has final authority and is the only stakeholder who can commit the organization to action, such as hiring someone, spending money, or making a legally binding agreement. Generally, the D role is held by one person. But a board of directors in which each member has voting power can be a collective D as well. (Ultimately, if the committee head is a true D, it's better to be explicit up front. Everyone knows where the power lies, anyway.)

- **P stands for *perform*.** Once a decision has been made, Ps carry it out. Often, those who are Ps are also Is.

The acronym RAPID captures a key benefit of the tool—the ability to make decisions more swiftly—but it's important to note that the name can also suggest that decision-making processes should be rushed, which they should not be.

Side Effects and Tradeoffs

There is no denying that implementing decision-making maps and instruments can be messy. In the short term, the tool will test the resilience of the management team, particularly if it exposes an existing process that is convoluted or sorely imbalanced or reveals a complete lack of process. And its tradeoffs can make people uncomfortable.

Implementing tools like RAPID, for example, can mean trading a highly participatory decision-making culture for a faster and more efficient one. The nature of the decision determines whether the tradeoff is appropriate. Sometimes a decision is better made by consensus (where everyone is an A), or even by voting (such as requiring 51 percent of the board for a D). But most organizational decisions are best made quickly and efficiently, using one D and only a few As. Consider an executive director who needs to select and hire key staff members at his discretion. In this kind of situation, a clear, streamlined decision process is likely the best alternative.

Using decision-making maps also means trading ambiguity for transparency. Some organizations prefer to leave some control issues ambiguous. For example, what constitutes a *strategic* change (that needs to be reviewed by the board) versus a *tactical* decision that is within the purview of the executive director? In reality, each decision requires a judgment call. Someone must decide whether to move a decision into the RAPID process. Once a tool is introduced, ambiguity is no longer an option.

"This tool was pretty important to us because we were moving from having only a few senior staff who had worked together for a while to becoming a bigger organization with a matrix structure and more senior staff."

—Aspire CEO Don Shalvey

Lessons Learned

What follows are lessons we've learned in our experience with RAPID and from our observation of other organizations using RAPID.

Make the case for the tool before you introduce it. First, act like an R. Outline what you want to do and why, the process, the instrument to be used, and inform stakeholders when they will be involved. Make sure that everyone understands the tool.

Start by carving out a few key decisions. It's great to start by tackling a handful of decisions that cause the most pain. But at the outset, don't put more than a dozen on the list; overloading may cause the process to stall. Your organization will not miss the irony if the exercise you've introduced to improve decision making merely creates analysis paralysis.

Pacing is important. Tool implementation is worth getting right, so lay out a formal work plan for the process. Decisions that result in big changes need managing, so you need to know when you will make key decisions and put them into action.

Stakeholder anxiety and adjustment are part of the process. In the case of RAPID, the process of assigning roles is best done iteratively and expeditiously. But without firm leadership, managing stakeholder inclusion can be tricky, not least because people can feel excluded when they are no longer involved in decisions. Others can be vulnerable because their power is exposed. One executive director described the process at his organization: At the beginning, when employees realized which role they were now expected to play, they expressed anxiety, asking, "So I am responsible for this myself?" And even when reassured that they would in fact be responsible for making the decision, staff members continued to ask, "Are you sure?"

Once any decision-making tool is in use, the genie is out of the bottle. Much of the value comes from unveiling how decisions are made.

Finalized decisions need to be communicated. Tools such as RAPID offer a simple way to diagnose and prescribe how to make decisions. But they do not tell you how to communicate those decisions. At one Justice Project staff meeting, for example, someone asked, "So who is responsible for communicating the decision to those who aren't involved in the decision making but still need to know the outcome (i.e., an R, A, P, I, or D)?" The executive director was quick to clarify that none of these roles had been assigned this responsibility; that decision would be made in a separate process.

Without firm leadership, managing stakeholder inclusion can be tricky, not least because people can feel excluded when they are no longer involved in decisions.

Once a decision-making instrument has been used, review the whole. Take the time to get distance and see how it all fits together. Does the new way of making key decisions make sense? Do responsibilities and accountabilities match roles? Does the work balance fairly? Do you have buy-in from key leaders?

Decision-making maps and diagnostic tools can be useful even when they are not used in their entirety. As we noted earlier, after introducing a tool, some organizations use it only for problem diagnosis. Others take these ideas and build on them to create their own unique decision-making processes. And some use the tools simply to map out how prior decisions have been made.

Once any decision-making tool is in use, the genie is out of the bottle. Much of the value comes from unveiling how decisions are made. And once roles are clear, it is hard to put things back under wraps. If your first foray with these tools is successful, however, your team will want to use them again. And if your organization is clear about where the power to make decisions sits, it can grow. Complexity can spark collaboration, not confusion. While some may feel excluded, we bet that the candor about decision making will engender respect. Your team can use its passion to strive for even greater impact.

RAPID IN PRACTICE: ASPIRE PUBLIC SCHOOLS

Aspire Public Schools, an organization that opens and operates public charter schools in California, initially used the RAPID (recommend, agree, perform, input, and decide) method as a diagnostic tool and then began to use it to plan future decision making. Aspire's experience demonstrates how the tool works in practice.

Founded in 1998, Aspire opened its first school in 1999 and grew quickly; by 2006, it operated 17 schools across California, primarily serving low-income students. One of the hallmarks of Aspire's culture was its mantra that everyone in the organization—teachers, principals, staff at the national level—was accountable for the schools' performance.

As Aspire grew, however, its leadership team—CEO Don Shalvey, Chief Academic Officer (CAO) Elise Darwish, COO Gloria Lee, CFO Mike Barr, and VP of Secondary Education Linda Frost—came to realize that while everyone felt a sense of accountability, allocation of responsibility was unclear.

When it came to making decisions about Aspire's high schools, the confusion was most acute. Aspire originally focused on elementary and middle schools and was successful using an outcome-based and process-driven academic model. The organization had expanded into high schools as more of its middle-school students approached high-school age. But producing top-tier educational outcomes at the high-school level presented a whole new set of challenges. High schools, for example, require curricula for many more subjects than do elementary and middle schools. And Aspire's high school-age students had more issues influencing academic performance than did middle school-age students.

The position of VP of secondary education had been created to guide the holistic development of the high schools. But the addition of a new person to the leadership team blurred already informal boundaries concerning decision making. For example, CAO Darwish, who had created Aspire's successful K–8 academic model and process, believed that a similar classroom model and process could work well at the high-school level. But it was unclear whether her role was to run the classroom model at the high-school level.While Frost agreed about the value of the model, she found herself swamped with school-level issues and responsibilities, such as establishing a college-bound culture, building relationships with local community colleges and businesses, and developing a standard model for the administration of the high schools in Aspire's portfolio. Both Darwish and Frost felt responsible for success and worked extremely hard. But their positions overlapped and also left gaps in responsibility.

The leadership team believed that RAPID could help clarify these positions' roles and responsibilities and create an organization-wide decision-making process for the future. And so, along with other members of Aspire's steering committee, they embarked on a process, in CEO Shalvey's words, to "decide how to decide."

The process began with several high-level conversations with the CEO, the COO, and the CAO about what makes high schools successful. These initial conversations resulted in a strategic context for Aspire's organizational processes. It became clear that, for Aspire, there were two different levels of success. There was success in the classroom, which included course materials, teaching methods, clear outcomes, and a process of testing and adaptation. And there was success throughout a school, which included the school's culture and operations.

Subsequently, the COO, the CAO, and the VP of secondary education engaged in additional discussion to define the CAO and VP roles more specifically. They realized that being responsible for and making decisions about these two spheres—in the classroom versus throughout the school—required different skill sets and that these two skill sets fit naturally with the CAO and the VP of secondary education roles.

This realization led the larger team to articulate an overall "accountability chain." The team didn't want to lose the idea that everyone was accountable for *something* (and thus was a stakeholder in Aspire's success). But they needed to create boundaries. Expressed in a chart, this accountability chain gave teachers responsibility for what happened in their classrooms, gave principals responsibility for what happened within their schools, gave the CAO responsibility for what happened within the classrooms throughout the entire network, and gave the VP of secondary education responsibility for what happened outside the classrooms within the high schools (see Figure 1, next page). It also clarified the responsibilities and boundaries that would accompany a new layer of positions—regional vice presidents—going forward.

As a result, it was easy for the CAO and the VP of secondary education to begin using RAPID to make decisions. It was now possible to assign RAPID roles, because it was easier to identify responsibility for decisions. A few areas, such as the professional development of teachers, remained gray and required the RAPID method to clarify what was needed to make a decision and why. But for the most part, decisions fit naturally into either the CAO's or the VP's court.

As CEO Shalvey sees it, RAPID helped Aspire at a critical inflection point in its growth. "This tool was pretty important to us at the time because we were moving from having only a few senior staff who had worked together for a while to becoming a bigger organization with a matrix structure and more senior staff," he says.

Category	Decisions	Home Office						Region		School	
		Board	CEO	CAO	VP Sec ED	Dir PD	COO	RVP	Coach	Principal	Lead Teacher
Class-room	Select course materials		I	D				I	I	I	I
	Define instructional guidelines		I	D				I	I	I	I
	Decide on approach to assessment		I	D				I	I	I	I
	Determine format for report cards			D	I					I	
	Decide on PD approach for teachers			D			R	I	I	I	I
	Other?										
School-wide culture and manage-ment	Develop ECHS policies and procedures re: entering into partnerships with universities	A	D	I	R,P		I	I		I	
	Decide on course selection and sequencing (secondary)			I	D			I	I	R	
	Develop SAT/ACT prep program			I	D			I		I	
	Determine grading policy (secondary)		A		D			I		I	I
	Select best practices for school-wide culture		I		I			R		D	
	Develop master schedule (secondary)				A			I		D	I
	Decide on approach to summer school			I	R			A		D	
	Other?										

Stanford SOCIAL INNOVATION REVIEW

This article originally appeared in the Summer 2006 issue of the Stanford Social Innovation Review.

The Leadership Deficit

One of the biggest challenges facing nonprofits today is their dearth of strong leaders—a problem that's only going to get worse as the sector expands and baby boom executives retire. Over the next decade nonprofits will need to find some 640,000 new executives, nearly two and a half times the number currently employed. To meet the growing demand for talent, the author offers creative ways of finding and recruiting new leaders from a wide range of groups, including business, the military, and the growing pool of retirees.

By Thomas J. Tierney

Nonprofit organizations depend on two resources to fulfill their missions. One, of course, is money. The other resource—just as vital but perhaps even more scarce—is leadership. Indeed, qualified leadership candidates may be even rarer than six-figure donors. As one highly respected executive director recently observed, "If I have the choice between spending time with a $100,000 donor or a potential candidate for a senior role, hands down it's the candidate."

Today, many nonprofit organizations struggle to attract and retain the talented senior executives they need to convert dollars into social impact. Searches for chief executive, operating, and financial officers often turn up only one to three qualified candidates, compared with four to six for comparable private-sector positions. The experience of a large nonprofit seeking a seasoned executive to guide its national expansion is typical: Only a single qualified candidate even considered the position. Like many other organizations in the nonprofit realm, this agency was one person away from a leadership crisis.

During the next 10 years, the nonprofit leadership deficit will become impossible to ignore. My Bridgespan Group colleagues and I recently carried out an extensive study of the leadership requirements of U.S. nonprofits that have annual revenues of more than $250,000. (We excluded hospitals and institutions of higher education because of their distinctive funding mechanisms, specialized pools of talent, and established infrastructure for developing talent.) As a group, the organizations we examined provide the bulk of American philanthropic programs in areas ranging from the environment, arts, and economic development to youth development, elder affairs, and other social services. Directly or indirectly, their activities touch almost every single American.

To offset executive transitions and build management depth, this echelon of nonprofits will need to add more than 56,000 new senior managers to its existing ranks in 2006 alone. (We define senior management as the organization's executive director and the people who report directly to him or her.) For the years spanning 2007 to 2016, these organizations will need to attract and develop a total of 640,000 new senior managers—or the equivalent of 2.4 times the number currently employed. To put the challenge in perspective, attracting that many managers is the equivalent of recruiting more than 50 percent of every MBA graduating class, at every university across the country, every year for the next 10 years.[1]

The experience of a large nonprofit seeking a seasoned executive is typical: Only a single qualified candidate considered the position. This agency was one person away from a leadership crisis.

To meet the need for new leaders, the nonprofit sector has little choice but to think and act in new ways. Board members and other recruiters will have to explore previously untapped networks of talent—women returning to the workforce after raising their families, baby boomers shifting out of corporate work, mid-career executives looking for a change, officers retiring from the military, and idealistic young graduates wanting to make their careers in the nonprofit sector. Equally important, nonprofits will have to work on retaining their best leaders, providing them with opportunities for career development and advancement, both within individual organizations and across the sector.

How the nonprofit sector responds to the leadership challenge will have an enormous impact on both individual organizations and the communities they serve. Scholars Paul G. Schervish, a professor of sociology at Boston College and director of the school's Center on Wealth and Philanthropy, and John J. Havens, associate director of the center, expect that during the next 30 to 40 years, $6 trillion in charitable bequests will flow to the nonprofit sector as wealth is transferred from the baby boom generation to its heirs.[2] And that's Schervish and Havens' conservative estimate.

Should the nonprofit sector be unable to fill its looming leadership deficit, much of that money will not be put to its best use, and society as a whole will be the poorer.

Short Supply, Expanding Demand

To understand the magnitude of the leadership deficit and why it will intensify, we need to examine what shapes the supply of, and demand for, nonprofit leaders. The supply side of the story begins with the baby boom generation. Because of the boom, the pool of American men and women of prime executive age (34 to 54 years) swelled to 35 million between 1980 and 2000.

But the first wave of this nearly 80 million-strong generation is now turning 60, and because the boomers did not have as many offspring as did their parents, the cohort that follows them has a lot fewer people. From 2000 to 2020, the number of people in the prime leadership age bracket of 34 to 54 will grow by only 3 million.[3]

Farsighted businesses have been preparing for this dramatic shift since the end of the 1990s[4] (the Partnership for Public Service began to address the federal government's anticipated brain drain back in 2002[5]), but nonprofits are only beginning to mount a response to this demographic threat. Their responses to date have not matched the scale of the problem.

In addition to the uptick in retirements, chronic nonprofit challenges also cut into nonprofits' supply of executives. Some leaders leave management for governance, consulting, or volunteer responsibilities within the social sector. Others leave the nonprofit world altogether, taking jobs in government or business. A study of 2,000 executive directors, conducted by the Meyer Foundation and CompassPoint Nonprofit Services, affixes numbers to these trends: Three quarters of respondents do not plan to be in their current job five years from now, and 9 percent are currently in the process of leaving their positions.[6] This study, "Daring to Lead 2006," suggests that the nonprofit leadership hole may be wider and deeper than anyone suspected. Although the results of this survey are open to differing interpretations, there is little doubt that there will be significant turnover in the sector's leadership ranks over the next decade.

Meanwhile, the demand for leadership is growing. Between 1995 and 2004 the number of larger nonprofit organizations (those with annual revenues exceeding $250,000) grew from 62,800 to 104,700—an annual growth rate of almost 6 percent (see graph, on the following page). Although there are far fewer larger organizations than smaller ones, the number of larger organizations is growing faster than the number of smaller ones. Because larger organizations often require more skilled leadership than do smaller organizations, the faster growth of larger organizations will only exacerbate the nonprofits' leadership crisis.

Every realm of charitable activity is feeding the growth of the social sector. Individual donations have increased as baby boomers age. Foundations have been multiplying, with an average of 2,900 new ones per year for the decade ending in 2002.[7] Social entrepreneurship is increasingly popular. Corporations are making social responsibility a greater priority. And government at all levels has steadily turned to nonprofits to deliver public services.

THE NUMBER OF NONPROFITS IS INCREASING ACROSS ALL SIZE RANGES

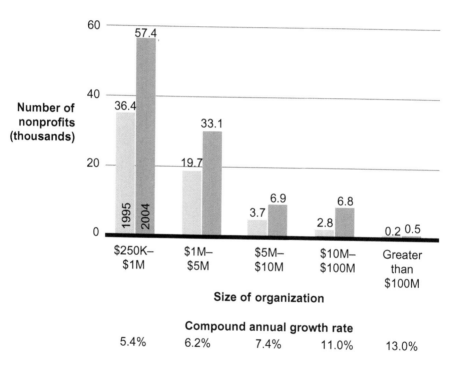

Data source: National Center for Charitable Statistics
(the data has not been adjusted for inflation)

Some knowledgeable observers label this growth "proliferation" and suggest that consolidation of the sector is in order. Others applaud the growth as a heartening voluntary response to unmet needs. Either way, the steady rise in the number of nonprofits and the commensurate need for more management talent show no sign of stopping.

Nonprofits are not only growing more plentiful; they are also being held more accountable. Under relentless performance pressure from donors, regulators, and the public, these organizations' management teams will have to expand to include executives with specialized skills. Do influential board members insist that the organization be run more like a business, with concomitant investment in capacity building? Then it will need to hire a chief operating officer. Are funders' reporting requirements growing more complex and rigorous? Then the organization probably needs a full-time chief financial officer, rather than a part-time bookkeeper. Is the agency stepping up its recruitment of frontline service providers? Then it's time to hire a human resources professional. Does the organization want to access more and deeper pockets? Then it will have to find skilled marketing, development, and communications executives. The need for additional management talent is unabating.

Trouble Ahead

To determine how many new senior managers nonprofits will need to hire by 2016, we first assumed that the sector would continue to grow at the same rates as it did from 1995 to 2004—a period that embraced a significant business cycle. We also assumed that retirement rates would remain constant from 1996 to 2016, save for a 6 percentage-point demographic boost from 2004 through 2009 due to baby boomer retirements. Our final assumption was that rates of other forms of transition out of nonprofit leadership positions would remain the same. (For a full discussion of the study's methodology and sensitivity analysis, please visit www.ssireview.org or www.bridgespan.org.)

On the basis of those assumptions, we project that nonprofits will require 78,000 new senior managers in 2016 alone, up from 56,000 in 2006 and more than a fourfold increase since 1996. When the leadership needs of each of the coming 10 years are added together, the total comes to 640,000 new senior managers—a 140 percent increase in the current population of nonprofit executives. This projected growth in the nonprofit sector's leadership needs breaks down into three categories (see graph, p. 200): Leadership transitions (for retirement or otherwise) account for 55 percent of the increase, the growth in the number of nonprofits makes up 42 percent, and nonprofits' trend toward having larger senior leadership teams accounts for the remaining 3 percent.

There is no guarantee, of course, that our assumptions are correct. The growth rates in the numbers of nonprofit organizations might decline dramatically because of sectorwide consolidation, changes in charitable funding, or even widespread failures of established nonprofits. Future turnover rates might fall below recent projections if existing senior managers delay retirement or turn down job opportunities outside the sector. Even using more conservative assumptions, however, we estimate that the sector will need some 330,000 new senior executives over the next decade. The leadership deficit might be mitigated or deferred, but it will not go away.

We believe it is more likely that the growth of nonprofit organizations will accelerate, driven by current momentum, increased reliance on nonprofits throughout society, and the effects of the coming wealth transfer. Factors like consolidation could easily increase the need for managers given the capabilities required to run larger organizations. Moreover, executive burnout and competitive bidding for talent will probably accelerate undesired turnover. If these more aggressive assumptions prove correct, the total need for new managers would increase from 640,000 to 1,250,000.

Forecasts are always imperfect. Nevertheless, the message in these numbers is clear: In the decade ahead, nonprofit organizations will need far more new senior leaders every year than they did in the past. Our leadership needs, it seems, are unprecedented.

THE NONPROFIT SECTOR WILL LIKELY NEED NEARLY 80,000 NEW LEADERS IN 2016

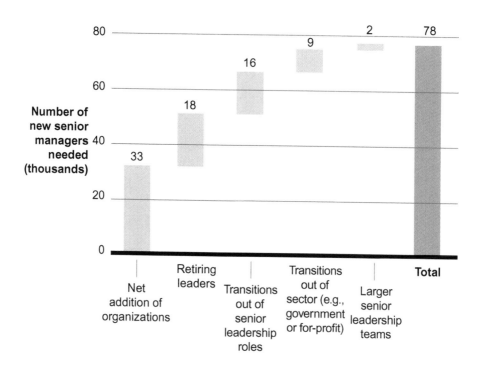

Finding the Talent

The very nature of nonprofits makes offsetting the sector's leadership deficit all the more difficult. Unlike businesses, most nonprofits cannot cultivate their own supply of future leaders. Successful companies routinely invest enormous amounts of time and money attracting talented junior managers and developing them into leaders. Most nonprofits (even larger ones) are too small to provide meaningful career development opportunities for their employees. Most cannot afford the huge investment in recruitment and human resources that such development requires—especially when boards, funders, and donors view such expenditures as wasteful overhead.

Consequently, nonprofits have little option but to search outside their own organizations for new senior managers. The best available data indicate that nonprofits fill only 30 to 40 percent of senior management positions with internal promotions, whereas businesses average 60 to 65 percent.[8] Without abundant firsthand experience in hiring, external recruiting is almost always riskier than internal sourcing. External hiring is also more expensive, often entailing costly executive searches. And as nonprofits compete with the corporate sector in the talent market, the cost of attracting leaders is likely to escalate.

Unfortunately, the short-term consequences of being light on leadership are tolerable. Nonprofits already do so much with so little—why not do a little more with a little less?

Nonprofits also lack the human resources infrastructure available to for-profit organizations. Business schools supply a steady stream of next-generation leadership to the private sector. The executive search industry has grown from modest beginnings a few decades ago to a multibillion-dollar business.[9] Internet job-posting platforms like Monster.com also aid the flow of talent, as do human resource organizations such as Hewitt Associates and Convergys. These services exist because profit-making businesses can amply reward those who help fill their leadership supply needs.

Without extra time and money to invest in finding talent, nonprofits simply cannot compete with the for-profit world when it comes to finding capable leaders. Most nonprofits lack the resources and experience to recruit effectively from colleges or graduate schools. The largest search firms devote only a tiny fraction of their staff to the nonprofit sector, and when they do, they typically focus on high-profile, high-paying executive director (CEO-level) jobs—an entirely rational approach given their financial incentives. A handful of medium-sized search firms, such as Isaacson, Miller, concentrate on nonprofits, but their clients are mostly larger institutions. (Approximately 60 percent of Isaacson, Miller's current business is in healthcare and higher education.[10]) Hundreds, perhaps thousands, of freelance recruiters do at least some work in the nonprofit sector, but they are constrained by limited resources and limited access to qualified talent. Internet-based organizations, such as Idealist.org, help nonprofits find talent, but to date their scale is dwarfed by the magnitude of the need.

Taking Action

Big problems often demand big solutions. To shore up the impending leadership crisis, both individual organizations and the nonprofit sector as a whole must take action. Board members, senior managers, and major donors must commit to building strong and enduring leadership teams within their own organizations. Across the sector, foundations, intermediaries, and associations need to collaborate to nurture a cadre of management talent that is as diverse as the country's population. In both cases, three broader actions must be undertaken: 1) invest in leadership capacity; 2) evaluate management compensation; and 3) enhance career mobility and explore new talent pools.

Invest in leadership capacity. Over the past decade, enhancing nonprofit management has become a front-and-center concern of the social sector. Sector leaders such as Paul Brest, president of the William and Flora Hewlett Foundation, Michael Bailin, former president of the Edna McConnell Clark Foundation, and Barbara Kibbe, former vice president of the Skoll Foundation, have argued the point forcefully. Funders created Grantmakers for Effective Organizations (GEO) in 1997 to enhance organizations' ability to measure results and to ensure sound financial oversight and organizational management. Venture philanthropists such as NewSchools Venture Fund, Venture Philanthropy Partners, and New Profit Inc. have put their money where their demand for good management is. And management advisers such as the Bridgespan Group, as well as the nonprofit practices at McKinsey & Company and the Monitor Group, have grown to assist more nonprofits in capacity building.

Those developments are a step in the right direction, but only a step. Foundations and nonprofits themselves must take the next steps. Only about 20 percent of all foundation funding in 2003 was dedicated to general operating support, with the remainder earmarked for specific programs.[11] That statistic reflects the implicit belief that spending on leadership—recruiting expenses, training costs, salaries, and benefits—should be held to a bare minimum, as should the number of senior positions. But not all overhead is equal. Leadership capacity is what matters most to the long-run effectiveness of any organization, including nonprofits. Consequently, foundations should ensure that their financial and other support for grantees includes resources for leadership development.

It takes time as well as money to build an excellent leadership team. Many successful business CEOs spend well over half their time on people-related issues. In contrast, the executive directors of nonprofits tend to devote the bulk of their time to fundraising.[12] To build stronger, higher-impact management teams, executive directors and other leaders within nonprofits must shift significant time to performance reviews, mentoring, training, succession planning, recruiting, and other human resource functions.

Evaluate management compensation. Talented managers don't join nonprofits to get rich. That doesn't mean, however, that compensation doesn't matter. There is inevitably—and properly—an economic component in a person's career choices, and, during times of increasingly intense competition for talent, even modest changes in compensation—whether up or down—can have a big impact.

Traditionally, nonprofit organizations have attracted outstanding leaders by offering a wealth of intangible rewards with a relatively modest amount of compensation. But that offer may no longer suffice. Nonprofit managers face increasingly complex challenges, both in fundraising and in operations, and they are being judged by much more rigorous performance standards. Nonprofits will have to pay more for leaders who are prepared for those challenges. The short list of candidates attracted to a chief operating officer job paying $90,000 looks dramatically different from the one for the same position advertised at $70,000. The additional $20,000 attracts candidates who not only are more seasoned, but who also have experience running more complex organizations.

Adopting a new approach to management rewards raises complicated issues, ranging from legal constraints on nonprofits to the public's perception that nonprofit executives already receive too much pay. Boards owe it to their organizations to face those issues squarely, matching increased accountability with increased rewards. They will have to resist hiring under-qualified candidates, accept the need to pay qualified candidates well, and fill key positions even if that means increasing "overhead" costs. Salaries must reflect the realities of an increasingly competitive marketplace and the preeminent importance of having the right people in leadership positions. To avoid distorted decision making, overhead costs such as occupancy cannot be lumped together with leadership development-related expenditures. Explicit goal setting and formal performance reviews are two tools that can be commonly employed to ensure that the actual performance of leaders meets the expectations inherent in those leadership expenditures.

Explore new talent pools. Greater investment in management and more attractive rewards for managers will not, by themselves, solve the leadership crisis. The nonprofit sector also needs to expand its recruiting networks and to foster greater career mobility for the talented people already at work within the sector.

Up to now, nonprofits have tended to draw their leaders from a relatively small circle of friends and acquaintances. Although personal networking is an essential element of any recruiting process, it will not produce all the leaders needed in the coming decade. We simply don't know enough people. As competition for leadership talent intensifies, nonprofits will need to expand their recruiting horizons by looking beyond their immediate circles of contacts.

Three significant pools of new leadership talent are already available. One is the baby boom generation. A recent study by the MetLife Foundation and Civic Ventures concludes that, contrary to conventional wisdom, many baby boomers want to continue to work after retirement age. Two-thirds of the 50- to 70-year-olds surveyed said they intend to continue working; fully half of them (and nearly three-fifths of those in their fifties) hope to work in organizations with social missions.[13]

In addition to the boomers, many people at the midpoint of their professional lives are thinking about finding new outlets for their talents. By reaching out to midlife career-changers, the sector would both gain new sources of leadership talent and provide collegial resources for existing leaders.

The third untapped pool of potential leaders is young managers in training. In 1990 there were 17 graduate programs in nonprofit management in the United States. Today, there are well over 90, and more than 240 programs offer nonprofit courses.[14] The young people who follow such courses of study not only are committed to serving the nonprofit sector, but are also more qualified to do so as a result of their training.

Nonprofits can also cast their hiring nets among groups that have been systematically excluded from the recruiting process because of their lack of social sector connections. Such groups include veteran business managers, experienced civil servants, military officers transitioning to civilian life, and women who want to re-enter the workforce after working at home to raise a family. By changing their assumptions about recruiting, and by experimenting with part-time positions, flexible career paths, job sharing, and training and mentoring, nonprofits and their boards can open up substantial new streams of leaders. They could also increase the diversity of their workforces.

In addition to attracting new talent, the nonprofit sector needs to build the infrastructure required to ensure that its existing talent is visible and mobile. A handful of such initiatives is already under way, including American Humanics, an alliance of colleges, universities, and nonprofits that aims to educate and prepare professionals to lead nonprofit organizations; CompassPoint's Executive Leadership Services and Executive Transitions division; Bridgestar, an initiative of the Bridgespan Group that focuses on talent matching for senior leadership; and Idealist.org, a project of Action Without Borders that connects nonprofits and individuals eager to serve. In building the sector's management ranks, much will depend on how quickly and effectively infrastructure-related initiatives can increase their scale.

While the sector stumbles, the deepest suffering will be visited upon the millions of people who rely, directly and indirectly, on the services that nonprofits provide and the social value they create.

What If?

Unfortunately, the short-term consequences of being light on leadership are tolerable. Nonprofits already do so much with so little—why not do a little more with a little less? Yet day after day the leadership deficit will take its toll as organizations across the sector fall short of their potential. Staff will become frustrated, donors discouraged, and reputations tarnished. And while the sector stumbles, the deepest suffering will be visited upon the millions of people who rely, directly and indirectly, on the services that nonprofits provide and the social value they create.

There is another future—one in which a robust nonprofit sector effectively addresses society's needs and achieves ever-higher levels of performance, where the escalating wealth transfer generates exceptional social return. In this future, the leadership crisis is averted, or at least mitigated. A new generation of leaders emerges from within nonprofit organizations, while diverse cadres of senior talent enter from without.

Both futures are possible. We can shift our talent to help the sector meet society's escalating demands, or we can allow its leadership deficit, with its debilitating consequences, to widen. The choice is ours.

PUNDITS WEIGH IN

Paul Brest, president, *the William and Flora Hewlett Foundation*
"The value of increasing the availability of high-quality nonprofit leaders ultimately depends on whether they are attracted to the organizations that need them. A strategically oriented organization that has adequate resources and considerable autonomy over their deployment is likely to attract talented leaders who, in turn, can achieve real impact. And funding practices can significantly affect these organizational characteristics."

Geoffrey Canada, president and CEO, *Harlem Children's Zone Inc.*
"It's also becoming increasingly obvious to us that there are young talented program people in our organization who could—if given help and support—become senior management. We will have to go out of our way to provide them with opportunities and experiences that they would not organically get in their present positions. We need to expose them to areas such as development, budgeting, and working with trustees, and to provide workshops where they can begin to stretch their skill set. These younger program people absolutely need these kinds of experiences over the next five to seven years to ensure that they can effectively take over the reins of leadership."

Jim Collins, *author and consultant*
"What to do? I'm more of a researcher than a practitioner, so allow me to offer a method of analysis that might shed light on the question. I might suggest an analysis of effective nonprofit leaders, with a special emphasis on comparing leaders who made a successful shift from business to nonprofits in contrast to others who did not make a successful shift in comparable circumstances. Why did some succeed and others not? What does this teach us about what separates those who become effective nonprofit leaders from those who do not? And how can those lessons best be deployed to create a vast army of effective nonprofit leaders?

"Whatever the answer, I'm convinced that Tom has identified the right question. Those who build greatness in any human system understand that it all starts—first, foremost, and always—with getting the right people into the key seats. First Who!...Then What. Money is a commodity; talent is not. Time and talent can often compensate for lack of money, but money cannot ever compensate for lack of the right people, especially in the key leadership seats. In the end, the most important thing is 'The Who Thing.'"

Ami Dar, *founder, Action Without Borders/Idealist.org*

"We also agree that what is often lacking is willingness from nonprofits and funders alike to invest in professional development and salary packages to both draw great people into the sector and sustain them throughout their careers. In some cases, it seems to be against senior management's self-interest to address this issue. They are in a position to protect their own salaries and they can rely on a steady stream of entry-level employees who often leave after a couple of years. In other organizations, funding and reporting pressures make staff development very difficult. In both cases, the development of managers and leaders is not a priority, and as often happens in our sector, there are few if any personal incentives in place for senior managers to try to hire the best people they can find."

Kathleen P. Enright, *executive director, Grantmakers for Effective Organizations*

"Effective leadership is at the heart of every innovation and every bit of progress the nonprofit sector makes. Yet we consistently and habitually neglect the sector's most valuable resource: its people. The result, as Tom Tierney's paper suggests, is an impending tragedy of the commons in which the demand for nonprofit management talent will greatly outstrip the supply. Nonprofits will battle and poach for experienced people—leaving no organization properly deep. Valuable energy will be wasted in countless leadership transitions, and very few organizations will have the depth of leadership to survive a crisis."

Marc Freedman, *president and founder, Civic Ventures*

"There is one place we need to concentrate our quest for talent: the vast population of aging boomers now moving into their 50s and 60s.

"We won't find the numbers anywhere else. ...And it's not just about warm bodies. We've invested an enormous amount in building up the human capital of this newly aging generation. We couldn't build campuses fast enough in the 1960s and 1970s when they were starting out. Why not recapture these investments—many made with public dollars—in a way that strengthens the greater good?

"There are two additional reasons to think this direction makes sense. First, changes in the numbers of Americans over 50 are matched by transformation in the nature of the post-midlife period. Buoyed by gains in longevity and health, this new generation of 50- and 60-somethings is poised to invent a new stage of life, and of work. "Second, there is growing evidence that a significant segment of these individuals is yearning to renegotiate its relationship with work, in a way that not only is more meaningful personally, but means something beyond themselves."

Brian Gallagher, *president and CEO, United Way of America*
"As a sector we must do a great deal more work identifying the predictors of success of our future leaders, especially those who come from outside the sector. Many of the skills required to lead a successful for-profit business, for instance, do not necessarily translate to leading a major nonprofit. Just as I could not easily go and run a major software company, the opposite is also true.

"Developing a set of research-based senior leadership competency models would allow us to develop executive training strategies that were more likely to succeed. There have been some very high profile failed executive search placements in major nonprofits recently because the parties did not clearly understand the political and operating complexities of the nonprofits involved and the skills that were transferable (or not) from other sectors."

David Gergen, *professor of public service and director, Center for Public Leadership, John F. Kennedy School of Government, Harvard University*
"As bracing as the study's conclusions are, however, it probably understates the leadership deficits that could be just over the horizon for nonprofits. The fact is that the federal government has entered into such dire financial straits that in future years we will probably invest an even smaller percentage of our national resources on health, education, and environmental programs for the underserved population—and create an even greater need for nonprofits to expand.

"At the beginning of this decade, we thought we had sufficient surpluses to pay for a transition from today's Social Security and Medicare systems to ones that might be more affordable. But those surpluses have now disappeared, and the front edge of the baby boom generation is only five years away from reaching 65. How will Washington pay for its retirement and still respond generously to the social needs of the young? It probably won't. And we will want an even bigger nonprofit sector to make up the difference."

Paul C. Light, professor, *Robert F. Wagner School of Public Service, New York University*

"The nonprofit sector's leadership deficit is both a cause and consequence of continued public doubts about charitable performance. The leadership crisis creates inevitable meltdowns in nonprofit performance, which reduce public confidence, which whets the appetite for further investigations, which weakens the case for decent compensation and increased operating support, which in turn creates greater leadership turnover and vacancies. It is a classic vicious circle.

"The sector must do much more than make its call to leadership more appealing. Although debt relief, decent compensation, and a welcoming embrace of for-profit executives who wish to cross over into the sector will increase the pool of potential talent, the sector must also make the leadership more inviting by building stronger organizations both before and after the new leaders arrive. The allure of leading what Tierney describes as a 'life-transforming' nonprofit may be strong, but the administrative infrastructure cannot be so weak that talented leaders see nothing but repairs ahead."

Jan Masaoka, *executive director, CompassPoint Nonprofit Services*

"One area that goes overlooked is that of racial and ethnic diversity in tomorrow's nonprofit leadership. Many studies, including CompassPoint's 'Daring to Lead 2006,' show that nonprofit executives continue to be largely white/Anglo. It is troubling that our sector, where so many civil rights movements have been nurtured, does not seem to be taking advantage of the talented and capable leaders of color who are ready to step into leadership."

Jon Schnur, *CEO and co-founder, New Leaders for New Schools*

"While Tierney's paper speaks of the need for 640,000 managers, my focus is on the star senior leadership and management team members who can take 50 high-performing social enterprises to great scale and change America and the world. We can use the looming 'shortage' as an opportunity to transform the way high-performing nonprofits can be managed and led to scale."

Lorie Slutsky, president, *New York Community Trust*

"Many people are unaware of the complex operations some nonprofits run and the need for specialized talent. They may not know that workforce development entails working with prospective employers, following business trends, and training undereducated people to fill jobs successfully. They may not realize that financing and building housing is no different from what it is for private developers, except it is harder because it must be affordable for those with modest and low incomes. The list of nonprofit operations that require expert staff is very long."

Roxanne Spillett, *president, Boys & Girls Clubs of America*
"Tom Tierney makes a clear and compelling case that unless there is intentional and widespread intervention beginning now, the nonprofit sector will soon encounter a leadership deficit of dramatic proportion. What makes the need to act even more urgent is the simple fact that the quality of executive leadership is the single greatest factor in predicting the future success of an organization. It follows then that developing and recruiting top executive leadership is one of the greatest priorities for the nonprofit sector. This is in fact the position and the priority for the Boys & Girls Club Movement."

Tom Vander Ark, *executive director, education, Bill & Melinda Gates Foundation*
"This report is one of the first attempts to quantify the mounting challenge of developing nonprofit leaders. Investing in leaders, improving compensation, and expanding recruiting efforts are important parts of the solution. Nonprofit organizations have the potential to build the civic and educational infrastructure our children deserve, but only if they have the leadership to achieve their missions."

Author Biographies

Jeffrey L. Bradach is managing partner and co-founder of the Bridgespan Group.

Paul Carttar, a co-founder of the Bridgespan Group, today serves as director of the Social Innovation Fund established by the Obama Administration.

Barbara Christiansen, a former Bridgespan consultant, works as an independent consultant to urban school districts.

Susan J. Colby, founding partner of Bridgespan's San Francisco office, today leads the firm's work in education.

Susan Wolf Ditkoff is a Bridgespan partner.

William Foster is the head of Bridgespan's Boston Office and leads the firm's work on nonprofit funding models.

Ann Goggins Gregory is Bridgespan's director of internal knowledge.

Don Howard is a Bridgespan partner and head of the firm's San Francisco office.

Jon Huggett is a former Bridgespan partner and independent advisor to non-governmental organizations.

Peter Kim is a Bridgespan case team leader.

Kirk Kramer is a Bridgespan partner and leads the firm's work in organization.

Katie Smith Milway is a Bridgespan partner and heads the firm's knowledge unit.

Alex Neuhoff is a Bridgespan manager.

Gail Perreault is manager of Bridgespan's funding and youth development areas.

Robert Searle is a Bridgespan partner and leads the firm's work in environment.

David Simms is a Bridgespan partner and heads the firm's leadership initiative.

Daniel Stid is a Bridgespan partner.

Nan Stone is Bridgespan's founding knowledge partner.

Thomas J. Tierney is chairman and co-founder of the Bridgespan Group.

Carol Trager, formerly senior director of marketing and communications for Bridgespan and Bridgestar, serves as vice president of strategic marketing at the Jewish Community Centers of Greater Boston.

Caitrin Moran Wright is a Bridgespan manager.

Endnotes

STRATEGY

More Bang for the Buck

1   Notable studies in public sector and for-profit service industries, besides those mentioned elsewhere in this article, include Vernon Altman, Marty Kaplan, and Ravi Vijayaraghavan, "The Challenge of Cutting Costs," Tele.com (May 2003); Theodore Levitt, "The Industrialization of Service," *Harvard Business Review* (September 1976); Theodore Levitt, "Marketing Intangible Products and Product Intangibles," *Harvard Business Review* (May 1981); Brent Keltner, David Finegold, Geoff Mason, and Karin Wagner, "Market Segmentation Strategies and Service Sector Productivity," *California Management Review* (Summer 1999); and Ashish Nanda, "Scale and Scope in Professional Service Firms," Harvard Business School Publishing (April 2006).

2   Among studies illuminating effective cost management in the public sector is John Drew and Nina Bhatia, "Applying Lean Production to the Public Sector," *The McKinsey Quarterly* (June 2006).

3   For further research on the value of introducing technology to transaction-level processes in a service organization, see Michael Van Biema and Bruce Greenwald, "Managing Our Way to Higher Service Productivity," *Harvard Business Review* (July 1997).

4   For additional reading on spreading best practices in the service sector, see Theodore Levitt, "Production Line Approach to Service," *Harvard Business Review* (September 1972).

5   The service-profit chain provides a comparable framework for understanding the link between employee satisfaction, profit, and growth. See James Heskett, Thomas Jones, Gary Loveman, W. Earl Sasser Jr., and Leonard Schlesinger, "Putting the Service-Profit Chain to Work," *Harvard Business Review* (March/April 1994).

6   For further research on the measurable impact of using benchmarks to improve performance and reduce employee turnover, see Fred Reichheld and Christine Detrick, "Loyalty: A Prescription for Cutting Costs," *Marketing Management* (September/October 2003).

7   For additional research discussing the challenges in integrating performance metrics that tie to the organization's strategic goals, see Keith Leslie and Catherine Tilley, "Organizing for Effectiveness in the Public Sector," *The McKinsey Quarterly* (2004).

8   For additional reading on economies of scale and the experience curve, see Pankaj Ghemawat, "Building Strategy on the Experience Curve," *Harvard Business Review* (March/April 1985); and Bruce Henderson, "The Experience Curve Reviewed," *Perspectives* (1973).

9   For a more complete discussion of funding sources, see William Foster and Gail Fine [Perreault], "How Nonprofits Get Really Big," *Stanford Social Innovation Review* (spring 2007).

10 System costs are the total costs required to achieve the target outcome. Teach for America, for example, does not pay the cost of its teachers' salaries; these are covered by the school systems where its teachers serve.

Zeroing in on Impact

1   "Habitat for Humanity Fact Sheet," http://www.habitat.org/how/factsheet.aspx.

2   Natural Resources Defense Council's IRS Form 990 (2001).

3   Average of Ford and GM's advertising expenses in 2002, as reported in U.S. Securities and Exchange Commission filings.

4   HCZ's IRS Form 990 (2002).

5   The 1990s were a period of unprecedented growth for nonprofits. Between 1987 and 1997, private contributions to nonprofits increased from $95 billion to $133 billion, according to the Independent Sector's New Nonprofit Almanac & Desk Reference. During that same time span, according to the almanac, government contracts and grants to nonprofits increased from $115 billion to $206 billion. Today, this pattern has sharply reversed, as philanthropic resources have flattened. Charitable giving (excluding bequests) amounted to $184 billion in 2002—a decrease of 0.9 percent from 2001, adjusted for inflation (Giving USA 2003). According to the *Chronicle of Philanthropy*, "Toward a Cautious Optimism" (February 19, 2004), charities saw only modest gains in giving during 2003. Government funding has also been shrinking dramatically. The Chronicle reported that "state and federal money is expected to be flat or face cuts." In a June 26, 2003 article, "Charities Brace for Shakeout," it reported that "major cutbacks by state governments pose a big problem for many charities."

6   Two of the authors of this article are currently affiliated with the Bridgespan Group; the third is a co-founder and former partner. Several nonprofits mentioned in this article—Larkin Street Youth Services, the Natural Resources Defense Council, and Harlem Children's Zone—have been Bridgespan clients.

7   Social scientists in a variety of fields have used the term "theory of change" for several years; there is no common definition. We borrow the term here to apply to nonprofit strategy specifically as discussed in this article. We are not familiar with other uses of the term "intended impact."

8   "Larkin Street Youth Services: A Case Study in Sustaining Success," http://www.bridgespan.org/LearningCenter/ResourceDetail.aspx?id=876.

9   Harlem Children's Zone, Inc. Growth Plan FY2001-FY2009, http://www.bridgespan.org/WorkArea/linkit.aspx?LinkIdentifier=id&ItemID=1030.

Going to Scale

1   Olson, Lynn. "Growing Pains," *Education Week,* Nov. 2, 1994, p. 29.

2   Letts, Christine; Grossman, Alan; and Ryan, Bill. "Virtuous Capital," *Harvard Business Review,* March-April 1996.

3   It is important to remember that many social ideas spread spontaneously, through the dissemination of a set of principles, the best example being Alcoholics Anonymous. Sometimes a loose "learning network" links programs doing similar things that might subscribe to common principles or goals. See Taylor, Melissa; Dees, J. Gregory; and Emerson, Jed. "The Question of Scale: Finding the Appropriate Strategy for Building on Your Success," in Dees, J. Gregory; Emerson, Jed; and Economy, Peter, *Strategic Tools for Social Entrepreneurs: Enhancing the Performance of Your Enterprising Nonprofit* (John Wiley & Sons, 2002).

4   For a detailed analysis of franchising in the for-profit sector, see Bradach, Jeffrey L. *Franchise Organizations* (Harvard Business School Press, 1998).

5   David Hunter, director of evaluation and knowledge development at the Edna McConnell Clark Foundation, has stimulated my thinking on this subject in very helpful ways. To see how the Clark Foundation addresses this important topic, go to www.emcf.org.

6   See "City Year: National Expansion Strategy (A)," *Harvard Business School case study, HBS 0-496-001,* 1995.

7   See "Habitat for Humanity International," *Harvard Business School case study, HBS 9-694-038,* 1993.

8   See "Spreading the Gospel: D.A.R.E.," *John F. Kennedy School of Government case C16-91-1029.0.*

9   See "STRIVE," *Harvard Business School case study, HBS 9-399-054,* 1998.

10 See "Growing Pains: The Story of Summerbridge," *John F. Kennedy School of Government, case C16-94-1267.0,* 1994.

11 For a discussion of different kinds of networks, see Grossman, Allen and Rangan, V. Kasturi. "Managing Multi-Site Nonprofits," *Nonprofit Management and Leadership* 11, no. 3 (spring 2001).

12 By contrast, the typical for-profit franchisee pays from 5 to 7 percent of its revenue to the center. If its annual sales are $1 million, it is returning $50,000-$70,000 for its use of the brand and related services. In chains that do significant advertising, there are advertising fees (often 3 to 5 percent) in addition to the franchise fee.

FUNDING

The Nonprofit Starvation Cycle
1 See also Kennard Wing, Tom Pollak, and Patrick Rooney, *How Not to Empower the Nonprofit Sector: Under-Resourcing and Misreporting Spending on Organizational Infrastructure,* Washington, D.C.: Alliance for Nonprofit Management, 2004. Wing, Pollak, and Rooney are three of the lead researchers on the Nonprofit Overhead Cost Study.

2 William H. Woodwell Jr. and Lori Bartczak, *Is Grantmaking Getting Smarter? A National Study of Philanthropic Practice,* Washington, D.C.: Grantmakers for Effective Organizations, 2008.

3 Kennard Wing and Mark Hager, *Who Feels Pressure to Contain Overhead Costs?,* Paper presented at the ARNOVA Annual Conference, 2004.

4 Holly Hall, Harvy Lipman, and Martha Voelz, "Charities' Zero-Sum Filing Game," *The Chronicle of Philanthropy,* May 18, 2000.

5 White House Office of Management and Budget, *Circular A-122 (Revised): Cost Principles for Nonprofit Organizations.*

6 Jeanne Bell, Richard Moyers, and Timothy Wolfred, *Daring to Lead 2006: A National Study of Nonprofit Executive Leadership,* San Francisco: CompassPoint Nonprofit Services, 2006.

Ten Nonprofit Funding Models
1 In a November 2008 Bridgespan survey of more than 100 nonprofits, leaders were asked which of eight different and often conflicting fundraising tactics would play some role or a major role in their approach to addressing the downturn. Nearly half (48 percent) of respondents said that six or more would.

2 For example, see Thomas Malone, Peter Weill, Richard Lai, et al., "Do Some Business Models Perform Better Than Others?" *MIT Sloan Research Paper* No. 4615-06, May 2006.

3   For an early framework looking at "donative" vs. "commercial" nonprofits, see Henry Hansmann, "The Role of Nonprofit Enterprise," *Yale Law Journal,* 89, 5, April 1980.

4   William Foster and Gail Fine [Perreault], "How Nonprofits Get Really Big," *Stanford Social Innovation Review,* spring 2007.

Money to Grow On

1   "Subject Focus of Grants Awarded by Size of Foundation," FC Stats: The Foundation Center's Statistical Information Service, 2005. http://foundationcenter.org/findfunders/statistics/gs_subject.html.

2   Bridgespan analysis, conducted in 2006, drawn from research conducted by the Center on Philanthropy at Indiana University.

3   PricewaterhouseCoopers/National Venture Capital Association MoneyTree Report, August 2007.

4   FC Stats: Foundation Center's Statistical Information Service. http://foundation center.org/findfunders/statistics/pdf/07_fund_tos/2006/15_06.pdf.

5   To explore the role of philanthropic investors, see Christine W. Letts, William Ryan, and Allen Grossman, "Virtuous Capital: What Foundations Can Learn from Venture Capitalists," *Harvard Business Review,* March 1997, which brought this topic squarely into nonprofit discussions. In more recent years, George Overholser has made vital contributions calling for much clearer measurement and accounting of such differences; see Overholser, "Defining, Measuring, and Managing Growth Capital in Nonprofit Enterprises: Building Is Not Buying," Nonprofit Finance Fund; and Clara Miller, "The Equity Capital Gap," *Stanford Social Innovation Review,* Spring 2008.

6   *The New York Times,* December 21, 2007.

7   I am a first-grade youth soccer coach, and I believe that the sport is great for kids.

8   CIS completed the first two phases of a five-year study with the Caliber Group in 2007.

How Nonprofits Get Really Big

1   The Bridgespan Group agreed not to reveal the name of the nonprofit.

2   The Bridgespan Group is a 501(c)(3) nonprofit applying management strategies, tools, and talent to help other nonprofits and foundations achieve greater social impact.

3   The Bridgespan Group, "Growth of Youth-Serving Organizations," March 2005.

4   *The NonProfit Times* 100, 2003.

5 For an excellent discussion of the differences between for-profit and nonprofit funding, see Clara Miller, "The Looking-Glass World of Nonprofit Money: Managing in For-Profit's Shadow Universe," *Nonprofit Quarterly,* Spring 2005.

6 The Bridgespan Group, "Funding Patterns" white paper, September 2003.

7 Exceptions to this cross-socioeconomic characteristic include selected faith-based organizations, such as Habitat for Humanity and the Christian Foundation for Children and Aging, which have a focus on lower-income beneficiaries and receive high levels of individual support.

8 Data for the years 1977 to 1997 are from *The New Nonprofit Almanac and Desk Reference* (Jossey-Bass, 2002). Data for 2002 are from the National Center for Charitable Statistics, Giving USA, and the Foundation Center.

9 Ibid.

10 For a discussion of the complexities of earned-income ventures, see "Should Nonprofits Seek Profits?" *Harvard Business Review,* February 2005.

11 National Center for Charitable Statistics, Center on Nonprofits & Philanthropy, and Center on Philanthropy at Indiana University, "Nonprofit Fundraising and Administrative Costs Study," 2004.

12 "Small" gifts were designated as gifts under $10,000. Data were not available for Focus on the Family, which could be an exception to the pattern described.

13 Foundations provide about 2 percent of overall funding in the nonprofit sector, but about 5 percent for the domains that Bridgespan covered in this study (which exclude hospitals and colleges).

14 National Center for Charitable Statistics.

LEADERSHIP

Leadership Priorities: What Facets of Management Shouldn't You Delegate?
This article was originally published by the Bridgespan Group in February 2010.
This article draws on knowledge shared in a number of Bridgespan pieces, noted below.

Kirk Kramer, "The Effective Organization: Five Questions to Translate Leadership Into Strong Management," *The Bridgespan Group,* November 2008. http://www.bridgespan.org/LearningCenter/ResourceDetail.aspx?id=2624.

"James O'S Morton: Life as a Nonprofit CEO," *Bridgestar,* January 2010. http://www.bridgestar.org/Library/CareerPaths/PractitionerMorton.aspx.

Simms, David and Carol Trager, "Finding Leaders for America's Nonprofits,"
The Bridgespan Group, April 2009.
http://www.bridgespan.org/finding-leaders-for-americas-nonprofits.aspx.

"Considering and Evaluating Internal Candidates for Senior-Level Nonprofit Roles,"
Bridgestar, August 2008.
http://www.bridgestar.org/Library/ConsideringInternalCandidates.aspx.

"Hiring a Bridger," *Bridgestar*, October 2006.
http://www.bridgestar.org/Library/HiringBridger.aspx.

Ann Goggins Gregory and Don Howard, "The Nonprofit Starvation Cycle," *Stanford Social Innovation Review*, Fall 2009.

Daniel Stid and Regina Maruca, "Self Enhancement, Inc.: From Strategy to Implementation," *The Bridgespan Group*, September 2008.
http://www.bridgespan.org/LearningCenter/ResourceDetail.aspx?id=2104.

Daniel Stid and Jeffrey L. Bradach. "Strongly Led, Under-managed,"
The Bridgespan Group, July 2008.
http://www.bridgespan.org/learningcenter/resourcedetail.aspx?id=312.

Amy Saxton and Mike Perigo. "Aspire Public Schools: Building the Organizational Capacity for Healthy Growth," *The Bridgespan Group*, February 2008.
http://www.bridgespan.org/LearningCenter/ResourceDetail.aspx?id=416.

Finding Leaders for America's Nonprofits
This report was originally published by the Bridgespan Group in April 2009.

Strongly Led, Under-managed
This article was originally published by the Bridgespan Group in July 2008.

1   See Jim Collins, "Good to Great and the Social Sectors," self-published monograph, 2005.

Who Decides? Mapping Power and Decision Making in Nonprofits
1   RAPID is a registered trademark of Bain and Company.

The Leadership Deficit
1   The National Center for Education Statistics reports that 120,785 MBA degrees were conferred in the 2001-02 school year.

2   Schervish, P. and Havens, J. "New Findings on the Patterns of Wealth and Philanthropy," Social Welfare Research Institute (June 2003).

3   "Cracks in the Education Pipeline: A Business Leader's Guide to Higher Education Reform," Committee for Economic Development (May 2005).

4 Chambers, E., et. al. "The War for Talent," *The McKinsey Quarterly* no. 3 (1998).

5 www.ourpublicservice.org.

6 Peters, J.; Moyers, R.; and Wolfred, T. "Daring to Lead 2006: A National Study of Nonprofit Executive Leadership," A Joint Project of Compass Point Nonprofit Services and the Meyer Foundation (2006).

7 "Foundation Yearbook: Facts and Figures on Private and Community Foundations," Foundation Center (2004).

8 Charan, R. "Ending the CEO Succession Crisis," *Harvard Business Review* (February 2005); "The CFO Turnover Study," Russell Reynolds Associates (May 2005); "Daring to Lead: Nonprofit Executive Directors and Their Work Experience," CompassPoint (August 2001).

9 Association of Executive Search Consultants.

10 www.imsearch.com.

11 "Foundation Giving Trends, 2003," The Foundation Center (2003).

12 Bossidy, L. "The Job No CEO Should Delegate," *Harvard Business Review* (March 2001); "Daring to Lead: Nonprofit Executive Directors and Their Work Experience," CompassPoint (August 2001); Whelan, D. "Exploring a New World," *The Chronicle of Philanthropy* (Jan. 23, 2003).

13 "New Face of Work Survey," MetLife Foundation/Civic Ventures (June 2005).

14 Joslyn, H. "Gaining Success by Degrees" and "Young People Fuel Demand for Nonprofit Study," *The Chronicle of Philanthropy* (Jan. 8, 2004).

5757021R0

Made in the USA
Charleston, SC
29 July 2010